# Redefining Japaneseness

## Asian American Studies Today

This series publishes scholarship on cutting-edge themes and issues, including broadly based histories of both long-standing and more recent immigrant populations; focused investigations of ethnic enclaves and understudied subgroups; and examinations of relationships among various cultural, regional, and socioeconomic communities. Of particular interest are subject areas in need of further critical inquiry, including transnationalism, globalization, homeland polity, and other pertinent topics.

*Series Editor: Huping Ling, Truman State University*

Stephanie Hinnershitz, *Race, Religion, and Civil Rights: Asian Students on the West Coast, 1900–1968*

Jennifer Ann Ho, *Racial Ambiguity in Asian American Culture*

Haiming Liu, *From Canton Restaurant to Panda Express: A History of Chinese Food in the United States*

Jun Okada, *Making Asian American Film and Video: History, Institutions, Movements*

Kim Park Nelson, *Invisible Asians: Korean American Adoptees, Asian American Experiences and Racial Exceptionalism*

Zelideth María Rivas and Debbie Lee-DiStefano, eds., *Imagining Asia in the Americas*

David S. Roh, Betsy Huang, and Greta A. Niu, eds., *Techno-Orientalism: Imagining Asia in Speculative Fiction, History, and Media*

Jane H. Yamashiro, *Redefining Japaneseness: Japanese Americans in the Ancestral Homeland*

# Redefining Japaneseness

*Japanese Americans in
the Ancestral Homeland*

Jane H. Yamashiro

Library of Congress Cataloging-in-Publication Data

Names: Yamashiro, Jane H., author.
Title: Redefining Japaneseness : Japanese Americans in the ancestral homeland / Jane H. Yamashiro.
Description: New Brunswick, New Jersey : Rutgers University, [2017] | Series: Asian American studies today | Includes bibliographical references and index.
Identifiers: LCCN 2016015516| ISBN 9780813576374 (hardcover : alk. paper) | ISBN 9780813576367 (pbk. : alk. paper) | ISBN 9780813576381 (e-book (epub)) | ISBN 9780813576398 (e-book (web pdf))
Subjects: LCSH: Japanese Americans—Japan—Ethnic identity. | Japanese Americans—Ethnic identity. | Japanese Americans—Migrations. | National characteristics, Japanese. | Ethnicity—Japan. | Japan—Ethnic relations. | Transnationalism—Social aspects—Japan. | Transnationalism—Social aspects—United States. | Japan—Emigration and immigration—Social aspects. | United States—Emigration and immigration—Social aspects.
Classification: LCC DS832.7.A6 Y37 2017 | DDC 305.8956/073—dc23
LC record available at https://lccn.loc.gov/2016015516

A British Cataloging-in-Publication record for this book is available from the British Library.

Copyright © 2017 by Jane H. Yamashiro

All rights reserved

No part of this book may be reproduced or utilized in any form or by any means, electronic or mechanical, or by any information storage and retrieval system, without written permission from the publisher. Please contact Rutgers University Press, 106 Somerset Street, New Brunswick, NJ 08901. The only exception to this prohibition is "fair use" as defined by U.S. copyright law.

www.rutgersuniversitypress.org

Manufactured in the United States of America

*To my mother Christine T. Yamashiro, my late father Richard T. Yamashiro, and my husband and partner in life, Mark H. Fujiwara*

# Contents

Preface   ix
Acknowledgments   xiii
Note on Terminology   xix

Introduction   1

1   Japanese as a Global Ancestral Group: Japaneseness on the US Continent, Hawai'i, and Japan   24

2   Differentiated Japanese American Identities: The Continent versus Hawai'i   43

3   From *Hapa* to *Hāfu*: Mixed Japanese American Identities in Japan   64

4   Language and Names in Shifting Assertions of Japaneseness   98

5   Back in the United States: Japanese American Interpretations of Their Experiences in Japan   126

Conclusion   147

Appendix A: Methodology of Studying Japanese American Experiences in Tokyo   157
Appendix B: List of Japanese American Interviewees Who Have Lived in Japan   167
Notes   175
Glossary   189
Bibliography   191
Index   209

# Preface

Redefining Japaneseness refers to the process of rethinking what it means to be "Japanese." For Japanese Americans born and raised in the United States, what it means to them to be Japanese is shaped by American ideas about Japanese people and culture, including being treated in certain ways by other Americans. They have internalized these ideas and learned to see themselves and their Japaneseness in particular ways. When they go to live in Japan as adults, they bring these ideas with them. Yet, at the same time, they encounter new ideas in Japan about what it means to be Japanese there. The idea for this project emerged from my own experiences as a Japanese American who was born and raised in the United States and has lived in Japan for several periods of time as an adult. Two anecdotes from over the years raise questions and touch on issues related to race, nation, culture, identity, language, and symbolic boundaries that this book tries to address.

The first is a conversation that I had while visiting the Philippines in 1996. I had been residing in Japan for a year on the Japan Exchange and Teaching (JET) Program, as a Coordinator of International Relations (CIR) in a small city nestled in the "Japanese Alps" in the mountains of Nagano. Through a friend, I met a woman from the Philippines who was also living in this small city, married to a local Japanese man and raising a small child. She invited me to travel back to the Philippines with her to stay with her family since I had never been there, so I accepted her generous offer and stayed with her and her extended family in their home in Quezon City just outside of Manila for a couple of weeks.

The conversation that befuddled me was with one of her brothers. The family knew that we had met in Japan and was very friendly, making conversation and helping me to feel at home. When the brother in question introduced himself, he also asked about my background, as the natural flow of conversation would go. Since the conversation was twenty years ago, some of the details are fuzzy but I remember very clearly the final conclusion my interlocutor made.

"So, you live in Japan?"
"Yes."
"You speak Japanese?"
"Well, yes."
"Your blood is Japanese?"
"Yes, I guess you could put it that way."
"So you are Japanese."

Although going through the questions I had been answering truthfully, I was taken aback that he had come to such a conclusion. Growing up in California, I had always identified as Japanese American, differentiating myself from Japanese immigrants. I was even more surprised that I became speechless, unable to challenge his logic. Though I knew in my core that I was different from Japanese in Japan, based on his questions, I completely understood the logic of his conclusion: that I, in fact, must be Japanese!

The second is in regards to a comment that my five-year-old nephew in Berkeley made once I moved to Japan to conduct my dissertation fieldwork in 2004. During the first year of his life, I had lived nearby and had seen him daily. For the next four years, I had been living in Hawai'i to attend graduate school so I had seen him less often but had spoken to him regularly on the phone. When I moved to Japan in 2004, I visited home less frequently so most contact with family was through phone calls and I expected it to be similar to when I had lived in Hawai'i, as far as my nephew was concerned. After all, I might be moving around, but I expected it to be the same for my family—just another phone call. Once I moved to Japan, however, when my sister would ask my nephew if he wanted to speak with me he began to refuse. After this happened several times, I wondered if he was mad at me for moving so far away. When my sister finally asked my nephew why he refused to speak with me, to both of our surprise, he responded, "I don't speak Japanese."

While these two conversations took place among people in very different social and geographic contexts, they both highlight the same underlying idea, that people in Japan are Japanese and speak Japanese.

The first conversation with my friend's brother makes this point within a context of knowing that there are "Japanese" and "foreigners" in Japanese society. Since his sister had migrated to Japan, this man was familiar with the premise that Japanese society includes foreign residents from places such as the Philippines. So he asked a number of questions that he thought would help him to sort out whether or not I was a foreigner. He thought that if he knew what language I spoke, my ancestral background, and where I was living that he would be able to determine whether I was "Japanese" or "foreign," like his sister. The question he was missing was where I had been raised.

The second comment by my nephew is decidedly naïve but still reflects a quintessential US-based perspective on nation, culture, and migration. My nephew's confusion that his previously English-speaking aunt might only speak Japanese in Japan reflects a simple multiculturalist view that people in different countries speak different languages. After all, everyone knows that people in Japan speak Japanese. What my nephew had not yet been taught is that in every country, there is some linguistic diversity because of minority populations comprised of migrants and indigenous groups. He did not yet understand that migrating to a new society and learning the language does not cause the erasure of previous linguistic abilities or ways of thinking.

By studying Japanese American experiences in Japan, this book tries to address the common problem of oversimplified, static views of culture and society, especially in relation to international migrants and their descendents. I hope to challenge assumptions about national membership, in regards to both what it means to be Japanese as well as what it means to be American. The experiences of Japanese Americans in Japan raise questions about how we define membership in national, racial, and ethnic groups. Ideas about place, belonging, and authenticity shape how Japanese Americans and Japanese in Japan interpret each other and reconstruct boundaries around the groups with which they identify. While this is a project about transnational connections, it is also about social inclusion and exclusion and how people redefine who they are and how they are different from others they may have previously identified with as they have deeper, more sustained contact with them.

While the idea for this project began with my experiences, this book is a story about the Japanese Americans I interviewed and how they have adjusted to Japanese society in more creative ways than I could have ever thought possible. I hope that my descriptions and analysis can do justice to the complicated ways that Japanese Americans are navigating Japanese society and reconstructing identities in Japan.

# Acknowledgments

I have often heard that publishing your ideas is like having photographs taken of you—your ideas are constantly in motion and putting them in print documents a version of them at that time, even as they continue to transform and grow. If this book is like a photo of me, then the many people who helped me while I was writing it could be thought of as kindly pointing out that I have something in my teeth or that my shirt is inside out, as telling me to tuck in my tag or sit up straight, as reminding me to smile, or even as suggesting that I use a slightly different background. In other words, the photo is, indeed, of me, but many people behind the scenes have supported me and contributed to the production of the best possible version of this project.

With that said, writing acknowledgments is always bittersweet for me. I enjoy being able to publicly acknowledge the help that I have received in so many forms over the years, but at the same time I know that I am not able to thank everyone who has helped me. Please know that beyond those mentioned here by name, I greatly appreciate the support of many, many more people who have helped me along the way.

I must begin by thanking the hundreds of Japanese Americans I have met over the past twelve years, who were living in Japan and had lived in Japan, for sharing their time, thoughts, and experiences with me—without them there would be no stories of experiences to analyze for this book. Almost everyone is mentioned only with pseudonyms so this acknowledgment is the only way that I can publicly recognize them. In addition, many individuals helped me locate potential interviewees. Though I wish I could recognize each one of these people individually, they are too numerous. The kindness and generosity of all of these people was invaluable to the completion of my study and is sincerely appreciated.

Over the years that I have been working on this project, I have been fortunate to receive support from mentors and colleagues at institutions across the Pacific. Moving around for so many years, the people I have met at each institution and in each area have been instrumental in helping me develop a home base as I reoriented myself geographically, situated myself socially, and attempted to continue to progress academically and professionally, sometimes not knowing where I would be beyond a year or two at a time.

The first person to validate that this topic was worthy of academic pursuit was Christena Turner, my advisor from my undergraduate days at UCSD. I contacted her after two other professors had told me that their departments were not places for me to do this research. I will never forget Christena's reaction—that this was "cutting edge" research that crossed over Asian American and Asian Studies. Over the years as scholars in Asian American and Asian Studies have said that my research was not part of either field, I have remembered that early encouragement.

This book began as a dissertation project at the University of Hawaiʻi at Manoa (UH). I was fortunate to have a critical yet supportive dissertation committee that provided guidance and encouragement while also respecting my academic creativity. Pat Steinhoff was a strong chair who has always inspired me to work hard and do my best. Mari Yoshihara offered helpful advice and pushed me to explain as I wrote for an interdisciplinary audience. Candace Fujikane provided critical feedback and encouraging advice at just the right moments. Sun-Ki Chai was a wonderful source of practical advice and support. Finally, Guobin Yang has been a great resource and continues to provide friendly collegiality as well as helpful guidance. In addition, I learned much from Jon Okamura about ethnic identity and Japaneseness in Hawaiʻi. UH friends and colleagues who kept me mentally healthy include: Heng-hao Chang, Joyce Chinen, Soon Hock Kang, Shinji Kojima, Jinzhao Li, Serina Makaiwa, Kinuko Maehara, Quamrun Nahar, Lisa Pasko, James DeShaw Rae, Kiran Sagoo, Xiaodan Wang, Ying-shan Wei, and Rinda Yamashiro. Off-campus, the Honolulu JACL Board and members, as well as volunteering at the Japanese Cultural Center of Hawaiʻi (JCCH), helped me to learn about what it means to be Japanese American in Hawaiʻi.

Generous financial support greatly enhanced my ability to bring this project to fruition. The East-West Center (EWC) provided me with a Graduate Degree Fellowship that supported me during language study at the Stanford Inter-University Center (IUC) in Yokohama, and for the final year of dissertation writing. Mendl Djunaidy was always a friendly face at the EWC and I thank her for her kindness over the years. The Crown Prince Akihito Scholarship was my main source of funding while studying at the IUC and conducting fieldwork. Earl Okawa gave friendly encouragement and valuable contacts. The Professor Misawa Honjo International Fellowship and the Gary Sakihara Memorial Scholarship also helped me to finish up. I appreciate not only the monetary assistance, but also the encouraging recognition of my work that these awards provided.

While I was conducting fieldwork in Tokyo, institutional support was critical to the execution and completion of this project. At the University of Tokyo, it was a pleasure to be sponsored by Yujin Yaguchi, who was helpful throughout my stay. He and his students provided a home base for me while I conducted interviews and began writing in Tokyo, making me feel welcome in their *zemi* (seminar classes), their Hawai'i *kenkyū kai* (research group), and at their social gatherings. One student, Yoko Tsukuda, assisted me in sorting through the literature in Japanese on Japanese Americans. At Sophia University, David Slater kindly sponsored me. His practical advice and collegial encouragement while I was collecting data and beginning to write helped me work though various chapter ideas. Presenting my initial findings at his monthly fieldwork workshop also enabled me to meet a number of fellow graduate students with whom I exchanged writings and ideas. While I was at Sophia, Mariko Iijima and Tamaki Watarai were fantastic colleagues also studying *nikkeijin* (the descendents of Japanese emigrants). At International Christian University Naoki Onishi generously sponsored me for a library card.

When I returned to the United States, I was incredibly fortunate to find supportive and intellectually stimulating environments in Los Angeles. The faculty, staff, and students at Loyola Marymount University (LMU) provided a wonderful environment in which to teach and work on my writing. In particular, Ed Park offered much-needed guidance about research, teaching, and navigating academia. Many friends and colleagues made LMU feel like another home: Jennifer Abe, Maria Alderete, Danielle Borgia, Marne Campbell, Karen Mary Davalos, Liz Faulkner, Linh Hua, Joseph Jewell, Michelle Ko, Chan Lu, Alex Neel, Stella Oh, Anton Smith, and Curtiss Takada-Rooks. Darnise Martin continues to be an encouraging and inspiring sounding board. Thanks also to students Leslie Toapanta and Andrew Turner. At USC, Duncan Williams not only kindly and generously sponsored me, but also provided comments on the entire manuscript. Kana Sugita was always a friendly face on campus. UCLA has also provided a magnificent base for the final leg of revisions on the manuscript. My sincerest thanks to David Yoo, Gilbert Gee, and Melany De la Cruz-Viesca at the Asian American Studies Center for making this possible.

As I moved back and forth across the Pacific, numerous writing groups provided the critical feedback, moral support, and external deadlines necessary for finishing a project this daunting (and which will never feel finished). Skype and email allowed me to continue "meeting" with colleagues across locations and time zones. More than anyone else, Ryoko Yamamoto deserves special mention for her unwavering friendship and consistently helpful critical feedback on my writing (including comments on the entire draft). It is difficult to convey in words the depth and breadth of support she has provided over the years, and for which I am incredibly grateful. Regular meetings with Kyle Ikeda motivated me to keep progressing on this manuscript, and I have appreciated his critical feedback and encouragement (on the entire draft) over the years. Hugo Cordova Quero was a superb writing partner in person in Tokyo and virtually, as we both crossed oceans to different parts of the Americas. While based in Tokyo, Jeffrey Maret and David Cannell helped me work through various fledgling ideas as they took shape, and Greg Dvorak helped make the dissertation writing process more social. Once I moved back to California, Rachel Washburn provided consistent encouragement and much needed sociological perspectives on my work. Helene Kim Lee read through multiple book chapters and I learned much from reading her work on Korean American migration to South Korea. Lisa Hirai Tsuchitani carefully read through the entire manuscript and has been a great source of support since we first met.

In addition, a number of people have generously provided comments that improved this book. Many thanks to Nahum Chandler, Cindy Nakashima, Koz Sato, Lily Welty Tamai, Josh Paddison, and David Brunsma for reading book chapter drafts and Sharmilla Rudrappa for reading a book proposal draft. I also appreciate Stephen Murphy-Shigematsu and the anonymous reviewers for their feedback on the entire manuscript. Lynn Ritter's feedback improved the clarity and readability of the manuscript. Conversations with Pawan Dhingra, Nadia Kim, and Michael Omi have also greatly improved this work. Sonali Jain and Leslie Wang provided helpful advice about how to title this book.

I would also like to thank the various editors at Rutgers University Press who have helped me turn my manuscript into a book: Katie Keeran, Leslie Mitchner, Lisa Boyajian. Carrie Hudak, and Jaya Dalal provided great copyediting. Thank you also to the Japanese American National Museum (Gift of Hideo Date, 99.111) for permission to include Hideo Date's striking abstract piece *Mandara* in my book's cover design. Part of Chapter two was previously published in *Ethnic and Racial Studies*.

ACKNOWLEDGMENTS xvii

Support and encouragement have come in various forms over the years. Glen Fukushima generously helped me in a variety of ways, including inviting me to attend and present my work at his Japanese American Study Group in Tokyo. I also received materials and assistance from: Sherman Abe, Brent Ackerman, Adrian Favell, Donna Fujimoto, Eric Han, Evelyn Hu-DeHart, Kathryn Ibata-Ahrens, David Ida, Craig Ishii, Laura Kusaka, Rika Lee, Kathy Masaoka, Fuminori Minamikawa, Jim Minamoto, Mike Morizumi, Jean Oda Moy, Rika Nakamura, Art Nomura, Mytoan Nguyen-Akbar, Daniel Rosen, Susie Sakayori, Ed Sumoto, Okiyoshi Takeda, David Takeuchi, Michelle Mayo Tovik, J. K. Yamamoto, Ryan Yokota, Kosaku Yoshino, and Henry Yu. I have been able to present my work to diverse audiences thanks to Dean Adachi, John Campbell, Lon Kurashige, Gary Mukai, David Swanson, and Gabriele Vogt. Special thanks to Deborah Yamasaki, Lynn Sugiura, Makoto Takeda, the Kazuto Ezawa family, and Geoff, Diana, and Nicky Yeo/Lock.

Family has always been important to me and they have sustained me over the course of this project. My mother Christine has encouraged and supported my work in more ways than she probably realizes, as she provided rides to and from the airport and to interviews when I was in town visiting, told her friends about my research, and always seemed so excited to hear that my research and writing were progressing. She and my late father Richard have always encouraged me even when they haven't completely understood what I was doing or why I was doing it. My sisters Julie and Amy and their families, Mike, Brian, and Tracy; and Jason, Kalen, Alton, and Revin, have provided much-needed breaks from research and writing, while also making me feel supported and encouraged to keep working hard. They, along with other relatives and friends in the Bay Area, remind me that I have a community in Berkeley to which I will always belong. Thank you to the extended Fujimoto, Fujiwara, Lustig, Otani, Spielman, and Weitz families and the late Yamashiro uncles and aunts for being consistent sources of friendly encouragement. Uncle Bob deserves special mention for helping me maintain a transnational lifestyle over the years. Cousin Valerie graciously helped me find the cover art for the book. The late Shig Fujiwara and the Fujiwara family—Ruby, Gail, Rodney, Jill, Noah, and Kai—have supported me in numerous ways over the years, for which I am extremely grateful. Last but not least, thank you to Mark, perhaps the only person in the world who is more relieved and more satisfied than me that this book is finally in print. You constantly amaze me with how hard you work and the sacrifices you make to support me in pursuit of my goals.

# Note on Terminology

In this book, I use the term "Japanese American" to refer to US citizens of Japanese ancestry and focus on Japanese Americans born and raised in the United States. However, I recognize that Japanese Americans include people who are not US citizens and who may not have been born or raised in the United States. Thus, the Japanese Americans I focus on in this book are part of a larger ethnic Japanese population in the United States. I define Japanese American in this way because of my study's focus on experiences in Japan, rather than the United States; in the United States Japanese immigrants are included as Japanese Americans, while in Japan they are not, instead, typically considered Japanese living overseas.

In discussing Japanese migration to the United States, I use the terms "prewar" and "postwar" to describe major waves and the descendents of migrants from these time periods. I use "prewar wave Japanese Americans" and "prewar Japanese Americans" interchangeably, and "postwar wave Japanese Americans" and "postwar Japanese Americans" interchangeably.

Following conventions in sociology, I do not capitalize "white" or "black" in reference to racial categories. For the same reason, I also do not capitalize "issei" (first generation), "nisei" (second generation) or other generational markers for Japanese Americans, though I recognize that it has been a convention for scholars of Japanese American studies to do so.

When discussing Japanese Americans of mixed heritage, I refer to them as "mixed" rather than as "mixed-race" or "mixed-ethnicity" to focus on the mixed Japaneseness itself, rather than whether Japanese should be considered a race or an ethnicity. I use the terms "mixed-ancestry," "mixed-heritage," and "mixed" interchangeably. I avoid the language of mixed-race and mixed-ethnicity because in the United States and Japan constructions of race and ethnicity—and mixes of them—are categorized and given meaning

xix

differently. When interviewees use certain terms to refer to themselves, however, I adhere to their language.

I use the term *nikkeijin* to refer to the descendents of Japanese emigrants in the context of Japanese society. People in Japan and Japanese emigrants themselves tend to refer to Japanese emigrants as *nihonjin* so I do not include them as *nikkeijin*. In the US context *nikkei* is used more interchangeably with "Japanese American" and includes Japanese emigrants but it is important to note that these are two different terms used in different ways in Japan and in the United States.

At times I use the terms "America" and "American," though I recognize that this is a problematic term because many countries comprise the Americas. As much as possible, I try to be specific and use "United States" or "US citizen."

I put Japanese words in italics and do not capitalize them, though when interviewees had different ways of writing, I kept their original style to show that variations exist. I follow the Hepburn style of Romanization, where macrons indicate long vowels. In words commonly used in English, however, macrons are omitted (e.g., Tokyo instead of Tōkyō).

# Redefining Japaneseness

# Introduction

As he sat on the Narita-bound plane headed to Tokyo for a year of study abroad at International Christian University (ICU), Kevin finally had a moment to stop and think.¹ What had he gotten himself into? He only had a few years of college Japanese classes under his belt and had never lived in a foreign country before. His friends and immediate family were all in the United States. At the same time, Kevin was excited to have an adventure experiencing life outside of the United States. While he saw Japan as a foreign country, it was not just any foreign country since he had ancestral ties to it. His aunt had written down contact information for some distant relatives in Hiroshima. Were they his grandparents' cousins? Or were they his great-grandparents' cousins? In any case, he hoped to meet them during one of his school breaks in order to learn more about his family heritage.

Moreover, part of Kevin wondered if in Japan, he might finally feel "at home" and escape the microaggressions and racism he experienced in the United States. Although Kevin was born and raised in San Diego, other Americans often perceived him to be a foreigner. When they asked, "Where are you from?" and were not satisfied with "San Diego" as his response, Kevin knew that they were fixated on his East Asian phenotype and did not hear his native English, particularly his California accent. Being of Japanese ancestry and looking phenotypically similar to most Japanese people, he wondered if in Japan these same traits that marked him as a minority in the United States might finally lead to his acceptance as part of the majority in Japan.

After living for a while in Tokyo, Kevin found that his situation was much more complicated than he had expected. Sometimes he was interpreted as being Japanese, while at other times he was interpreted as being foreign. Sometimes he felt Japanese, and other times he felt foreign. When sitting on a train, he could blend in as part of the crowd, which made him feel like he was just another Japanese person in Japan. But sometimes he got lost riding the orange Chuo Line trains because he could not read all the signs or understand all the announcements. More than once, he accidentally got on an express train and missed his station, only accessible from a local train, which reminded him of his limited social knowledge and Japanese language ability and made him feel like he did not belong. Comments from Japanese people reflected similar fluctuations between being perceived as Japanese or foreign. For example, in some situations, he was complimented on his use of chopsticks (implicitly pointing out that he must not be Japanese), while in others, he was told how his "Japanese blood" explained his fondness for green tea. Similar to the United States, Japan has a particular set of social categories and meanings. And similar to his experiences in the United States, in Japan, Kevin felt a gap between how he saw himself and how others saw him within these larger social classifications.

Contrast Kevin's feelings with those of Cheryl, who grew up in Hawai'i. While Kevin romanticized Japan as a place where he might finally fit in, Cheryl imagined a relatively smooth transition to Japanese society because growing up in Honolulu, she was exposed to Japanese food, language, and culture in her everyday life. Like many Japanese Americans, Cheryl was familiar with Japanese concepts such as *gaman* (endurance), and *enryo* (holding back), so she did not expect much culture shock in Japan. But perhaps even more importantly, Cheryl never felt like a racial or ethnic minority in Hawai'i because of the large population of ethnic Japanese and their strong representation in mainstream society and culture.[2] So in contrast to Japanese Americans such as Kevin from the US continent, instead of being asked, "Where are you from?" and having to explain how she was born and raised in the United States, Cheryl was more used to having people in Hawai'i assume she was local and inquiring about which high school she had attended.

Thus, when Cheryl went to Japan as an Assistant Language Teacher (ALT) in the Japan Exchange and Teaching (JET) Program in a prefecture neighboring Tokyo, she was somewhat surprised at her inability to seamlessly melt into Japanese society. Similar to Kevin, she had some difficulty with everyday tasks such as maneuvering trains and reading restaurant menus. However, once Cheryl revealed she was from Hawai'i, the positive responses she received differed from the confused reactions from Japanese people when Kevin revealed that he was from the continental United States.

Unlike Kevin and Cheryl, who could phenotypically blend into crowds in Japan because of their black hair and dark brown eyes, Jocelyn, whose ancestry was a mix of Japanese and European, had a different experience due to her sandy blond hair and hazel eyes. Growing up in Oakland, California, Jocelyn had been involved from a young age in the local Japanese American community, attending a local Buddhist temple and learning traditional Japanese dance. She was excited to live in Tokyo, take Japanese language classes, and learn more about her mother's country. Similar to Kevin and Cheryl, she was sometimes interpreted as being Japanese and other times interpreted as being foreign. But for Jocelyn, sitting on trains and not speaking to anyone was when she was treated most like a foreigner, not a Japanese person. With a mother of Japanese ancestry from Japan and a father of mixed-European ancestry from the United States, it was only when she spoke Japanese or revealed her Japanese middle name that people in Japan became aware of her ancestral connections to Japan. And even then, rather than being mistaken for a Japanese person, Jocelyn was usually asked if she was *hāfu* (half Japanese).

Kevin, Cheryl, and Jocelyn's stories point to the complicated relationships and connections to Japan that shape how Japanese Americans experience living there. On the one hand, later-generation Japanese Americans may have little cultural knowledge about Japanese society and feel like they are living in a completely foreign country. On the other hand, being of Japanese ancestry and having grown up exposed to different forms of Japanese culture, they might go to Japan expecting cultural similarities. For those who are phenotypically similar to most Japanese and have experienced racial discrimination on the US continent, living and working in Japan offers the possibility of escaping to a land where they can physically blend. But for those who do not phenotypically blend in Japan, it is a struggle to have Japanese people acknowledge their shared ancestral ties.

Kevin, Cheryl, and Jocelyn's experiences raise questions about how Japanese American experiences in Japan are shaped by their perceived relationships to Japanese people and culture, including expectations of how Japanese people will treat them, as well as how they themselves will interpret and respond to how they are treated. Over time, as Japanese Americans become more familiar with the Japanese language and with Japanese cultural frameworks through repeated interactions with Japanese people in Japan, how might they alter their ways of identifying and create strategies for negotiating Japanese social categories? More broadly, how does the experience of Japanese Americans migrating to and living in Japan affect their understanding of Japaneseness and their identification as Japanese Americans?[3]

This book examines the contemporary experiences of US-born and raised Japanese American adult migrants residing in Tokyo in terms of how individual ways of identifying are shaped by larger social structures.[4] I investigate how Japanese Americans broaden their cultural "tool kit" (Swidler 1986) or repertoire of social knowledge that informs their behavior, as they learn about Japanese social classifications and the related expectations. Focusing on how Japanese American migrants perceive interactions in Japan, this book combines a micro-level approach with a transnational and global framework to show how the individual-level interaction of international migrants in the postmigration society (Japan) reflects the meeting of not only two societies but also of two systems of social classification. Ien Ang has commented that "the relation between 'where you're from' and 'where you're at' is a deeply problematic one" (Ang 2001: 30). In this study, I investigate the further complications that arise when you go "where you're from."

The migration of Japanese Americans to Tokyo is most commonly perceived as an example of a "return" to the homeland, of the "diaspora" "going back" to Japan, but this type of narrative masks some of the complexities of their experiences. The "return of the diaspora" paradigm (e.g., King and Christou 2010a, Lake 1995, Munz and Ohliger 2003, Tsuda 2009b) highlights the connections that Japanese Americans have to Japan since they can trace their family histories to ancestors in Japan. Indeed, most Japanese Americans I interviewed said that the connections they had to Japan mattered in choosing it as a destination. However, while ethnic ties mattered, for the majority of my Japanese American interviewees, multiple factors shaped the decision to live in Japan, with ethnic ties not being the determining one. In fact, the infrastructure of Tokyo, a global city which has businesses, educational institutions, and neighborhoods that rural areas do not (see Appendix A), was a major factor facilitating Japanese American migration to Japan. In contrast to most "ethnic return migrants" or "ethnic migrants," who take advantage of special visas acknowledging ancestral ties offered by the homeland government (Kulu 2001, Munz and Ohliger 2003, Tsuda 2009a), most Japanese Americans are residing in Japan through other kinds of visas (e.g., student, work, or spouse). This also differentiates them from the large population of Japanese Brazilians in Japan, most of whom do get visas as descendants of Japanese citizens.

As I discuss further below, Japanese American migration to Japan is best understood not as a "return of the diaspora," but as what I call an *ancestral homeland migration*. This concept avoids the connotation of "return" evident in the more common terms such as "ethnic return migration" and "diasporic return." I argue that the relationship of Japanese Americans to Japan is not that of a "diaspora" and a "homeland," but of different branches of what I call a *global ancestral group*. To see people of Japanese ancestry around the world as a global ancestral group is to see ancestral ties that link them, while at the same recognizing the diversity in the group caused by their history and socialization in specific societies. This concept also differs from diaspora because it makes no assumptions about how people of shared ancestry identify with each other or with the ancestral homeland. Moreover, using this framework of ancestral homeland migration and global ancestral groups enables discussion of Japanese American identity constructions in Japan that are transnational and, sometimes but not always, diasporic.

Japanese American identity constructions in Japan are transnational because they are shaped by social classification systems in both Japan and the United States. More specifically, I focus on how structures of race intersect with notions of culture and nation to cause shifting symbolic boundaries that include and exclude Japanese Americans depending on the context. Racial formation theory tells us that "our ability to interpret racial meanings depends on preconceived notions of a racialized social structure" and that "we expect people to act out their apparent racial identities" and "become disoriented when they do not" (Omi and Winant 1994: 59). In this light, Japanese American defiance of commonsensical expectations in Japanese society regarding the behavior and knowledge of "Japanese people" reflects their ambiguous positioning in the racial formation in Japan. Based on five years of ethnographic fieldwork in the Tokyo area and conducting more than 80 formal and many more informal interviews with Japanese Americans (see Appendices A and B for more on methodology), I investigate how residence in the ancestral homeland impacts perceptions of self in terms of race, ethnicity, and nation, as well as the relationship to the ancestral homeland.

## Global Ancestral Groups

I use the term *global ancestral group* to refer to a population that claims shared ancestral ties, is dispersed across multiple societies and nation-states, and includes people who are both oriented and not oriented toward the ancestral homeland. In this regard, a global ancestral group encompasses, but is not limited to, people with diasporic stances–it also includes people exhibiting nondiasporic stances. Members of a global ancestral group are historically and culturally linked, but their histories and identities have diversified due to different local contexts and the fluidity of culture in general.[5]

My concept of *global ancestral groups* addresses the limitations of applying a diaspora framework to Japanese American migration to and identity formations within their ancestral homeland of Japan. These limitations include the lack of a distinction between ancestry and homeland orientation; the inherent, contemporary centering of the ancestral homeland; and subsequent cultural essentialization, as well as the naturalization of migration to the ancestral homeland as a fulfillment of "diasporic return." Below I discuss how the concept of global ancestral groups 1) separates ancestry from identification with the ancestral homeland, 2) decenters the ancestral homeland as the contemporary cultural center, 3) provides a framework for comparative analysis by asserting that racial formations help explain the heterogeneity among branches of the global ancestral group, and 4) recasts migration to the ancestral homeland as a movement from one branch of the global ancestral group to another through the concept of *ancestral homeland migration*.

This framework provides the background for understanding why Japanese Americans in Japan learn to identify differently from their Japan-based counterparts and why there are further differences between identity constructions of Japanese Americans from the US continent and Hawai'i. Taken together, these aspects of a global ancestral group help to explain the simultaneous similarities to and differences from Japanese cultural forms in Japan that Japanese American migrants encounter and how these encounters shape their experiences and identity formations in Japan.

*Separating Ancestry from Identification with the Ancestral Homeland*

A global ancestral group is different from a diaspora because no assumptions are made about how members identify. Within a global ancestral group, some members exhibit diasporic homeland orientation, while other members do not. By acknowledging that some people of shared ancestry do not have a diasporic orientation, this concept distinguishes between being of a certain ancestry and being oriented toward the ancestral homeland, a distinction that is often missing from discussions framed by the concept of diaspora.

One limitation of the term diaspora as used in academic discourse is the attenuation in meaning where no distinction is made between people of shared ancestry who have a homeland orientation and those who do not (see Brubaker 2005, Dufoix 2008). Studies that examine "the ___ diaspora" are typically examples of this (see, for example, Adachi 2006, Cohen 1997, Sheffer 2003). Brubaker intervenes by proposing that only those who have a homeland orientation should be considered to be making diasporic claims because "not all those who are claimed as members of putative diasporas themselves adopt a diasporic stance" (Brubaker 2005: 12).[6] Since a population of shared ancestry is not the same as the subsection within it that has a "homeland orientation," it is only by making this distinction that we can empirically study the latter (Brubaker 2005: 13).

Following Brubaker, I distinguish between people of shared ancestry and the subgroup within that population that identifies with the ancestral homeland, recognizing the former to be a global ancestral group and the latter to be people with a diasporic stance. Making this distinction enables discussion about a population that claims shared ancestry and is dispersed globally—without making assumptions about how its members identify. Moreover, people of Japanese ancestry who do not exhibit a diasporic orientation would be a population without a name if we follow the aforementioned request by Brubaker to not call this population a "diaspora." By making this distinction, these nonhomeland-oriented, ethnic Japanese become a visible population within the global ancestral group.

"Ancestry" refers to claims of descent from a common homeland (Cornell and Hartmann 1998: 19).[7] In other words, perceived common descent from an identified, shared homeland constitutes the ancestral group. In this respect, Japanese Americans, as people from the United States who claim Japanese ancestry, all claim descent from people who have inhabited the geopolitical space currently referred to as "Japan."

To be clear, global ancestral groups is a concept that can be used for analyzing experiences and ways of identifying; it is not a way that people identify. Brubaker has pointed out that "we need to break with vernacular categories and common-sense understandings" to conduct our analyses (Brubaker 2002: 165). Thus, in stating that Japanese are a global ancestral group, I am not arguing that all people of Japanese ancestry globally identify with each other. Rather, I am asserting an analytic conceptualization of people who claim Japanese ancestry. Following Barth's view of ethnic groups as constructed against one another, I posit that once "Japan" was constructed as a nation, members of that nation were constructed as "Japanese," especially to outsiders. When people from Japan emigrated to other nations, "Japanese" as a category was constructed against other categories in places outside of Japan. So regardless of whether or not people across the globe who claim Japanese ancestry see themselves as a group, I call these people a Japanese global ancestral group in order to analyze them as a group.

People who claim Japanese ancestry represent a global ancestral group because they share claims to Japan as an ancestral homeland (as opposed to claims to somewhere else), even though the meaning and salience of "Japanese" as a group varies from place to place. Members of the Japanese global ancestral group are not all the same; the societal contexts in which they have grown up and been socialized make them different. Although a cultural and ethnic identity, rather than a political one such as "Asian American," the use of "Japanese" as a shared identity enables people "to understand unequal circumstances and histories as being related . . . but it may also inadvertently support the racist discourse that constructs [Japanese] as a homogeneous group" (Lowe 1996: 71). Especially in light of the discourse on Japanese homogeneity that has marginalized minority groups in Japan and of notions of racial purity that have marginalized Japanese Americans of mixed ancestry in the United States, it is important to see that this category is not homogeneous, even if we discuss it as a single category.

### Challenging the Ancestral Homeland as the Contemporary Cultural Center

To recognize both a shared past and diversity created through migration and history, drawing from Stuart Hall (1994), I conceptualize global ancestral groups as simultaneously exhibiting internal similarities and differences.[8] Members of a global ancestral group share claims to ancestry, culture, and history that are based in the past, but not necessarily in the present.[9] For some, identification with the ancestral homeland and its contemporary cultural forms is also based in the present, but this is only a subsection of the group who demonstrate a diasporic stance. In addition to those with a diasporic orientation, coethnics without a homeland orientation do not see the ancestral homeland as their contemporary cultural center.

Up to the point of emigration or displacement from the ancestral homeland and the emergence of separate branches of a global ancestral group, members of the group shared a common historical past and body of cultural references in the homeland. For ethnic Japanese in the United States, the shared past extends to the Meiji period in the late 1880s, when the first mass migration from Japan to Hawai'i and the US continent began. While they shared a past in Japan, with emigration and new experiences outside of the ancestral homeland, Japanese ancestry and culture took on new meanings as they were reconstructed against different groups in each racial formation, and "Japanese" people developed new histories and new ways of identifying, as a result.

Ien Ang rightly points out that the concept of diaspora highlights shared qualities and identities across or despite spatial distance, rather than differences among people who share ancestry. Challenging this idea of "sameness-in-dispersal" (2001: 13) centered in the ancestral homeland, Ang protests that "Being Chinese outside China cannot possibly mean the same thing as inside. It varies from place to place, moulded by the local circumstances in different parts of the world where people of Chinese ancestry have settled and constructed new ways of living. There are, in this paradigm, many different Chinese identities, not one" (Ang 2001: 38).

In the same vein, being Japanese outside Japan cannot possibly mean the same thing as being Japanese inside Japan. Japaneseness varies from

INTRODUCTION                                                                9

place to place, shaped by where people of Japanese ancestry have settled and developed new communities. As Arif Dirlik points out, by focusing on place, identities are historicized and located within specific societal contexts (Dirlik 1999: 47). The point that there are many different Japanese identities, not just one, is illustrated by how Japanese identities reference overlapping yet different meanings on the US continent, in Hawai'i, and in Japan, as discussed further in Chapter One.

I conceptualize global ancestral groups as being comprised of "branches," with the ancestral homeland as one of many branches. This is in contrast to the concept of diaspora, which separates the homeland from populations abroad in a bifurcated fashion. My formulation of ancestral groups at the global level that have diverse "branches" is similar to Barth's discussion of an ethnic group "spread over a territory with varying ecologic circumstances" that exhibits "regional diversities" (Barth 1969: 12).

Branches of a global ancestral group are societies, not necessarily limited to nation-states. Here I take seriously Wimmer and Glick Schiller's (2002) critique that social scientists presume nation-states to be the basic unit of analysis for studying international migration. In my formulation, Hawai'i and the US continent are two different branches of the Japanese global ancestral group despite being in the same country.

Making the ancestral homeland one of many branches of the global ancestral group effectively decenters it as necessarily being the contemporary cultural center, while still recognizing its critical role in the past. If the ancestral homeland is seen as the authentic cultural center, then populations outside of it will always be seen as inauthentic, lacking, and diluted. A diasporic framing perceives coethnic populations outside of the homeland to be extensions of the homeland, not as ontologically distinct, unique communities that have created their own "authentic" cultural forms (see Ang 2001). As Chapter Five will demonstrate, my Japanese American interviewees asserted that Japan is not always a cultural center of Japaneseness for them.

The global ancestral group concept also decenters the ancestral homeland by recognizing how coethnic cultural forms reference and center cultural forms from different historical periods. Even in Japan alone, the meaning of Japaneseness has changed over time and is constantly reconstructed. The multiplicity of Japanese identities across the globe derives from the particular historical and material circumstances in which they were created, as Japanese emigrants brought historically situated cultural forms with them and also developed new ones, as well as from the historical and cultural change within Japan. Lisa Lowe observes, "The making of [Japanese] culture includes practices that are partly inherited, partly modified, as well as partly invented;

[Japanese] culture also includes the practices that emerge in relation to the dominant representations that deny or subordinate [Japanese and Japanese American] cultures as 'other'" (Lowe 1996: 65). Here Lowe is pointing out that power dynamics, as well as the political and economic structures in which identities are constructed and associated with a minority or majority positioning, also matter.

### *Heterogeneity and Comparative Racial Formations*

Examining the migration experiences of Japanese Americans in Japan highlights the heterogeneity among branches of a global ancestral group caused by different "racial formations" or "racialized social structures." These formations or structures are hegemonic, institutionalized, racial classification systems that vary according to society (see Bonilla-Silva 1997, Omi and Winant 1994). Diverse socio-historical constructions of race (e.g., as based on phenotypical characteristics, socioeconomic status, and perceived "bloodlines") shape how branches of an ancestral group are interpreted and positioned within each social hierarchy (see Braziel 2008: 135). Moreover, seeing the heterogeneity caused by racial formations enables comparative analysis of ethnic forms.

In the United States, race tends to be understood largely in terms of phenotypical differences (e.g., Cornell and Hartmann 2007, Feagin and Feagin 1999, Schaefer 2011). This is partly due to the fact that in the US context, racial categories are panethnic, where ethnicity is equated with nationality. In other words, the scholarship on race in the United States typically views ethnonational groups as aggregated within larger racial groups, associating racial lines with phenotypical differences (also acknowledging ancestry as relevant per the one-drop-rule).

But this is not the only way to conceive of race—in other countries, including Japan, race is often understood in terms of national differences.[10] In Japan, rather than phenotype alone, race incorporates ideas of both ethnicity and nation (Morris-Suzuki 1998, Sugimoto 2010, Yoshino 1992). Analyzing Japanese American migrant experiences in Japan illuminates the gap between understanding race largely in terms of phenotype in the United States and understanding race as nation in Japan, where phenotypically similar groups, such as Koreans, Chinese, and Japanese, are treated as being racially different.

To highlight societal processes of racialization, other work has investigated the racialization of multiple ethnic groups within a single nation-state, but this study takes a different approach by focusing on one ethnic group across societies. Research has shown how ethnic identity options for people

INTRODUCTION

of Chinese, Japanese, and Korean ancestry are limited by racialization within the US context (Kibria 2002a, Tuan 1998). In contrast, my project explores how the structural incorporation of an ethnic group differs from society to society by focusing on people of Japanese ancestry on the US continent, in Hawai'i, and Japan.

The formation of different Japanese American migrant identities in a new racial context illuminates the construction of social categories, boundaries, and meanings (Cornell and Hartmann 2007, Lamont and Molnar 2002) by showing how the same bodies are differently racialized and categorized in the United States and Japan. When Japanese Americans migrate from the United States to Japan, most shift from being racial and ethnic minorities to being part of the racial and ethnic majority, reflecting movement between branches of the global ancestral group. Kevin, whose story began this chapter, is one example. At the same time, the study of migration from multicultural Hawai'i, where ethnic Japanese are not a minority, to "monoracial" Japan reveals further differences in meaning attached to Japaneseness. These varied constructions of Japaneseness reflect varied structures of race more broadly and systemically, including the specific ways in which race intersects with the concepts of ethnicity and nation in each society.

The unevenness between branches of a global ancestral group shapes and is shaped by relationships to indigenous populations and related minority or majority positioning in each society. On the US continent, Japanese Americans are part of the larger Asian American racial minority group, one of many groups "of color." Even though Asian Americans are a settler population on the US continent, because of the way the racial formation on the US continent has taken shape in relation to white supremacist and settler politics, native peoples are typically grouped with settler racial minorities as "people of color."[11]

However, in Hawai'i the relationship of Japanese to Native Hawaiians is sometimes differentiated as settler versus native. Japanese settler history is more contentious because of the prominent position and larger population of ethnic Japanese in Hawai'i. Progressive activists and scholars often point out that as settlers with strong political representation and cultural power, Japanese in Hawai'i should be seen as settler colonials, rather than more benignly as "locals" or a "multicultural" group where natives and settlers are perceived to be equally invested in the future of Hawai'i (see Fujikane and Okamura 2000, 2008). Thus, even though people of Japanese ancestry are not a numerical majority in Hawai'i, their status as part of the power majority differently influences their relationship to indigenous and other populations.

Similarly, in Japan, Japanese also have a contentious relationship with the indigenous populations. The myth of Japan as being racially homogeneous has led to the denial of indigenous (and racial minority) populations, including the colonization of the Ainu in the north and Okinawans in the south (see Cotterill 2011, Hein and Selden 2003, lewallen 2008, Lie 2001, Morris-Suzuki 1998, Rabson 2012, Siddle 1997, 2009).

Finally, the heterogeneity of a global ancestral group, caused by different racial formations, can further be conceptualized in terms of mixed ancestry. Japanese in the United States have been a mixed-ancestry community since the early settlers in the late nineteenth century (Nakashima, Welty, and Williams 2013). Moreover, Japanese are increasingly a mixed-ancestry population in Japan, Hawai'i, and on the US continent (Dariotis 2003, Lise 2011, Okamura 2002b, 2008). Anyone with Japanese ancestry is part of the Japanese global ancestral group. However, at the same time, people of multiple ancestries are part of multiple global ancestral groups. It is also important to note that ancestral claims are not the same as ethnic identity claims. That is, someone can be of a particular ancestry but not necessarily ethnically identify with it. For example, transracial adoptees not raised within families or communities of shared ancestry may not grow up identifying with their biological parents' heritage and cultural forms.

Studies of diaspora have not explicitly included populations of mixed ancestry, but the ways in which global coethnics imagine ties to each other are shaped by the history and politics of what is considered "racial mixing" in each society. Moreover, examining the experiences of mixed-ancestry Japanese Americans in Japan along with those who claim only Japanese ancestry highlights how much phenotype and name markers of Japaneseness shape strategies for interacting with Japanese people and limit options for identification. As mixed Japanese populations in the United States, Japan, and elsewhere continue to increase, this mixedness will become more and more central to Japanese American studies, Japanese studies, and discussions of Japaneseness.

## Ancestral Homeland Migration

*Ancestral homeland migration* refers to the movement of global coethnics to their ancestral homeland, regardless of whether or not the migrants identify with it. I conceptualize Japanese American migration to Japan as an ancestral homeland migration, rather than as any type of "return" migration, including "ethnic return" and "diasporic return."[12] Avoiding the paradigm of "return" recognizes how some global coethnics do not identify with the ancestral homeland even though they migrate and live there.[13]

One problem with the paradigm of "return" migration is that it is applied unevenly across ancestral backgrounds, reflecting constructions of race and ethnicity more than an actual linkage to the ancestral homelands. For example, in the United States, Asian Americans who go to Asia or African Americans who go to Africa are commonly described as "going back," even when they were born and raised in the United States and have never been to their ancestral homelands. In contrast, European Americans who go to Europe are rarely perceived through the same paradigm of "return."[14] What ideological and discursive assumptions are being made when people born and raised in the United States are described as "returning" to a country in which they have never lived?

When mainstream discourse perceives migration to the ancestral homeland to be a "return," it essentializes members of the global ancestral group as the same regardless of place and socialization and expects these migrants to have a relatively smooth transition "back home." This suggests that for some ethnic and racial groups in the United States—but not others—there is a presumed connection to their ancestral homelands that is perceived to persist regardless of generations removed. As Andrea Louie has pointed out, for Chinese Americans, the US multiculturalist discourse "both excludes them from cultural citizenship in the United States and associates them, willingly or not, with their ancestral homeland" (Louie 2004: 96). Indeed, the perception of immutable ties to the ancestral homeland is related to presumptions of disconnect from other Americans and of exclusion from full cultural and racial citizenship in the United States.

When the migration of Japanese Americans to Japan is seen as movement between branches of a global ancestral group, as I have posited, rather than from "overseas" to the homeland, the paradigm of "return" is not imposed. This paradigm shift allows for different types of analysis, including the migration of global coethnics to global cities within the ancestral homeland, rather than only to ancestral villages. That is, Japanese American migration to the Tokyo area can be analyzed differently from migration to more rural areas to which most ethnic Japanese—in and outside of Japan—claim ancestral ties. Ancestral ties are often conceived of in terms of nations but within the nation, living close to the ancestral village—or not—also matters.

In addition, the concept of ancestral homeland migration recognizes generational diversity in this migration. Some generational diversity has been acknowledged within the "return" paradigm but focuses only on differences between the "return" migration of first-generation emigrants who are physically returning and the "ethnic return" of second- and later-generation people born and raised outside of the ancestral homeland (e.g., Tsuda 2009b). Notions of diaspora and related concepts such as Appadurai's (1996) "ethnoscapes" do not account for the generational differences within a group caused by multiple waves of ancestral homeland emigration. For Japanese Americans, this is the divide between Japanese immigrants in the prewar and postwar periods, cut into two major waves due to US immigration policies that terminated large-scale immigration from Japan between 1924 and 1952. Among the descendents of emigrants, generational diversity shapes ancestral homeland migration experiences. As described in Chapter Five, Japanese American ancestral homeland migrants with and without parents raised in Japan differ in how they interpret their experiences in Japan.

Finally, my study highlights the gap between the abstract and sometimes idealized notion of diaspora among scholars and coethnics residing outside of the homeland and the lived realities of negotiating social categories in the homeland. By focusing on the lived experiences and social interactions of Japanese Americans in Japan, it becomes clear how they and other global coethnics do not fit easily into Japan-based social categories. Rather than decontextualize coethnics by using a diasporic lens, this book examines global coethnics specifically within the homeland's social classification systems to see how they negotiate that society, as well as how people in the homeland perceive them.

## Transnational Ancestral Homeland Migrant Identities

Once Japanese is seen as a global ancestral group, the migration of Japanese Americans to Japan becomes an ancestral homeland migration—and the identities that they construct in Japan are transnational, not necessarily diasporic. In this context, "transnationalism" refers to contemporary "lived" connections between international migrants and the societies from which they came, while "diaspora" implies orientation specifically toward one's national homeland. This distinction is important to make because it includes analysis of Japanese Americans who, in the United States, have not previously identified with Japan and would not have been considered diasporic or transnational before migrating to Japan (see Tsuda 2012).

Using a transnational lens to understand identity construction for Japanese American migrants in their ancestral homeland combines the basic sociological premise that individuals comprise and are shaped by social structures with the acknowledgment that societies are linked to one another through international migrants. If individuals embody societies (Cooley 1902, Mead 1934), since through socialization they internalize the social norms of a particular place, then when they migrate and interact with people in a new society, this individual-level contact is actually the meeting of two different societies and cultures, including two racial formations (see Joseph 2015, Kim 2008, Louie 2004, Roth 2012).

With this in mind, it is clear that Japanese Americans construct transnational identities through individual interactions in Japan. Identities are created through social interaction, a dialectical process of social categorization by others and individual identity assertion (Barth 1969, Cornell and Hartmann 1998, Goffman 1959, Jenkins 2004, Mead 1934). Social categorization by others within the new postmigration society occurs according to the norms of that society. Individual identity assertion may reflect the social position in the premigration society, since individuals embody larger social structures. Identities are multiple, fluid, and contextual, making identity formation an ongoing process of construction, reconstruction, and negotiation of both past and present perceptions of self, as well as social categories. This process continually incorporates changes in context, including time and place (Giddens 1990). Using a transnational framework to understand Japanese American identity formation in Japan means situating interactions within social categories in both Japan and the United States, enabling comparative analysis of their social classification systems.

In contrast to most research on transnational migrant identity formation, which focuses on movement to the United States to become racial and ethnic minorities, this book examines the transnational identity formation of Japanese Americans specifically as ancestral homeland migrants from the United States who become part of the racial and ethnic majority in Japan. A transnational framework highlights how Japanese Americans remain connected to the United States even when they go abroad to their ancestral homeland because they embody an American cultural framework. Seeing them as transnational migrants highlights this deterritorialized national identity and linkage to the United States (the premigration society), even as Japanese Americans live and interact with people in Japan (the postmigration society).

At the same time, however, the Japanese heritage of Japanese Americans certainly affects how people in Japan perceive and treat them, as well as how they interpret their migration to and experiences in Japan. In this way, they also need to be seen as "ancestral homeland migrants" or later-generation ethnics who migrate to their ancestral homeland. Depending on whether emphasis is placed on migrant connections to the premigration society or to the postmigration society, either national ties to the United States or ancestral connections to Japan become more significant. In reality, both types of linkages shape Japanese American interactions in Japan, making them what I call transnational ancestral homeland migrants.

## Transnational Racial and Ethnic Identity Formation

Most research on transnational racial and ethnic identity formation has investigated how people migrate to the United States and are put into US racial categories to become racial minorities in the United States: "black," "Hispanic/Latino," "Asian," and "white" (Cobas, Duany, and Feagin 2009, Foner 2005, Kim 2008, Rodriguez 2000, Roth 2012, Waters 1999). This research has tended not to look at migrant flows in the opposite direction or at the process of becoming part of the racial majority. This body of work can be enriched by an examination of how US racial categories continue to shape migrant experiences and identities outside of the United States when Americans migrate abroad and adapt to new social classifications. Further ramifications can be unveiled by investigating the racialization processes involved in shifting from being a racial and ethnic minority to being part of the racial and ethnic majority.

In contrast to unidirectional immigration studies that focus on adaptation, acculturation, and integration to the postmigration society (e.g., Alba and Nee 2003, Gordon 1964, Portes and Zhou 1993), a transnational framework illuminates how people can be connected to multiple places at the same time. Individuals interpret conversation and other forms of social interaction according to the societies in which these exchanges take place, but a transnational framework recognizes that international migrants also continue to be influenced by previous societies in which they have resided. This "challenge[s] our previous conflation of geographic space and social identity" (Basch, Schiller, and Blanc 1994: 8). For Japanese Americans in Tokyo, this means that even as they navigate Japanese society, American ways of thinking, acting, and interpreting the world continue to influence them and the identities they claim in Japan.

American ways of interpreting the world include mixed messages about people of Asian descent in the United States. In the US context, constructions of Americanness simultaneously reject and incorporate Asianness (Lowe 1996, Palumbo-Liu 1999). Historically, by defining "the American *citizen*" against "the Asian *immigrant*" in legal, economic, and cultural terms, "Asian immigrants [are cast] both as persons and populations to be integrated into the national political sphere and as the contradictory, confusing, unintelligible elements to be marginalized and returned to their alien origins" (Lowe 1996: 4; italics in original). The United States has a history of including people of Asian descent through labor participation in the building of the nation, while at the same time repudiating them due to racism and xenophobia. As a result, Japanese Americans sometimes think of themselves as Americans and sometimes do not.

Recognizing the identities that Japanese Americans construct in Japan as being transnational reveals how US cultural frameworks for understanding the world extend beyond the geopolitical space of the United States and explores the ability of a minority to represent the United States in an international context. Studies of cultural imperialism tend to examine inequalities in global influence through critical analyses of media representation, global capitalism, and modernity (Tomlinson 1991), typically focusing on textual or structural processes. The experience of Americans migrating abroad adds to this work by analyzing the social positioning and interactions of Americans outside of the United States. Japanese American interpretations of Japanese society, people from other countries, and international events reflect American attitudes and perspectives.

At the same time, Japanese interpretations of Japanese Americans as being Americans, Japanese, or otherwise, draw from knowledge about the United States. When a Japanese person is told that a Japanese-looking person is an American, s/he often responds with a question about who in the family is American (i.e., "white"). Another example is my acupuncturist in Shibuya, who, in 2009, told me he was impressed that the United States had a black president. Such comments reflect interpretations of Americanness, which are typically racialized white. This book examines how Japanese Americans respond to these questions and comments, as well as how Japanese understandings of Americanness shape Japanese American understandings of what it means to be Japanese as well as of what it means to be American. In addition, these interactions reveal the broader construction of Americanness outside of the United States.

### Ancestral Homeland Migrant Identity Constructions

At the same time that transnational processes continue to link Japanese Americans back to the United States, ancestral ties and interactions with Japanese shape their experiences in Japan. To see Japanese Americans as ancestral homeland migrants illuminates the general experiences and social processes of descendents of emigrants migrating to their ancestral homelands—within both general patterns as well as those pertaining to Americans in particular. In addition, Japanese American ancestral homeland migrant experiences can be contextualized within larger migrant flows to Japan, comparing them to most other foreign nationals in Japan, including *nikkeijin* (descendants of Japanese emigrants) from other countries. Placing Japanese Americans in these various migration streams points to their unique positioning as Americans of color migrating to their ancestral homeland, another highly industrialized nation.

Previous research has found that when people migrate to their ancestral homelands, it becomes clear how they are different from local residents (Kim 2009, Tsuda 2003), but these studies have assumed that nations were the appropriate unit of analysis for understanding these differences. Takeyuki Tsuda points out that "during the migratory process, the emphasis shifts from race to culture as the main determinant of ethnic inclusion or exclusion" (2009a: 326) because ancestral homeland migrants "strengthen their nationalist attachments to their countries of birth in response to their ethnic and socioeconomic marginalization in their ancestral homelands" (2009a: 334). But even if ancestral homeland migrants feel marginalized in the ancestral homeland, nationalist attachments are not the only forms of identification which may become stronger (see, for example, Takenaka 2009). In Chapter Two, I examine how Japanese American ancestral homeland migrants from Hawai'i and the US continent develop different ways of identifying in Japan, neither of which are simply national identities as "Americans," even though both groups are from the United States.

Comparative studies have found ancestral homeland migrations to be hierarchically organized, whereby migrants from the Global North tend to enjoy better employment, housing, and other social privileges and opportunities than migrants from the Global South (Lee 2009, Seol and Skrentny 2009, Yamashiro and Quero 2012). Most research on ancestral homeland migration has examined movement from less industrialized, peripheral countries to more highly industrialized, core nations, characterized by economic disparities between premigration nations and the ancestral homeland (e.g., Cook-Martín and Viladrich 2008, Song 2009, Tsuda 2003).

In contrast, studying American ancestral homeland migrations can shed light on a more privileged migrant experience. For example, the ancestral homeland migrations of US citizens to India (Jain 2011, 2012), China (Louie 2004, Wang 2016), Vietnam (Nguyen 2014), and South Korea (Kibria 2002b, Kim 2009) invert typical migration patterns by focusing on movement from the Global North to the Global South. Studies on American ancestral homeland migrations have highlighted the global status associated with Americanness, especially in terms of economic capital and potential to contribute to economic development in the ancestral homeland (Bruner 1996). But the movement of ancestral homeland migrants between the two highly industrialized core nations of the United States and Japan highlights different intersections of race and nation at the top of the global economic hierarchy, where the gap between national economies is not as large and the economic strength of the United States is relatively less salient.

Among migrants specifically to Japan, Japanese Americans sit at an unusual, privileged intersection as ancestral homeland migrants from the United States. Ancestral homeland migrants in Japan are known as *nikkeijin* and are overwhelmingly from Brazil, where they are typically middle class.[15] But in Japan, they perform blue-collar work in factories, mostly in industrial areas, because the pay is better. As Portuguese speakers from a less industrialized nation, they lack the cultural capital afforded to English speakers and Westerners. Despite having middle-class occupations and lifestyles in Brazil, the great majority do not transfer their skills and educational background to take on white-collar employment in Japan (see Yamashiro and Quero 2012). Moreover, with the difference in national economies, while working in factories in Japan, most can earn five to ten times what they earned in white-collar jobs in Brazil (Tsuda 2003). Since most Japanese Brazilians migrated to Japan by taking advantage of the "long-term resident" visa, which is available to people of Japanese ancestry up to the third generation, their presence in Japan has been understood to be related to the privileging of their ancestral ties to Japan (see Sellek 1997, Yamanaka 1993) and as a form of "ethnic return" migration (Tsuda 2003).

In contrast, US citizens make up a large proportion of the population of Westerners who overall can be found as students and white-collar workers in various professions. In Japan, particularly in urban areas, being a native English speaker is a form of cultural capital that provides access to white-collar work (such as teaching English) that values Western (particularly US) college degrees. Thus, in some ways, Japanese Americans are similar to other highly skilled Westerners concentrated in Tokyo, but they are not white (though some are mixed). In fact, within the Western expatriate communities, Japanese Americans are racial and ethnic minorities. To see them as *nikkeijin* is to acknowledge their ethnic similarities to Japanese, but unlike the majority of *nikkeijin* in Japan, they are performing skilled work and are concentrated in Tokyo. In addition, most are not on a *"nikkeijin* visa" (i.e., long-term resident visa).

Finally, unlike other international migrants in Japan, who are neither ethnically Japanese nor from Western, highly industrialized countries and who tend to have tenuous visa statuses and experience various forms of discrimination, Japanese Americans are privileged in terms of both race and nationality. Hence, the migration of Japanese Americans highlights the multiple and intersecting hierarchies of nationality, race, and class in migrant flows to Japan, manifested in residential patterns, employment opportunities, and the transfer of human capital skills.

## Ethnicity, Diaspora, Transnationalism, and Asian Americans

The concepts of global ancestral groups and ancestral homeland migrations are useful in discussing not only Japanese Americans and their migration to Japan, but other Asian American experiences and ways of identifying as well. Considering Asian American connections to global coethnics in terms of global ancestral groups and migrations to Asia as ancestral homeland migrations addresses some problems with existing frameworks for discussing Asian American relationships to Asia.

Since the 1990s, Asian American Studies scholars have been critically discussing ways to rethink the connection between Asian Americans and Asia. The dominant framing of Asian Americans since the establishment of the field in the late 1960s and early 1970s has been to establish their histories and identities in the United States as US-based, even as solidarity with people outside of the United States was being expressed (Wong 1995: 3). In response to the mainstream racialization of Asians as foreigners despite generations of developing local communities in the United States, Asian American scholars and activists have emphasized that Asian immigrants and their descendents are Americans. While US-born and raised Asian Americans can be seen as American due to citizenship and upbringing, Asian immigrants are also included as American because they have chosen to live in the United States and become part of this country. In other words, where one chooses to reside supposedly reflects how s/he identifies.

As globalization, transnationalism, and diaspora have become popular analytical frameworks across academia and as post-1965 Asian migration to the United States has created vibrant, immigrant-replenished communities, research on Asian Americans has framed them as more connected to Asia. In response to this literature casting Asian Americans as diasporic and transnational, critiques have also emerged. Dirlik, for instance, warned that the idea of diaspora abolishes the difference between Chinese Americans and Chinese (1999: 44) and "distances the so-called diasporic populations from their immediate environments, rendering these populations into foreigners" (1999: 47). In her influential essay, "Denationalization Reconsidered," Sau-ling Wong expressed concern that recognized the problem mentioned earlier in this Introduction: that it is unclear whether the concept of diaspora implies ethnicity alone or if it also suggests a homeland orientation. While some Asian immigrants and their transnational children may demonstrate a homeland orientation, Wong pointed out that if US-born Asian Americans are cast as diasporic, they "may be left without a viable discursive space." That is, since "diasporic" typically refers to the immigrant generation, "what would be the meaning of preferring a diasporic outlook for the American-born generation?" (Wong 1995: 16).

Moreover, in developing frameworks that connect Asian Americans to Asia and bridge the epistemological gap between Asian American and Asian Studies, scholars have proposed the terms "Asian diaspora" (Chuh and Shimakawa 2001) and "Asian diasporas" (Parreñas and Siu 2007). These concepts attempt to rethink in creative ways how Asian Americans and Asians in Asia can be analyzed within a single framework, but by building on the concept of "diaspora," both of these concepts inadvertently center Asian homelands, separate them from populations abroad, and continue to obscure the complicated relationships and ways of identifying expressed by Asian Americans who are sometimes homeland-oriented but other times not.

I offer the concept of global ancestral groups as a way to analyze Asian Americans and Asians in the same framework without centering Asia or assuming that Asian Americans identify with their ancestral homelands. For example, the notion of global ancestral groups can be applied to Asian Americans to illuminate the similarities and differences among global ancestral Filipinos, Vietnamese, or Indians. How have emigration and changes in the ancestral homeland differently shaped forms of culture and identification for populations of shared ancestry? By recognizing the difference between ancestry and identity, in addition to factoring in socialization in particular places, the concept of global ancestral groups can also account for adoptees from places such as South Korea or China who are spread out globally.

The concept of global ancestral groups also differentiates between ethnic and diasporic identities in the United States. Ethnic identities are focused on and based in US ethnic communities as well as on their shared history. Diasporic identities are oriented toward the ancestral homeland. This, of course, is an analytic distinction that is not very clear-cut in everyday life. Nonetheless, whether Asian Americans are identifying with forms of identity and culture that are based in the United States or in Asia, or often times a mix of the two, it is important to point out the distinction, especially as Asian American identities become increasingly complex and transnational in the modern era of globalization.

Finally, the concept of ancestral homeland migration enables analysis of Asian American migrations to Asia that recognizes the varied reasons why people migrate and ways that they identify in the context of their ancestral homeland. As more and more Americans work abroad, Chinese Americans are finding work in Beijing (Wang 2016); Korean Americans are moving to Seoul (Lee 2009); Vietnamese Americans are working in Ho Chi Minh

City (Nguyen-Akbar 2014), and Indian Americans are finding employment in places such as Mumbai and New Delhi (Jain 2010, 2011). While some of these migrants, especially those who are second-generation, may identify with their ancestral homelands and move there due to diasporic longings, the concept of ancestral homeland migrations provides an epistemological framework that also accounts for those who migrate for other reasons.

## Overview of Remaining Chapters

Chapter One provides the background for the rest of the book by juxtaposing constructions of Japaneseness in the continental United States, Hawai'i, and Japan. Japanese Americans bring internalized notions of what it means to be "Japanese" with them from the US continent and Hawai'i to Japan, where they encounter a different form of Japaneseness that sometimes does not include them. This chapter prepares the reader to understand Japanese American encounters in Japan, as well as the reflections on their experiences in Japan that Japanese Americans have after they return to the United States.

Together, Chapters Two, Three, and Four focus on how Japanese Americans negotiate everyday experiences in Japan. They examine the shifting ways that Japanese Americans identify as they interact with Japanese people and navigate interpretations of them based on social categories and boundaries in Japan. These detailed descriptions of their experiences in Japan lead into the discussion of how Japanese Americans who return to the United States view and sometimes learn to differentiate between forms of Japanese culture.

Specifically, Chapter Two concentrates on national and racial identities. Most strikingly, Japanese Americans from Hawai'i and the US continent who phenotypically blend in Japan learn to reconstruct different kinds of identities. That is, ethnic Japanese from the US continent who are phenotypically similar to most Japanese but not culturally or linguistically competent in Japanese society reconstruct identities as "Japanese Americans," in contrast to ethnic Japanese from Hawai'i who reconstruct "Hawai'i" identities. These two different identities that Japanese Americans construct in Japan reflect how geopolitical distinctions in the Japanese global ancestral group can be reconstructed abroad.

Chapter Three investigates the experiences of Japanese Americans of mixed heritage in Japan. I begin with an overview of *hāfu* and *hapa*, terms that are commonly used to refer to mixed Japanese in Japan and the United States, respectively. Then I present five narrative portraits of Japanese Americans of mixed ancestry whose experiences showcase similarities because they claim Japanese and other ancestries, as well as differences due to phenotype; the knowledge level of Japanese language, culture, and society; and the number of generations removed from Japan.

Chapter Four delves into how Japanese Americans use linguistic and cultural knowledge to manage Japanese expectations of them. Depending on their Japanese language fluency, immersion in Japanese society, and length of residence in Japan, Japanese Americans selectively use Japanese and English in a variety of ways. Using the multiple Japanese alphabets, they also present themselves strategically, highlighting their Japaneseness or foreignness through the usage of *kanji* (Chinese characters used by most Japanese in Japan) and *katakana* (used for foreign words). Phenotype and other factors also affect Japanese American language usage in Japan.

Through interviews with Japanese Americans who have returned to the United States, Chapter Five follows Japanese Americans back across the Pacific to shed light on how residing in Japan has shaped their sense of Japaneseness and relationship to Japan. Generational and gendered factors influence how Japanese Americans reflect on their experiences in Japan.

Moreover, the ways in which Japanese Americans relate to Japan are reflective of their geographic diversity. After living in Japan, Japanese Americans who are enmeshed in large, Japanese American communities identify with Japanese American culture as being ontologically distinct from Japan-based culture. However, Japanese Americans who do not live near or feel connected to large, Japanese American communities see Japan as their cultural center of Japaneseness. In addition, Japanese Americans from Hawai'i ontologically distinguish between forms of Japaneseness in Hawai'i, the US continent, and in Japan.

Finally, in the Conclusion, I discuss what Japanese American identity formations in Japan and the concept of global ancestral groups reveal about the relationship between ancestry, identity, and place and how they facilitate discussion about the reconstruction of different types of identities in Japan, ending with comments on how this study challenges the boundaries of Asian American and Asian Studies.

CHAPTER 1

# Japanese as a Global Ancestral Group

## JAPANESENESS ON THE US CONTINENT, HAWAIʻI, AND JAPAN

When Japanese Americans migrate to and live in Japan, they encounter a new form of Japaneseness that has been created within a different social structure. Due to the varied social formations in which it has been constructed, "Japanese" takes on different meanings on the continental United States, Hawaiʻi, and Japan. In order to understand Japanese American experiences in Japan, it is necessary to understand the larger social formations of both the places from which and into which they migrate, especially the disparate notions of what it means to be Japanese in each place. Japanese American interactions with *nihonjin* (Japanese in Japan) are shaped by these larger social contexts, as *nihonjin* interpret Japanese Americans within normative social categories in Japan. At first, Japanese Americans interpret and respond to *nihonjin* based on the commonsensical views that they have internalized and brought with them from the United States. Over time, as subsequent chapters will show, Japanese Americans acclimate to Japan-based notions of Japaneseness and adapt their strategies for interpreting situations and strategically presenting certain pieces of information about themselves.

This chapter provides an overview of these contexts between which my Japanese American interviewees are migrating, describing the multiple constructions of Japaneseness on the continental United States, Hawaiʻi, and Japan. Rather than attempt to provide a comprehensive historical comparison, I review the three forms of Japaneseness to show how each context has differently shaped what it means to be Japanese. I theorize Japaneseness in each of these social formations as branches of a global ancestral group that claim shared ancestry and are historically and culturally linked, but factors such as local geopolitical, historical, and power contexts also make them distinct. Since global ancestral group is an analytic construct, it is a way of thinking about and discussing Japaneseness on a comparative basis. It does not reflect how individual people of Japanese ancestry identify and see connections to one another. After reviewing the distinct, empirical forms of Japaneseness, it will be easier to understand why the Japanese Americans I interviewed learn to identify in Japan as not Japanese. It will also help explain why Japanese Americans from the US continent and Hawai'i construct different ways of identifying in Japan.

### Ethnic Japanese on the US Continent

On the US continent, ethnic Japanese are a numeric minority, as well as a minority in terms of power and representation. According to US Census data, there are 1,043,168 (US Census Bureau 2013) people residing on the US continent who claim Japanese ancestry alone or in combination with other ancestries. This is only 0.3 percent of the population of the US continent (i.e., not including Hawai'i).[1]

People of Japanese ancestry on the US continent are concentrated in the state of California, with a population of 435,588. The greater metropolitan areas on the US continent with the largest populations of ethnic Japanese (in descending order) are Los Angeles, New York City, San Francisco, San Jose, Seattle, San Diego, Washington, D.C. and Baltimore, Chicago, and Sacramento (Shinagawa, Wang, Lee, and Chen 2011).[2] Most of my interviewees were from the greater Los Angeles, New York, and San Francisco areas, in line with the above demographics (although they are not a representative sample).

The representation of Japanese Americans in mainstream American media on the US continent is often stereotypical and conflated with other Asian ethnic groups. Along with other people of Asian ancestry, Japanese Americans are portrayed in many ways, including as nerdy computer geeks and scientists, sexy dragon ladies, kung fu masters, sneaky foreign villains, or the model minority (see Espiritu 1992, Gee et al. 1995, Lee 1999, Ono and Pham 2009). Moreover, outside of areas with large Japanese American or other Asian American populations, many Japanese Americans grow up being one of the few Asians (specifically Japanese Americans) in their class, neighborhood, or school. Many of these Japanese Americans are made to feel different from their white peers, especially when they are phenotypically different. Despite their tendency to identify as "Americans," even later-generation US born and raised Japanese Americans are commonly racialized Asian and assumed to be foreigners (Tuan 1998). This makes them feel like they have to represent their ethnic and racial groups, as well as their Japanese cultural backgrounds even when they have minimal cultural knowledge. In Japan, most Japanese Americans from the US continent experienced not being a racial and ethnic minority for the first time in their lives.

### *Japanese Americans as Asian Americans*

In response to negative categorization by mainstream American society, from the 1960s, people of Asian ethnic backgrounds have come together to assert "Asian American" counter-identities (Espiritu 1992). Challenging stereotypical representations, young, primarily US-born activists claimed identities based in the United States, replacing older, more derogatory labels such as "Mongloid" and "Oriental." This panethnic identity not only creates solidarity between people of Japanese ancestry and people of other Asian ancestries, but also provides a single identity with which people of mixed Asian ancestries can identify.

In comparing Japaneseness on the US continent and in Japan, different relationships between Asian ethnics in the two contexts become clear. In Japan, ethnic Koreans or Chinese might be phenotypically mistaken for ethnic Japanese, but everyone in Japan is aware that these groups are located differently within Japan's social formation. Histories of colonialism and war, as well as linguistic and cultural differences, have built strong boundaries between Japaneseness and Koreanness, Chineseness, and other Asian ethnic groups in Asia.

However, an Asian American grouping and identity in the United States brings together people of diverse ethnonational backgrounds under a single panethnic label. This shared political identity was only able to emerge once there was a significant US-born generation that shared a language (i.e., English), a US-based identity, and common historical experiences as racial and ethnic minorities in the United States (Espiritu 1992). Over time, these later generations have sometimes placed at least as much if not more importance on Asian American identities than on separate ethnic ones (see Kibria 2002a). Many of my Japanese American interviewees from the US continent described identifying as Asian American in the United States but this kind of panethnic identity was not a viable option in Japan because it does not exist in the Japanese societal context.

## Prewar and Postwar Waves of Migration

The migration of people from Japan to the United States has taken place in two major waves, typically described as "prewar" and "postwar," referencing World War II as a major point in Japanese American history when migration from Japan to the United States was officially ceased. More precisely, the prewar wave refers to migration from 1885 until the Immigration Act of 1924 ended large-scale migration of Japanese to the United States. The Walter-McCarran Act of 1952 officially eliminated racial bias in immigration and naturalization, restarting immigration from Japan and many other Asian countries.

The first wave of immigrants from Japan tended to be farmers, merchants, and students, with farmers primarily going to Hawai'i. They came primarily from Hiroshima, Wakayama, Kumamoto, Fukuoka, Yamaguchi, Okayama, Nagasaki, Saga, Kagoshima, and Okinawa prefectures in southwestern Japan (Spickard 2009).[3]

Early Japanese migration to the US continent and Hawai'i consisted of two different flows because Hawai'i was legally a separate nation until it was annexed as a US territory in 1898.[4] From 1885, Japanese migration to Hawai'i consisted mainly of contract laborers on plantations, while migration to the United States was more commonly represented by student-laborers (Ichioka 1988).[5] The Organic Act of 1900 applied US law to Hawai'i, outlawing the contract system and thereby encouraging secondary migration to pursue opportunities on the US continent, where pay was typically better.[6]

As a result, in the prewar period, migration from Japan to the United States can be understood in two phases: before 1900 and after 1900. Yuji Ichioka explains that from 1891 to 1900, 27,440 Japanese were admitted to the United States, most as laborers. From 1901 to 1907, "42,457 more persons were admitted, augmented by upwards of 38,000 laborers who entered the United States via the Hawaiian Islands" (Ichioka 1988: 51–52). In 1907, Theodore Roosevelt issued an executive order "prohibiting those aliens whose passports had been issued for destinations other than the United States, from entering the country via insular possessions, the Canal Zone, or other nations ... This meant that any Japanese who possessed a passport issued for the Hawaiian Islands no longer could enter the continental United States" (Ichioka 1988: 52). In other words, even after Hawai'i legally became part of the United States, migration to Hawai'i had a slightly different flow than migration to the US continent.

This first generation from Japan was eventually regarded as *issei*, while their US-born children are *nisei*.[7] In addition to nisei who were born and raised in the United States, *kibei nisei* refers to nisei born in the United States then raised partly in Japan. Nisei were sent to Japan as children in a variety of scenarios, most commonly migrating with parents, but also including being sent by parents for education and to live with relatives (Azuma 2005). In the Japanese American community, kibei nisei are commonly discussed as a subset of nisei since birthplace and generations removed from Japanese immigrants are the main criteria by which Japanese American generational labels are given (e.g., Kitano 1993).[8] However, if we think about Japanese American generations in terms of early experiences living in Japan and comfort in speaking Japanese, issei and kibei nisei experiences actually overlap quite a bit, causing some similarities in the children of these two groups. In Chapter Five, when I discuss the children of people socialized in Japan, these are the children of both issei and kibei nisei.

The prewar Japanese American experience is largely defined by the mass, forced removal and incarceration of Japanese Americans during World War II by the US government. Since Franklin D. Roosevelt's February 19, 1942 Executive Order 9066 required all people of Japanese ancestry to evacuate areas on the West Coast designated "military areas," issei and nisei experiences generally include this past. The violation of civil rights and stigmatization of Japaneseness that the forced removal and incarceration caused are commonly referenced in community and individual narratives about what it means to be Japanese American. Older *sansei* (children of nisei) were born in these camps surrounded by barbed wire. Much research has touched on the legacy of this history in terms of the physical and mental well-being of those who were incarcerated as well as on the effect on subsequent generations of the trauma experienced by their parents (e.g., Holsapple 1999, Tanaka 1992). One legacy of the incarceration of US-born and raised nisei is the emphasis placed on their Americanization, including not passing on Japanese language and culture to the third and later generations.

Before World War II, Japanese American communities were clustered in areas known as Japantowns all over the West Coast. When the war ended and Japanese Americans resettled, many returned to these neighborhoods, but some also moved east. While there used to be over forty Japantowns in California alone (Graves and Dubrow, Pease 2008), now there are only three official Japantowns remaining in the entire United States: Los Angeles, San Francisco, and San Jose. Since the passing of the issei generation, the descendents of the prewar migration wave from Japan have been a predominantly monolingual, English-speaking community, except for kibei nisei. As I discuss in Chapter Five, having a parent raised in Japan who speaks fluent Japanese shapes how Japanese Americans interpret their experiences living in Japan.

In addition to the prewar wave (and descendents) of Japanese Americans, there has also been immigration from Japan in the postwar period. To differentiate this wave from the prewar period, academics and community organizations use the prefix "shin," meaning "new." Thus, the new, postwar issei are *shin-issei*, with their children being *shin-nisei*. The earliest group is typically referred to as "war brides" or "military brides" (Ward Crawford, Kaori Hayashi, and Suenaga 2010) since they met and married American military personnel in Japan, including Japanese Americans, then came to the United States as spouses of US citizens once it became legal to do so (Tsuchiya 2011). Other migrants from Japan have had varied occupations, ranging from business expatriates to the various owners and employees of institutions created to support their needs (Befu 2010). Since the 1980s, many of the Japanese citizens who migrate to the United States are residing here only on a temporary basis, as exchange students and Japan-based company employees who plan to return to Japan. Most of these temporary migrants from Japan in the United States identify as "Japanese" and not as "Japanese American" or shin-issei. It has been pointed out that it is not until there is a US-born second generation that a first-generation "Japanese" is redefined as an issei.

Representations of Japanese American history and identity overwhelmingly focus on prewar migrants and their descendents. But Japanese American histories are quite diverse and even contradictory (Yamashiro 2016). Japanese American history is typically represented by the experience of being incarcerated during World War II in rural areas away from the West Coast. In stark contrast, postwar migrants and their descendents remember wartime experiences in terms of surviving fire bombing in Tokyo, the atomic bombs in Hiroshima and Nagasaki, and the Battle of Okinawa. One goal of this book is to include US-born descendents of both prewar and postwar migrants as we consider Japanese American relationships to Japan, to flesh out some of these complexities and contradictions about what it means to be "Japanese American."

### *Speaking and Learning Japanese on the US Continent*

Japanese Americans have different relationships to the Japanese language, not only in terms of exposure to it, but also in terms of the language as a pragmatic tool for communication versus as a symbol of Japaneseness. When Japanese Americans study Japanese on the US continent, it is both a minority language and their heritage language. As a minority language, Japanese is not taught at most schools and is not understood by the majority of the population of the United States. Most commonly, Japanese Americans who learn Japanese as children are exposed to it in the home or in the ethnic community. Japanese American usage of the Japanese language varies by the number of generations the speakers are removed from native Japanese speakers. Differences in the exposure of children of Japanese ancestry on the US continent to formal education in Japanese reflects the generational gap between prewar and postwar Japanese American populations in the United States.

On the one hand, the children of Japanese immigrants, as well as immigrant children, are more commonly exposed to Japanese not only in the home environment but also through some form of Japanese school, most typically weekly Saturday school called *hoshūkō*. These schools originally targeted temporary Japanese expatriate communities and incorporated Japan-based curriculum so that Japanese citizen adults temporarily living overseas could keep their children educated in Japanese and up-to-date with Japanese curriculum to ensure a relatively smooth transition when they eventually moved back to Japan. Over time, however, various studies show that because many Japanese migrants residing in the United States have become long-term and even permanent residents, the hoshūkō have needed to adjust their curriculum to accommodate diverse language backgrounds and learning needs (Kataoka, Koshiyama, and Shibata 2008).

On the other hand, most later-generation Japanese Americans (i.e., third, fourth, fifth generations) on the US continent do not grow up speaking Japanese, as they do not learn it through their families or take formal Japanese language classes. However, in areas with historically large Japanese American populations, such as the Los Angeles and San Francisco areas, there are "Japanese American heritage schools" that teach language in addition to cultural practices, songs, cooking, and other activities. Daruma no Gakko, located in Berkeley, California, is an example of this type of school, describing itself as a "non-profit parent cooperative which offers a four-week Japanese cultural education program in the summer for K-6 students." Its mission is "to develop and maintain an educational program which fosters an appreciation of Japanese American culture." It does this by helping to "build strong positive self-images and identities through learning and engaging in the study of Japanese and Japanese American history, literature, language, music, art, food, field trips and community activities" (Daruma no Gakko 2015).

However, it must be pointed out that the study of Japanese language in this context is more symbolic than functional. Students spend fifteen minutes per day of the four-week session with a Japanese language teacher. This amount of time is enough to learn some words and phrases, but students do not become conversational in Japanese. The structure of this school reflects a "symbolic" Japanese American identity (Gans 1979) that is not necessary in everyday life.

This annual summer program teaches children about Japanese American heritage and "Japanese American culture" and serves to promote a sense of pride since mainstream school curriculum and society do not provide this kind of education in the continental United States.

The range of Japanese language abilities among Japanese Americans in the United States is, not surprisingly, similar to that of Japanese Americans living in Japan. Some speak almost no Japanese, while others are quite fluent. In addition to exposure to the Japanese language as children, many of my interviewees took Japanese classes in college. As we will see in later chapters, attitudes about the language and expectations about their Japanese language abilities both affect how Japanese Americans use—and do not use—Japanese when communicating with people in Japan.

## Ethnic Japanese in Hawai'i

In contrast to ethnic Japanese on the US continent, who are a minority in terms of both numbers and power, and to ethnic Japanese in Japan, who are clearly the majority in terms of both numbers and power, ethnic Japanese in Hawai'i are a numeric minority but are part of the majority in terms of power and representation. The US Census reports 311,653 people claiming Japanese ancestry alone or in combination with other ancestries residing in Hawai'i (US Census Bureau 2013), comprising 22 percent of the total population of the state of Hawai'i. No ethnic group is a numeric majority in Hawai'i, but 56 percent of the population of Hawai'i reports being of Asian ancestry (US Census Bureau 2013), so in contrast to the US continent, Asians are not a racial minority.

Politically, economically, and culturally, ethnic Japanese are part of the majority in Hawai'i. Politically, they are well represented "among elected and appointed officials at the state and county levels such that they have greater political power than most ethnic groups" (Okamura 2008: 127). Since local Japanese "dominate state institutions and apparatuses like the State Legislature and the Department of Education," they author state and federal legislation as well as other forms of public policy (Fujikane 2000: 39). In addition, local Japanese, along with Chinese and whites, "are able to maintain if not increase their socioeconomic status because most families have the financial resources to reproduce themselves socially in succeeding generations" (Okamura 2002a: xi). Culturally, as well, Japanese American influence is strong in Hawai'i. Mainstream culture in Hawai'i includes "things Japanese," such as Japanese foods at grocery stores, Japanese food at restaurants, and Japanese customs, such as taking off one's shoes indoors (Hazama and Komeji 1986: xix–xx). While Hawai'i is ethnically diverse with no numerical ethnic majority, ethnic Japanese clearly occupy a privileged position in the socioeconomic and political power hierarchy.

As a result of the powerful positioning of Japanese Americans in Hawai'i society, Japaneseness is not constructed as a minority identity in opposition to other identities. Since Japanese Americans see themselves as "a socioeconomically successful ethnic group in Hawai'i, they do not actively construct an identity with a more specific meaning than that." That is, due to their "already dominant socioeconomic status in the islands, they do not need to articulate an ethnic identity that can be used to advance their economic and political interests" (Okamura 2008: 126).

Since the social positioning of Japanese Americans in Hawai'i can be understood in terms of privilege, referring to Peggy McIntosh's well-known list of the effects of white privilege is instructive here.[9] Included in her list are experiences such as: "5. I can turn on the television or open to the front page of the paper and see people of my race widely represented," and "7. I can be sure that my children will be given curricular materials that testify to the existence of their race" (McIntosh 2007: 179). Thus, despite ethnic Japanese not being the numerical majority in Hawai'i, their representation in positions of power and in the history of Hawai'i associate Japanese identity in Hawai'i with privilege. As Sarah Manyika puts it in her discussion of how whiteness is associated with the power majority in South Africa, Zimbabwe, and America, despite whites not being a numeric majority in South Africa and Zimbabwe, "to discuss race comparatively, it is the question of power and where that power resides rather than a comparison of numbers that is most important" (Manyika 2003: 76).

The high social positioning of Japanese Americans in Hawai'i affects how they see themselves in relation to others and the normative connotations associated with Japaneseness. This contrasts with the lower social positioning and minority status of Japanese Americans on the US continent, which is similarly reflected in their experiences in Japan.

### *The Postwar Socioeconomic Rise of Japanese Americans in Hawai'i*

Japanese Americans were not always part of mainstream society in Hawai'i.[10] One major explanation for the socioeconomic rise of Japanese Americans in Hawai'i is their World War II experience, which sharply contrasted with that of Japanese Americans on the US continent, the majority of whom lost significant assets through forced relocation and incarceration. In the prewar and even into the early postwar period, Japanese Americans in Hawai'i were mainly employed in blue-collar work, particularly on plantations. But by the

1970s, they had become significantly represented in professional and managerial work (Okamura 2000). What happened in between? One answer is that Japanese American war veterans played an important role in the social changes in postwar Hawai'i. As veterans funded by the GI Bill, they were able to attend college. Many of them went to elite US colleges, law and graduate schools, transforming them into "a major pool of social, educational, business, and political firepower" (Odo 2004: 253). In the prewar period, very few nisei had the financial resources to attend prestigious universities, but after the war many attended schools such as Yale, Northwestern, Columbia, the University of Minnesota, the University of Illinois, and the University of Chicago, attaining law, doctoral, and MBA degrees.

These skilled and well-educated Japanese American veterans—17,000 of them (Boylan 1985: 65)—became a dominant force in challenging the primarily white elite from the US continent who had maintained political and economic power in the Islands for centuries. A turning point was certainly the 1954 "Democratic Revolution" that ushered in fifty years of continuous Democratic domination in the state and was responsible for the rise of Japanese American political power in Hawai'i. According to Okamura, "For Japanese Americans, statehood resulted in further political power and economic mobility" (Okamura 2014: 103). He explains that as a state, Hawai'i elected its own governor, leading to the election of George Ariyoshi (2014: 103–104), and that the 1960s economic boom was "a result of Hawai'i becoming further integrated into the national economy with statehood" (Okamura 2014: 104). John A. Burns, who eventually became governor in 1962, extensively recruited Japanese American veterans into the Democratic Party. In fact, Japanese American veterans' clubs "provided ready-made organizations for political use" (Boylan 1985: 66).

The majority of famous Japanese American politicians have been from Hawai'i. These included Senator Daniel K. Inouye, US Congressperson Patsy Takemoto Mink, US Senator Spark Matsunaga, Governor of Hawai'i George Ariyoshi, and numerous politicians at the state and local levels. Though Hawai'i Japanese Americans are usually included with the larger Japanese American population in the United States, considering them separately could change the way Japanese American accomplishments are perceived. In addition, though not a politician, Ellison Onizuka became nationally known as one of the astronauts to orbit the earth in 1985, before tragically perishing in the Challenger space shuttle disaster one year later.

The prominence of Hawai'i Japanese Americans in Hawai'i, as well as nationally, shapes what it means to be Japanese in Hawai'i, associating Japaneseness with the mainstream rather than with a minority group. At the same time, when Hawai'i Japanese Americans live on the US continent, they often experience racism for the first time and develop a firsthand understanding of a different meaning attached to being Japanese. In this regard, when Japanese Americans go to Japan, they bring with them their different experiences as part of the majority in Hawai'i or as a minority on the US continent.

## *Local Identity*

In contrast to their counterparts on the US continent and in Japan, ethnic Japanese in Hawai'i construct their identities in relation to the Hawai'i-based category of "local." While people of Japanese ancestry in Hawai'i are considered Japanese Americans or Asian Americans by people on the continent, at the local level and in everyday use, ethnic Japanese in Hawai'i do not use these terms or identify in these ways. Typically, they refer to themselves simply as "Japanese" or "local Japanese" (Okamura 1994: 161). This can be explained in at least two ways. First, in contrast to the continental United States, where many people have trouble distinguishing between Americans of Asian/Japanese ancestry and migrants from Asia/Japan, most people in Hawai'i recognize that the people of Hawai'i—those born and raised in the Islands—include people of Asian ancestry. So there is no need to qualify "Japanese" by adding "American" to emphasize their identification with the United States. Second, ethnic Japanese in Hawai'i distinguish themselves from continental Japanese Americans, who are often deemed "haolified" and differentiated from local people.[11] That is, many people from Hawai'i do not culturally identify with being American in the same way that people on the continent do.

"Local" is a broader category that includes Japanese, differentiating Hawai'i Japanese from people of Japanese ancestry from other places, such as Japan or the continental United States. According to Chinen and Hiura, "In matters of personal identity, most sansei, yonsei and gosei view themselves as 'locals' first, integral members of multicultural Hawai'i—fully Americanized, yet distinct from Japanese Americans on the U.S. continent, Japanese from Japan, or 'mainstream' white American culture" (1997: 92). It is important to note how the salience of identities is rank ordered in this statement such that place-based identity takes precedence over an exhnic one.[12]

In addition, "local" is a relational category that has been constructed against "nonlocal." The "commonsense meanings" are "someone born and raised in Hawai'i, or who has lived in Hawai'i for a sufficient length of time, and is thereby familiar with what is thought to be the distinctive lifestyle of the islands"; as not white; as not military; and as not immigrant (Okamura 1980: 128–129). Local identity continues to be significant due to Japanese investment in the late 1980s, the expansion of the tourist industry in Hawai'i, the Native Hawaiian sovereignty movement, and an increasing social cleavage between Japanese Americans and other ethnic groups (Okamura 1994). Since the mid-1990s, "local" is contrasted with and constructed against not only whites, immigrants, and the military but also against tourists and Japanese foreign investors. In other words, "Local identity is a matter of positioning oneself in relationship to power and place" (Rosa 2000: 101).

For the ethnic Japanese population, asserting a local identity is not only an expression of collective identity, but according to Okamura (1994) also allows them to downplay their Japanese background, which has become increasingly controversial and problematic in recent decades with the rise of local Japanese political power and socioeconomic status in Hawai'i. In other words, claiming a local identity is a way to maintain solidarity with other ethnic groups, despite a growing gap in socioeconomic status and access to power in Hawai'i. Some scholars have attempted to address this distinction by rethinking the category of local as including both settlers and indigenous peoples.[13] Positioning oneself as local Japanese is not only about who is or is not local to Hawai'i, but also about what this particular construction of local implies and what sort of vision of Hawai'i it suggests. The salience of local identity and the practice of claiming a Hawai'i-based identity before migrating to Japan contributes to the tendency of Hawai'i Japanese Americans to claim Hawai'i-based identities in Japan as well.

## Ethnic Japanese in Japan

The boundaries around the meaning of Japaneseness in Japan contextually shift to sometimes include and sometimes exclude Japanese Americans living in Japan. Depending on the context, the word "Japanese" can refer to a person's citizenship, ancestry or "blood," cultural and linguistic background, or social knowledge. *Nihonjin* (literally, Japan person) are presumed to have all of these Japanese traits, while *gaijin* (foreigners) are presumed to have none of them. In addition, Sugimoto (2010: 193) has observed how birthplace and current residence can factor into whether or not one is considered *nihonjin* by mainstream Japanese society.

### *Japaneseness as Homogeneous Race, Culture, and Nation in Japan*

In Japan, Japanese is a national identity that conflates race, culture, and nation in addition to a discourse of homogeneity and uniqueness. While notions of Japaneseness have fluctuated over time, since at least the 1970s, the dominant discourse of Japanese national identity has been one of homogeneity, as expressed in hundreds of works known as *nihonjinron* (see Hayashida 1976, Mouer and Sugimoto 1986, Yoshino 1992).[14] The idea of Japanese homogeneity is that Japanese people generally look, speak, and act the same. For example, according to University of Tokyo political science professor Takeshi Ishida, in Japan, it is "known" (*kimatte iru*) that Japanese people all have the same hair and eye color, speak the same language, and live similar lifestyles. Thus, to be Japanese does not require any consciousness or effort—rather, it is considered "natural." It is only when they go overseas that Japanese become aware that their hair color and lifestyle are different from those of "*gaikokujin* [foreigners]" (Ishida 1973: 172).[15] In other words, the homogeneity of Japanese people is constructed against foreigners—the boundaries around Japaneseness become evident in contrast to people from outside of Japan, presumably without any "Japanese" traits. Alternative perspectives do exist, but the mainstream view of Japaneseness in Japan continues to be one of Japanese as homogeneous, conflating notions of culture, language, race, and citizenship.

"Authentic" or unquestionable *nihonjin* have all of these traits, perhaps most importantly Japanese "blood." There is a strong association between Japanese blood/race, language, and culture. Kosaku Yoshino explains: "At the base of the *nihonjinron* is an assumption concerning the 'racial' nature of Japanese identity. Built on this assumption is belief in the uniqueness of Japanese culture" (Yoshino 1992: 22). Exemplifying this perspective, Ishihara Shintaro, who later became governor of Tokyo, proudly wrote, "There is no other country like Japan, people who are virtually mono-ethnic, who speak the same language which is like no other country's, and which has a unique culture" (Oguma 1995: 358). Jennifer Robertson further remarks, "Blood remains an organizing metaphor for profoundly significant, fundamental, and perduring assumptions about Japaneseness and otherness; it is invoked as a determining agent of kinship, *mentalité*, national identity, and cultural uniqueness" (Robertson 2005: 329, italics in original). Using the symbolism of blood that references a presumed genetic or rigid biological difference, this construction of Japanese national identity implies that to be a true Japanese citizen, one has to be of Japanese ancestry. As Cullen Hayashida explains, "Japanese national identity is primarily perceived along racial rather than ethnic lines . . . this racial emphasis is being legitimized by a blood ideology in contemporary Japan that elaborates on the meaning and the significance of their sense of uniqueness" (Hayashida 1976: 211).

## Japanese Americans and the Boundaries of Japaneseness

Notions of Japaneseness based on blood should include Japanese Americans as fellow people of Japanese ancestry, but in Japan the conflation of ancestry with culture, language, and citizenship, along with the presumption that Japanese are homogeneous, consequently excludes the majority of Japanese Americans, who lack other Japanese traits.

In Japanese society, ancestry is only one component of larger conceptions and criteria for defining Japaneseness, in contrast to the United States where ancestry is the main criteria. Statistics on "Japanese" populations in Japan and the United States reflect this gap. The Statistics Bureau of Japan reports that the "Japanese" population was 125,359,000, comprising about 98 percent of the population of Japan (Statistics Bureau of Japan 2011), but these numbers refer to something different from the previous two US-based cases. These Japanese Census figures report people with Japanese *citizenship*, not people claiming Japanese ancestry. While most Japanese citizens are of Japanese ancestry, technically people of any ancestry can naturalize to Japanese citizenship as long as they meet the qualification criteria. Unfortunately, the Japanese government collects data only on citizenship—not on race or ethnicity. This gap between populations described in census counts reflects the complicated intersection of traits that comprise Japaneseness in Japan, as compared to places such as the United States. Moreover, while ancestry is perhaps the most important factor overall in determining Japaneseness in Japan, the fact that it is not always what makes a person "Japanese" means that Japanese Americans are not always considered Japanese within Japanese society.

Although I have been referring to ethnic Japanese in Japan as *nihonjin*, it is worth pointing out that sometimes *nihonjin* is used to refer to people not of Japanese ancestry and some ethnic Japanese living in Japan are not consistently considered *nihonjin*. An example of a situation where someone not of Japanese ancestry is referred to as *nihonjin* is included in the above discussion of Japanese census data.

Examples of ethnic Japanese living in Japan who are typically differentiated from *nihonjin* include *kikokushijo* and *zanryūkoji*, as well as *nikkeijin*. *Kikokushijo* are usually the children of two Japanese citizens (of Japanese ancestry) and have been partially socialized overseas during childhood—this term implies that migration was a family move decided by the parents, as opposed to study abroad students migrating individually and voluntarily (Fry 2009, Goodman 1990, Kanno 2000, Kidder 1992, Maher and Macdonald 1995, White 1988). Zanryūkoji refers to Japanese citizens who were orphaned in China during World War II (Efird 2010, Itoh 2010, Tamanoi 2006, Ward 2006).[16] Finally, *nikkeijin* literally means "people of Japanese ancestry" and thus could technically include *nihonjin*. But in practice, *nikkeijin* refers to the descendents of Japanese emigrants, who were previously assumed to be living outside of Japan. Since the early 1990s, this group also includes the large population of later-generation Japanese Brazilians who are currently residing in Japan (Yamashiro 2008b).[17] Despite this slippage, I will continue to use *nihonjin* interchangeably with "ethnic Japanese in Japan" since this is the most conventional usage.

### *Japanese and the Hierarchy of Foreignness*

"Japanese" and "foreigner" are the two major categories for social identification in Japan. With this sort of dichotomization, much like the categories of "self" and "other," the two classifications are assumed to be mutually exclusive and diametrically opposed. In other words, "Japanese" is constructed against "foreigner," though the boundaries and contents of each category continue to change over time. "Japanese" refers to people who are presumably not foreign in any way, while "foreigner" likewise describes people who are supposedly "not Japanese." Moreover, foreignness is organized hierarchically in terms of nations and races, in what I call the *hierarchy of foreignness*.

In addition to the broader distinction most Japanese make between "Japanese" and "foreigners," a more complicated relationship between the two groupings can be visualized as two perpendicular axes. Constructed as a homogeneous group, Japanese are spread out along the horizontal axis, while foreigners are lined up along the vertical axis, hierarchically organized based on both phenotypical and national distinctions. The two axes do not meet; foreigners are either above or below Japanese in the social hierarchy. To understand how the relationship between Japanese and the hierarchy of foreigners has taken shape in contemporary Japan, it is necessary to understand how Japanese people have been constructed as homogeneous in contrast to foreigners and how foreigners are organized hierarchically in Japanese society.

In terms of their categorical relationship to foreigners, Japanese people can be visualized as horizontally related. This is not meant to challenge the characterization of Japan as a vertical society (*tate shakai*) (Nakane 1970), nor to ignore the class stratification that clearly exists in Japan (Ishida and Slater 2010). Rather, much of Japanese socialization focuses on in-group identification and distinguishes between insiders and outsiders (*uchi* and *soto*) (Creighton 1997, Doi 1973). This distinction continues to be an important aspect of how Japanese see themselves in relation to others.

For example, when a Japanese person meets another person, if the second individual is deemed a fellow Japanese, there is an instant sense of similarity, homogeneity, and relationship that is conceptualized horizontally in ethnic and national terms. This construction of homogeneity is part of the imagined community of Japanese and may not correlate to material reality, but it nonetheless shapes beliefs about ethnic and national stratification. Japanese are taught to relate to one another as "we Japanese (*ware ware nihonjin*)," downplaying the diversity among them when contrasted with foreigners.

However, when a Japanese person encounters someone whom they distinguish to be "foreign," that person is not usually considered to be of equal standing. Influenced by the long history of respect toward white Western nations and contempt for neighboring Asian countries, Japanese have learned to view foreigners as being unequal. In this way, one can imagine ethnic Japanese nationals from Japan interacting with one another on a horizontal axis, based on some perceived notion of sameness. At the same time, there is a vertical axis of foreigners who are hierarchically organized such that they are only above or below the stratum of Japanese. In this schema, when a Japanese assesses a stranger to be Japanese, then they both fit in the middle stratum. But if the stranger is perceived to be foreign, then s/he is recategorized on the vertical axis as being from a country either looked up to or down upon.

In contemporary Japan, foreigners continue to be seen as occupying higher or lower social positions in relation to Japanese people. This positioning is based on phenotypical, linguistic, and cultural traits, correlating not only with categories of race but also with occupation (Shipper 2002). In his research on images of foreigners in Japanese TV commercials, Michael Prieler (2010: 22) has found that "there is a clear hierarchical order of races" and that "whites" are depicted most positively and in varied ways, while "blacks" and "Asians" are portrayed more narrowly and stereotypically. Thus, physical blending in Japan does not always mean being able to fit in. That is, how Japanese people perceive race is not based on phenotype alone, as is evident in the case of Koreans and Chinese, as well as *Burakumin* or Eta (Takezawa 2005).[18]

All of this categorization depends on a complex web of intersecting characteristics that can be conceptualized in terms of spectrums. Multiple intersecting axes represent varying combinations of characteristics, such as phenotype, behavior, language ability, and citizenship. Each of these axes can be conceptualized as a spectrum of Japaneseness, with unquestionably Japanese "Japanese" at one extreme and unquestionably foreign "foreigners" at the other. Between these are "foreigners" with Japanese traits and "Japanese" with foreign traits. For example, a white American who is fluent in Japanese might be completely foreign (a foreign "foreigner" in terms of ancestry, "blood," and phenotype), but that person would be toward the "Japanese" end of the scale on the axis of language ability.

Another example would be an ethnically Japanese person who was born and raised abroad and lacks fluency in Japanese language and culture as a result. This person would be placed at the "Japanese" end of the ancestry, "blood," or phenotype spectrums but toward the "foreign" end of the culture and language measures. I picture spectrums because even a category such as citizenship, where one would seemingly be either counted in or out, can be complicated by those with dual nationality. A spectrum merely acknowledges that there is a blurred middle area that is at neither extreme.

The location of a person on each axis, as well as the intersection of the axes, may change according to context. For a phenotypically "Japanese" Japanese American, this would mean that the person may look more "Japanese" in a crowd among strangers but act less "Japanese" during face-to-face interactions when other factors are taken into consideration. Each characteristic scale operates in different ways and affects how the other characteristics are interpreted. For example, although the sumo wrestler Akebono is a naturalized Japanese citizen, he is not of Japanese ancestry and was not born or raised in Japan. By appearance alone, he could be deemed a foreigner. But in the 1998 Winter Olympics opening ceremony in Nagano, Akebono was chosen to ceremonially purify the grounds, representing Japan in international competition (Panek 2006). Due to his mastery of sumo, a traditional Japanese sport, in this particular context Akebono would be considered "Japanese."

More important than cataloging or naming each and every axis—as they could become infinite if one were to include characteristics such as birthplace and place of residence—is to understand that there are multiple axes. No single formula or definitive list can define Japaneseness since characteristics shift in priority and salience by context.

The hierarchy of foreigners also applies to other subsets of foreigners, including *nikkeijin* and mixed ancestry Japanese (*hāfu*). Both of these groups are internally stratified. *Nikkeijin* are hierarchically ordered by country in a similar fashion to the general foreigner population in Japan. In the same way that Western foreigners have more cultural capital in Japan than Latin American foreigners, Japanese Americans are higher in the social hierarchy than Japanese Brazilians (Yamashiro and Quero 2012). Similarly, *hāfu* or mixed ancestry Japanese are further racially and nationally stratified. For example, "white," Western mixed Japanese tend to be seen as more beautiful and are associated with a higher class status than black or African mixed Japanese.[19]

This conceptualization of an intersecting "Japanese/foreigner" distinction and a hierarchy of foreigners contributes to a more complicated and dynamic understanding of social categorization processes in Japan, specifically including the categorization of Japanese Americans. As the next chapter demonstrates, *nihonjin* categorize Japanese Americans in a variety of ways: as fellow Japanese; as Western, English-speaking foreigners; and as Asian foreigners. Categorization shifts due to a combination of the perception of others, social context, and how individuals strategically act to make different characteristics salient at different times.

This shifting categorization not only reflects assumptions about culture, language, and national background, but also different positioning in the intersecting Japanese/foreigner axes and the hierarchy of foreigners.

Conclusion

This chapter has provided the background contexts for both the United States, from which Japanese Americans migrate, and for Japan, into which they migrate. The varied meanings associated with Japaneseness on the US continent, in Hawai'i, and in Japan reflect their construction in different social formations. These differences become salient when Japanese Americans from the US continent and Hawai'i go to Japan. Incongruent notions of Japaneseness shape the interactions between Japanese Americans from both places and Japanese people, as discussed in the next four chapters.

The concept of global ancestral groups provides a framework for examining forms of Japaneseness on the US continent, Hawai'i, and Japan and for analyzing interactions between global coethnics when Japanese Americans from the US continent and Hawai'i migrate to Japan and interact with Japanese people in the context of Japanese society. Japanese Americans and Japanese people are part of the same global ancestral group. This explains the similarities between them as people of shared ancestry, even though they were born and raised in different societies. They share a common past in Japan up to the point of emigration. At the same time, coming from different branches of the global ancestral group, ethnic Japanese from different societies have internalized disparate notions of what it means to be Japanese based on the history and demographics of each place. As "Japanese" is constructed against different combinations of "other" groups, its meaning as a category as well as the boundaries around Japaneseness, have taken on varied shapes. Over time, cultural forms change and mix, such that "Japanese culture" relates to slightly different practices and meaning in each society.

Chapters Two, Three, and Four examine what happens when Japanese Americans migrate to Japan and are immersed in Japan-based forms of Japaneseness. Their everyday interactions in Tokyo and the transnational identities they construct illuminate how the meaning of Japaneseness is embodied differently by people from each place. Interactions between Japanese people and Japanese Americans reflect the meeting of these different embodied forms of Japaneseness. Chapter Five then describes how Japanese Americans make sense of their experiences and identity formations in Japan as they return to the United States and recontextualize Japan-based notions of Japaneseness back into US-based forms.

CHAPTER 2

# Differentiated Japanese American Identities

## THE CONTINENT VERSUS HAWAI'I

Even though they are from the same nation-state, Japanese Americans from the US continent and Hawai'i are interpreted differently in the ancestral homeland. Jay, a Japanese American from the US continent comments, "[In Japan,] there are clear-cut categories that people fall into. [For Japanese people] It's weird to have someone with Japanese ancestry but of American citizenship . . ." Meanwhile, Michelle, a Japanese American from Hawai'i observes, "In Japan, people are more likely to ask about Hawai'i than about being Japanese American." Both Jay and Michelle notice social categories and mainstream understandings of them in Japan, but based on their experiences they have come to different conclusions about what it means to be Japanese American in Japan. While they are both ethnically and phenotypically Japanese, the fact that they come from different places greatly shapes their interactions with *nihonjin*. Jay, who hails from the continental United States, comments that in Japan people find him confusing. In contrast, Michelle, who comes from Hawai'i, comments that Japanese seem to be more interested in where she comes from rather than her being Japanese American.

This chapter comparatively examines the ways that Japanese Americans from the US continent and Hawai'i learn to identify as a result of their interactions with people in Japan. How do Japanese Americans construct identities within the limitations of Japanese social categories? As discussed in the previous chapter, in Japan the main social classifications are "Japanese" and "foreigners"—categories that US citizens of Japanese ancestry inherently challenge by crossing over. What happens when Japanese Americans

43

can phenotypically "pass" but are not socially knowledgeable about Japanese society or fluent in Japanese? What kinds of options are there for these Japanese Americans to make themselves intelligible in Japanese terms? What can the ways they learn to identify tell us about the boundaries around and meanings of Japanese social classifications?

In exploring the process of identity formation for Japanese Americans in Tokyo, I view construction of identities as an interactive, ongoing process (Goffman 1959, Mead 1934) that reveals shifting symbolic and social boundaries. Symbolic boundaries are the analytic distinctions that individuals make when they categorize people, practices, objects, and places, while social boundaries are the material outcomes of these distinctions (Lamont 1992, Lamont and Molnar 2002: 168–169). Categorizations guide interaction through common sense rules about expectations of group members. Separating people into groups potentially causes inequality because through these distinctions, people can acquire or lose status and gain advantage to resources and opportunities (Lamont 1992: 12, Lamont and Molnar 2002: 168–169). So how *nihonjin* and Japanese Americans interpret and categorize each other reflects ideas about social membership and affects how Japanese Americans experience Japan.

A dialectical process of negotiation constructs and reconstructs boundaries that shape ways of identifying (Cornell and Hartmann, 1998, 2007). As others categorize us into socially recognizable groupings, they draw symbolic boundaries that include or exclude us. In turn we assert identities that confirm or challenge how we are interpreted. Through this back-and-forth manner, individuals learn to identify in relation to mainstream labels so as to become intelligible to others (even if rejecting mainstream categorization, one is still constructing identity in relation to it). With international migration, this process takes on an added dimension: the migrant encounters a new system of (racial) categorization. Furthermore, the way s/he asserts identity may reflect internalized notions of race, as well as other social classifications, from the premigration society.

In Tokyo, Japanese Americans reconstruct transnational identities that make sense within that context, at the same time that they are influenced by their upbringing in the United States. They initially interpret interactions with Japanese through an American understanding of race that deems them "Japanese" and conflates them with Japanese in Japan. However, over time, Japanese Americans learn that Japan-based notions of Japaneseness include more than just phenotypical characteristics. Specifically, Japanese language ability and social knowledge, or the lack thereof, are also relevant in shaping how they are understood in Japan.

Moreover, as their Japanese language ability and knowledge of Japanese social norms increase, Japanese Americans develop more complicated and strategic ways of asserting their identity in different situations, as well as a more nuanced sense of the limitations to developing a "Japanese" identity in Japan. Through trial and error, Japanese Americans learn how to describe themselves in ways that create the least confusion and the most positive reactions from their interlocutors. The differentiated ways that Japanese Americans from the US continent and Hawai'i construct identities in Japan emerge from a combination of how they identified themselves before they went to Japan and how they are stereotypically identified by *nihonjin* (mainstream Japanese in Japan), who clearly differentiate between people from the US continent and Hawai'i. The identities that Japanese Americans from the US continent and Hawai'i reconstruct in Japan illustrate how differences from within the nation-state can be reconstructed abroad.

## Categorized as "Japanese," Feeling Japanese

From the moment they first step off the plane, their black hair and brown eyes enable the majority of Japanese Americans in Japan to phenotypically blend, which in American terms implies fitting in "racially." On the US continent, these same phenotypical characteristics are what mark them as different—as "racially Asian" (see Espiritu 1992, Tuan 1998). In the United States, the concept of "race" implies phenotypical as well as genetic differences between "races."[1] That is, in most cases, it is believed that by looking at someone, you can tell what race s/he is (even if the "one-drop-rule," used to quantify one's blackness, means that phenotype is not the only way to sort people into racial categories). While Japanese Americans from the US continent who could visually blend in Japan tended to mention this as integral to their interactions in Japan, Japanese Americans from Hawai'i who could physically blend were less likely to bring up the subject since they were already used to looking similar to the majority of people in Hawai'i.

### *Japanese Americans from the US Continent*

Initially, most Japanese Americans enjoy this blending in on trains and in crowds because they interpret it as a form of acceptance by *nihonjin*. All of the Japanese Americans I interviewed from the US continent who can phenotypically pass in Japan mentioned physical blending as integral to their Japan experience.[2] This racialized dimension of their experiences enables them to take on a new "role" (Goffman 1959) as part of the visual majority, which is a novel experience for people who grew up in predominantly white suburbs or multiracial areas where they were one of few Asian Americans in their schools and neighborhoods. For these individuals, going to Japan represents the first time that they are able to visually blend into a crowd.

All Japanese Americans from the US continent with whom I spoke found this to be a new and positive experience, in contrast to the experience of being racialized a minority in the United States. People of all ages and generations commented on the demographic shift from being a racial minority and not being able to visually blend in to suddenly being able to not phenotypically stand out. Some characterized their newfound invisibility in Japan as "liberating" because attention is no longer arbitrarily drawn to them in public, as in the United States. Henry, a thirty-eight-year-old from the New York area, explains, "I feel like the spotlight has been taken off of me."

Masato, a thirty-six-year-old also from the New York area, expresses the same sentiment using the analogy of phenotype as a uniform, reminiscent of Robert Park's commentary that the main obstacle to the assimilation of Asians and blacks in the United States is "not mental but physical traits." That is, it is the "racial uniform" that makes them phenotypically distinguishable, which is not the case for Irish or other European immigrant groups (Park 1914: 610–611). Masato explains, "In America, the way you look is like your uniform . . . it's the first thing people notice, like if you were missing a leg or something." Park further adds how phenotypical differences from the majority population in the United States shape not only white attitudes toward racial minorities, but vice versa as well. "It puts between the races the invisible but very real gut of self-consciousness" (Park 1914: 611). In Japan Masato finds a refreshingly different situation: "In Japan you just fit in . . . the nice thing is in Japan I'm not wearing any uniform. If I'm in America, sometimes I'm a little too conscious about other people's judgment or if I'll influence that person's judgment about Asians . . . it's important that people have a positive view of Asians. In Japan I don't carry that burden. There's a little bit of freedom there in being in Japan." In feeling more anonymous, Masato believes that he is treated more as an individual in Japan. "I enjoy the freedom of being invisible here. There's no need to feel like I represent any class or group." Both Henry and Masato feel freer in Japan because they no longer feel self-conscious about representing all Asians due to their phenotypical salience.

Perceived racial acceptance in Japan also offers the possibility of national inclusion and no longer being limited by racial stereotypes. Jay, a twenty-five-year-old from California, reflects, "In the United States, the thought of blending in never occurred to me. Psychologically it's comforting to know that if I want to I have the potential of being an average Joe . . . to be on the inside looking out . . . it's superficial but . . . it's important for me . . . because it's the first time in my life I can do that." Though Jay recognizes the superficiality of visual blending, for him it represents more than just daily anonymity. Visual blending represents the psychological comfort that accompanies being part of the unmarked racial majority (see Osajima 2007). In the United States, being nonwhite and having "Asian" phenotypical characteristics (regardless of being born and raised in the United States and being a native English speaker) led to being racialized "foreign" and "other" (see Kibria 2002a, Lee 1999, Tuan 1998). But in Japan, these same phenotypical traits no longer mark them as different; rather they afford them a different symbolic positioning as part of the mainstream society.

In *Turning Japanese*, David Mura linked his excitement at visual blending in Japan to possible future opportunities, juxtapositioning this to the institutional racism that limits opportunities for people of color in the United States. "*What do I find here? Thousands of faces that look like mine . . . I feel a wave of happiness coming over me . . . a smile and a voice that says, You are unnoticeable here, . . . you can stand not uttering a word and be one of this crowd, and in each job in this country, there is someone who looks like you, from the Emperor to the rock singers . . . and you are no longer budgeted by your color, parceled out into certain jobs, certain places of non-power . . .*" (Mura 1992: 42, italics in original). Even so, like Jay, Mura also recognizes how superficial this feeling is and how the opportunities are not as accessible as they appear initially because eventually other characteristics (e.g., linguistic and cultural deficiencies) become more salient and limiting.

Being categorized as Japanese by *nihonjin* leads many Japanese Americans to identify as Japanese. Ronald, a sixty-one-year-old from California, expressed that sometimes he feels Japanese: "because I don't feel noticeably different (visually) in Japan. I blend in." He explains that his visual salience in the United States makes his racial anonymity in Japan even more significant.

> If you live in America as a Japanese American, the Japanese part is emphasized. We're different from white Americans. But in reality if we're third or fourth generation Japanese American, we're no different from Italian Americans [i.e., ethnic white Americans]. But [in the United States] visually we're different. In Japan, visually we're the same . . . When I first got here, I was an American in Japan and emphasized the American side. But visually we're not noticeable. There's [a] certain anonymity here. I never realized that was an issue. . . . In Japan we blend in. I'm not noticeable until I open my mouth.

Like many of my interviewees, Ronald emphasized his American identity to Japanese people he interacted with when he first arrived in Japan.

If this identity had remained salient, he would have just developed a stronger national (US) identity (similar to the white Americans I interviewed). But once he realized that he physically blended and that his American identity was not apparent to others, Ronald began to feel more Japanese as a response to his being racially categorized as Japanese. In this sense, most Japanese Americans see their categorization as Japanese as being positive because it enables them to take on the role of a phenotypically unmarked member of society.

Some of my Japanese American interviewees commented on the importance of Tokyo as a context for this blending. Aaron was a twenty-one-year-old college exchange student from a rural area of California who had multiple piercings, including one between his bottom lip and chin that he had taken out in Japan. He reflected, "I don't know if it's being in Japan or if it's being in the city... Because being in a city you can fit in and just be lost in the crowd. And you can see someone and then never see them again." He contrasted this with "back home" which was much smaller, making him question whether the pertinent distinction was between Japan and the United States or a small town and a big city. He concluded, "I think I do feel like I fit in more here... just because there's so many people—in order to stick out you have to do something really extreme." For Aaron, the urban/rural difference mattered as much as the recontextualizing of his phenotypical traits in the journey from the United States to Japan as it relates to the ability to visually blend.

### *Japanese Americans from Hawai'i*

In contrast, Hawai'i Japanese Americans were less interested in physically blending in Japan because it was nothing new to them. Interestingly, when asked to compare their experiences of physically blending in Japan with their experiences in the Islands, Hawai'i Japanese Americans who look similar to most Japanese were more likely to contrast them to experiences in the continental United States. For example, Jimmy, a thirty-year-old from Hawai'i, juxtaposes the interpretation of his phenotypical traits in Japan and in the Midwestern United States: "Coming to Japan, even if you don't speak the language very well, by virtue of your face you blend in well." He then adds, "If it were Nebraska, I'd be the only Asian." In a similar vein, Bob, a fifty-one-year-old lawyer from Hawai'i, points out that in Japan, "people don't stare at you." He adds that sometimes in New York or the rural United States, people would stare at him.

These comments explicitly and implicitly tell us about the racialization of Jimmy and Bob in Japan, the continental United States, and Hawai'i.

Explicitly, both men relate how they are visually absorbed into crowds in Japan, suggesting categorization as a *nihonjin*. In contrast, in the continental United States they physically stick out and are categorized as Asian. Implicitly, by not mentioning Hawai'i in this discussion of racialization, Jimmy and Bob are revealing that their racialization experiences in Hawai'i sit somewhere between the extremes of the continental United States and Japan. The omission of Hawai'i represents the fact that they are not visually salient in that context, but at the same time, in Hawai'i, people physically do not look as much alike as in Japan. When asked about Hawai'i, Bob disclosed that he visually fits in there and does not think much about that fact—although he is aware of it.

It was typical of respondents from Hawai'i to mention blending in Japan, but not to mention such experiences in Hawai'i unless specifically asked. When questioned about how blending in Japan compares to experiences in Hawai'i, Jill, a twenty-five-year-old English teacher, responded, "Appearance matters more to me in Japan than in Hawai'i. In Hawai'i I never thought about my appearance." This is in contrast to continental Japanese Americans, who all pointed out how being in Japan was a very different experience because of their new ability to visually blend. In this way, the lack of interest that most Japanese Americans in Hawai'i expressed regarding their ability to physically blend in Japan reflects their comparatively privileged position within Hawai'i's racial formation.

Despite the relatively subdued attitude about being able to blend in, Hawai'i Japanese Americans still learn to identify with Japan when categorized as Japanese by people in Japan. Jill explains, "I feel Japanese when people think I am and when I sorta blend in and don't feel a need to correct them. When blending and walking around, I feel Japanese because everyone thinks I am." Jill's comments can be understood in terms of "the gaze," which implies interpretive power on the part of the viewer. Her ability to identify as *nihonjin* depends on her perception of the inability of the Japanese around her to notice that she is actually a foreigner. All the Japanese with whom I spoke, both formally and informally, have agreed that in daily life, they usually assume, at least initially, that in Japan people with Japanese phenotypes are, in fact, *nihonjin*.

As Goffman (1959) and Mead (1934) would point out, this categorization by others affects Jill's construction of herself as related to how others see her in a dialectic fashion. In this light, she and others could maintain a *nihonjin* sense of self if they could continue to be seen this way by people in Japan. However, once additional factors for determining Japaneseness are introduced to the equation, it becomes difficult for Japanese Americans—from Hawai'i or the continent—to keep identifying as *nihonjin*. Japanese Americans soon learn that in Japan, racialization (being associated with a particular race) factors in not only phenotype but language and behavior as well.

## Miscategorized as Asian Immigrants and Marginal Japanese

Looking similar to most Japanese in Japan does not always lead to categorization as mainstream Japanese. As Japanese Americans interact with people in Japan, they gradually reveal their linguistic and cultural differences. The categorization of Japanese Americans from the US continent and Hawai'i as mainstream Japanese described above is based on phenotypical characteristics alone. When their phenotypical similarity to most Japanese is combined with linguistic, cultural, and social incompetence, confusion reigns for most *nihonjin* because they subconsciously assume that someone who looks Japanese will also speak and act Japanese. Representative of Japanese people I spoke with, as well as numerous studies on Japanese identity in Japan (e.g., Dale 1986, Donahue 2002, Yoshino 1992), a Japanese man explained, "I don't know what [it means to be] Japanese but if you're Japanese, you're supposed to speak Japanese, it's supposed to be easy to communicate, and you should know social customs." Once they realize that Japanese Americans are not *nihonjin*, people in Japan tend to reread these individuals as Asian immigrants or mentally challenged or hearing-impaired Japanese.

Accented Japanese is often the first sign that Japanese Americans are not *nihonjin*. Bruce, a forty-seven-year-old lawyer from Hawai'i, says that people can usually tell he is not *nihonjin* by his accent. Once his language skills differentiate him from typical *nihonjin*, confusion results: "Generally, the assumption is that I am Chinese or Korean. However, I am sometimes asked if I am from the countryside. No one ever thinks I am American." So a Japanese face speaking in accented Japanese lead people to recategorize him most commonly as an East Asian immigrant.[3] Over a decade earlier, Dorinne Kondo described this as the "conceptual dilemma" she posed for the Japanese she encountered. Be it a taxi driver, a salesperson, or a bank clerk, her interlocutors would be surprised at Kondo's "linguistic mistakes," leading to a "series of expressions... bewilderment, incredulity, embarrassment, even anger, at having to deal with this odd person who looked Japanese and therefore human, but who must be retarded, deranged, or—equally undesirable in Japanese eyes—Chinese or Korean" (Kondo 1990: 11). While since the 1990s Japanese have become more exposed to foreigners at local and national levels, Japanese Americans continue to cause some confusion in initial encounters.

DIFFERENTIATED JAPANESE AMERICAN IDENTITIES          51

Interestingly, Bruce's Japanese language ability was quite advanced so some Japanese people attributed Bruce's accent to a rural Japanese upbringing.[4] This was not the case for most of my interviewees, however, whose Japanese was much less fluent. In any case, Bruce notes that people never assume he is American, most likely because of the strong image in Japan of Americans as being phenotypically white.

In addition to making them feel misunderstood, being mistaken for people from other parts of Asia allows Japanese Americans to experience firsthand the hierarchical treatment of foreigners. Henry says the first question most people ask is: "'Are you Chinese? Korean? Filipino?' Never oh, are you Japanese American? Never that." Indeed, when I asked Japanese people how they might interpret someone who looked Japanese but did not speak Japanese well, "Chinese" and "Korean" were typical responses. But once Henry is acknowledged to be Japanese American, as opposed to from a country in Asia, he has noticed differential, even more positive, treatment. Henry recalls being in a hardware store when the clerk asked him if he were Chinese and seemed suspicious of what he was doing. When he explained that he was Japanese American, he noticed that she "backed off." Several interviewees pointed out this "Japanese tendency to look down on [other Asians]" (Creighton 1997: 225), which can be explained by both Japan's imperial history in Asia, as well as the contemporary stereotype of Chinese in Japan as being associated with gangs and other criminal activities (see Yamamoto 2004, Yamamoto 2010).[5]

Many Japanese Americans noticed that Americans are generally more respected than Asian foreigners in Japan.[6] Russell, a thirty-nine-year-old from Hawai'i, points out quite directly and concisely the lower social status he has felt associated with when assumed to be Chinese or Korean, versus the higher status afforded to Americans: "In Japan they think you're lower if they think you're Chinese . . . when you're American, you're above them." In a similar vein, Grant, a forty-four-year-old from California, observed: "There is a double standard regarding how a Japanese person speaks to a Chinese person versus an American with the same language ability. Japanese look at Americans as equals. They show more respect to Americans than to Chinese people here. Chinese . . . are seen as belonging to gangs so [Japanese] talk down to them . . . Japan is playing catch up with America so people here respect America." Whether they perceive Americans as being treated as equal to or better than Japanese, my Japanese American respondents believed they received better treatment when identified as Americans, as compared to when they were believed to be Asian immigrants. When Grant says "Japan is playing catch up with America," he is alluding to Japan's position as a postwar vanquished power to the United States and its contemporary status as economically second (at the time of the interview) only to the United States. As Japanese Americans notice this distinction in treatment, most begin to think more strategically about their presentation of self in Japanese terms in order to avoid as much as possible feeling misunderstood and looked down upon.

From a Japanese perspective, encountering a Japanese American can conjure up not only confusion but also more complicated reactions. A Japanese woman told me, "We feel kinda betrayed when we find out that this person who looks like a Japanese turns out to be not Japanese." She explained the existence of an "unspoken understanding," implying a sense of comfort, when one Japanese person sees another. Kosaku Yoshino has described this perspective as "culturalism": "Explicit verbal communication is considered unnecessary because of the mutual sensitivity supposedly found in social interactions among the Japanese" (Yoshino 1998: 17). For example, when my Japanese interviewee sees an *obāchan* (older Japanese woman) speaking to a Japanese-looking stranger who then says, "Oh, I'm not Japanese" and responds in English or Chinese, she feels like "there is a wall that suddenly appears." This happens despite the attempt at communication that was extended by the obāchan once she discovers that her interlocutor is not a fellow Japanese.

A number of Japanese Americans mentioned being interpreted as mentally challenged. The combination of their less-than-fluent Japanese language skills and socially inappropriate behavior is no doubt the reason. Michelle, a twenty-seven-year-old from Hawai'i, thinks that sometimes people see her as mentally challenged. Once she was in a store trying to read the ingredients written in Japanese on a package. She noticed a store employee looking at her strangely and suddenly realized that she had been moving her lips while reading, which may have suggested to the clerk that she was a mentally challenged *nihonjin*.

In a similar vein, several people related an anecdote about a Japanese American woman who had been living in Japan before going into a line of work that required a security background check. The person doing the background check went to her former neighborhood to ask about her. It turned out that the woman's neighbors, landlord, and the local shopkeepers did not realize that she was Japanese American. Instead, all along they had thought she was mentally challenged but had never mentioned this in talking with her. So this woman found out how the people immediately around her felt about her only as a result of a background check. Numerous Japanese Americans from various parts of the United States related stories to me about being interpreted as mentally challenged in Japan—they said they could tell by the way people looked at them.

Miscategorization can occur in multiple forms for the same person. For example, at different times, Jimmy has been mistaken for being Korean or being hearing impaired. Both while an exchange student in Kobe (in western Japan) and then again near Tsukuba (a commutable distance from Tokyo), he was often mistaken for a Korean. In addition, Jimmy recalls being in a store conversing with a clerk and having trouble understanding the clerk, causing Jimmy to ask repeatedly, "Can you say that one more time, please?" (as students are commonly taught in beginning Japanese language classes). The store clerk responded, "Are you hard of hearing?" and did not seem to comprehend that Jimmy's poor language skills were a result of being nonnative and not yet very polished. If someone with a more obviously "foreign" phenotype had acted in the same way and said the same things, that person surely would have been perceived in a different way.

An additional distinction within the foreigner category is between different *nikkeijin* (descendants of Japanese emigrants). Compared to other foreign nationals, *nikkeijin* in general are seen more positively by Japanese people because of their shared ancestry. However, depending on their home country, *nikkeijin* are also perceived and treated unequally (Takenaka 2009, Tsuda 2009b, Yamashiro and Quero 2012). Tomoko Sekiguchi has found that in a neighborhood where Japanese Brazilians comprise 30 percent of the total residents, Japanese Americans are treated worse if they are thought to be Japanese Brazilian. "One *Nikkei* American resident of the area, who speaks limited Japanese but looks Japanese, claims being poorly served several times because he was mistaken as a *Nikkei* Brazilian. His claims gain credence because he once revealed that he was an American, to which a store clerk apologized saying, 'I am sorry, I thought you were a Brazilian ...'" (Sekiguchi 2002: 199).

It is important to note that a major difference between Japanese Americans and Japanese Brazilians in Japan is not only where they are from or what language they speak, but the relative size of their population in Japan, as well as their visibility and depiction in the Japanese media. Several Japanese people mentioned familiarity with a news story about a Japanese Brazilian or Japanese Peruvian in Japan who had committed murder.[7] When asked about her image of *nikkeijin*, one Japanese woman said that the first image to come to mind originated from one of these news stories. This illustrates how the images of *nikkeijin* and other foreigners can clearly be linked to their representation in the mainstream Japanese media.

Finally, the shifting ways that Japanese Americans are miscategorized reveal the multiple construction of "others" in Japan. *Nihonjin* is the dominant, normalized group in Japanese society, and historically marginalized populations include former Asian colonial subjects and mentally ill people (see Roth 2005, Ryang 2000, Weiner 1997). The interpretation of Japanese Americans by Japanese people in terms of these categories illuminates the multiple types of minority groups in Japan, as well the array of options for categories in which to interpret someone not resembling a typical *nihonjin*.

## Becoming Intelligible: Asserting Differentiated Identities

Once they realize they are being categorized in ways that do not benefit them, Japanese Americans assert alternative identities. Japanese Americans from the US continent tell people that they are "American," leading to questions and explanations about their Japanese heritage. In contrast, Japanese Americans from Hawai'i assert Hawai'i identities, which include recognition of their Japanese ancestry.

### *From the US Continent: American but Not White*

On the one hand, similar to most other Americans, the majority of Japanese Americans feel more "American" in Japan. In fact, as a racial and ethnic minority group, Japanese Americans feel more American and represent the United States while abroad in ways they previously could not have while in the United States. Alvin, a thirty-four-year-old Japanese American who grew up in California feeling like an outsider, feels more American in Japan than he did in the United States due to the salience of national (US) characteristics. "I honestly feel the most American when I'm in Japan. I also have less problems with America when I'm away . . . once, when I was on the JET program, a guy from Texas told me that I was totally American and no different from him. As messed up as this may be, it really felt good to have a white guy from Texas tell me this. When I'm in America, I'm always slightly on the outside (I feel like most white Americans look at me and want to ask me where I'm from—Japan? China? Korea?)." As an Asian American on the US continent, Alvin grew up feeling not fully accepted as American. However, in Japan, while on the JET (Japanese Exchange and Teaching) Program, he officially represented the United States. This part of his experience in Japan contrasted with his American experiences, where he was often questioned about his nationality and racialized as an Asian immigrant, based on "the assumption that all Asians in this country are newcomers" (Tuan 1998).

While not always positive, to be American is to be "a member of the most powerful nation on earth in political, military and economic terms" (Guibernau 2007).[8] For Japanese Americans, the motivation for asserting the role of "American" is often either better treatment or an easy out from restrictive Japanese social rules. One Japanese American said she sometimes speaks English in restaurants because she knows that she will receive better treatment as an (English-speaking) foreigner. While conducting fieldwork in Japan, anthropologist Matthews Hamabata found that rather than trying to present himself as an average Japanese, "The trick for a Japanese American ... is to present oneself as an American—to shake hands and use English—when meeting people for the first time" (Hamabata 1990: 8). This way, he explains, one can avoid rude treatment by and misunderstandings with Japanese people. These strategies reflect "transactional needs"—that people look for situations in which they can feel gratification (Turner 2002: 100). That is, interactions are not just about fitting in; they are also about what benefits can be gained from taking on different roles, recognizing that different characteristics have different values depending on the situation.

Despite asserting American identities, people who are phenotypically similar to most Japanese tend not to be readily accepted as Americans in Japan. Jay finds that being American and looking Japanese are contradictory characteristics to most *nihonjin*. "If I say I'm American they ask if I'm *hāfu* [half Japanese].[9] Or they'll say 'but you look Japanese.'" This conversation was typical among my Japanese American interviewees who visually blend in Japan.[10] Asking if he is *hāfu* implies that Americans and Japanese are phenotypically different. Since Jay looks Japanese yet asserts that he is American, Japanese people often interpret this as referring to mixed heritage. People also ask if he is Korean or Chinese; he answers that he is "*nikkeijin* [the descendant of Japanese emigrants]" and eventually recounts his California upbringing, also explaining his family immigration history until it becomes more comprehensible how he can be of all Japanese ancestry but also be American. After describing some incidents that occurred because of misunderstandings about his background, Jay concluded, "These are the kinds of problems that occur when you don't fit the self that others see you as." This "perceptual dissonance" (Rodriguez and Cordero-Guzman 1992) derives from the bundling of racial and national traits.[11]

Even in official situations, being phenotypically similar to most Japanese can complicate matters for Americans. Joe applied for a Japanese driver's license in Ibaraki (a rural prefecture from which people increasingly commute to Tokyo). He already had a California driver's license, and at the time, translating a US license to a Japanese one was easier than applying for a new Japanese license. When Joe submitted his application, he spoke in Japanese, which led to the clerk mistaking Joe for a Japanese national intentionally trying to fool the system by obtaining a license in the United States so he could avoid taking the Japanese test. Joe was appalled that someone thought his bad Japanese had been faked. Despite his nonnative Japanese and foreign driver's license, Joe's phenotypical characteristics (and Japanese-sounding name) led the Japanese clerk to categorize him as Japanese.

Similarly, a sansei from Hawai'i told me that once when she was at Roppongi crossing, she was asked by a police officer for her alien registration card (the identification card foreign residents were required to carry at the time), which she then provided while saying in Japanese, "Sorry, I don't speak Japanese." The police officer then proceeded to yell at her, accusing her of faking being a foreigner, even as she held the woman's alien registration card that included her photo and visa information. Thus, even when American traits are asserted—and official documentation provided—phenotypical categorization can still trump assertions of nationality and the lack of Japanese cultural fluency.

The strong image in Japan of Americans as "white" contributes to the exclusion of people with other phenotypes from being readily acknowledged as Americans.[12] This construction of Americanness as equaling whiteness has been demonstrated by numerous scholars in the US context (see, for example, Jacobson 1998, Lipsitz 2006, López 1996). Thus, when white Americans in Japan assert, "I'm American," this statement is rarely questioned because it meshes with the dominant image that Japanese have of Americans. Lynn, a twenty-nine-year-old American of German and Slovakian ancestry, thoughtfully responded that in Japan people do not ask her about race: "Usually [my] 'race' is apparent and is coded as 'white,' so no one asks. Sometimes I'm asked where I'm from. I say 'America' and then people usually say whether they've been there or not. Occasionally people ask me where my family is from and I say Germany and Slovakia (many people actually guess Slovakia from my last name) and they say it's interesting." Through these types of exchanges, white Americans reaffirm their (racialized) national identities as (white) Americans because they are racially accepted as Americans and are not questioned about how they can be American and still look white or be of European ancestry.

This is in stark contrast to the majority of Japanese American respondents who, like Jay and Alvin, said that stating "I'm American" typically led to further probing about how they could be both Japanese and American at the same time, encouraging them to explain their family histories of immigration to the United States from Japan. For Lynn, such follow-up questions about ethnic background may result in the reconstruction of ethnic identity, but this is different from racial minority identities based on exclusion from the national image. As Mary Waters (1990) has shown, ethnic identities for whites in the United States tend to be optional, while for racial minorities they are not. This also seems to be true in the Japanese context. By needing to explain how they are American despite looking Japanese, and how as Americans they can be of only Japanese ancestry, Japanese Americans see that they are excluded from mainstream Japanese representations of Americans.

As a result, as they lived in Japan, the majority of my Japanese American interviewees from the US continent who could visually blend in learned to identify as not just "American," but more specifically as "Japanese American."[13] Mark, a thirty-nine-year-old sansei from California, explained, "Most of the time, Japanese recognize me as Japanese American as opposed to white American." He added that younger Japanese people seem to understand once he explains his background, while older Japanese people have a harder time understanding, though they do seem to know about the US incarceration of Japanese Americans during World War II. Ryan, a shin-nisei/yonsei, made similar observations about generational differences noting that young people with international experience were especially quick to comprehend his "family's diasporic history."[14] As discussed above, within a framework of national identity, Japanese people understand that Mark is American but different from white Americans. Stephanie, a thirty-nine-year-old from the US continent reflected, "When I was blending in with the masses, I felt like I was regarded as another Japanese person . . . and oftentimes, I was trying to blend in. When I spoke, I felt and was treated as a foreigner, and I often had to explain that I was Japanese American or *nikkeijin*."

As these comments show, the reconstruction of Japanese American identities in Japan was due to a combination of categorization by Japanese people and identity assertion by Japanese Americans themselves. When Japanese viewed them as Japanese, my interviewees asserted that they were also American to avoid misunderstandings and benefit from positioning as English-speaking Westerners. But when Japanese Americans asserted American identities, in most situations, they had to further explain their Japanese ancestry to clarify why they "looked Japanese" and had Japanese surnames. This process illuminates the cultural and racial limitations of the roles that Japanese Americans are able to take on in Japan.

## *Hawai'i Identities*

In contrast to ethnic Japanese from the US continent who, in conversations with Japanese people, assert national identities as Americans, most Hawai'i Japanese Americans assert "Hawai'i" identities in Japan—for at least two reasons. First, people from Hawai'i themselves differentiate between being from Hawai'i or from the continental United States. Second, to most people in Japan, Hawai'i is a recognizable place that is distinct from the continental

United States and evokes a positive image. Though individuals may begin by making the distinction between being from Hawai'i and being from the United States, they eventually realize the cultural capital of the former in a Japanese context and are then encouraged to keep asserting Hawai'i identities for different reasons, as discussed below.

---

"Local" versus "The Continent": Why Hawai'i Is Distinctive. The significance of Hawai'i social categories—specifically the local/nonlocal distinction (discussed in Chapter One)—persists for people socialized in Hawai'i, even off-island. In Japan, Craig constructs his Hawai'i identity as different from both (continental) Americans in general and Japanese people in Japan. He explains: "I feel 'from Hawai'i' much of the time, and at such times, I feel I am different from both Americans and Japan[ese]—perhaps sort of a proverbial 'best of both worlds.'" By "Americans," Craig may be referring to either people from the US continent or specifically white Americans, perhaps even conflating the two. Like most people from Hawai'i, he distinguishes between "Americans" and people from Hawai'i. Though they also feel American in terms of language, culture, and citizenship, people from Hawai'i tend to differentiate between continental US and Hawai'i identities.[15]

A "Hawai'i" identity is different from both "American" and "Japanese" identities, yet for those of Japanese ancestry, it includes both American and Japanese aspects. In other words, a Hawai'i identity seems to overlap with or equal a "Japanese American" identity for many of my respondents. Craig further expands: "I never really thought much about saying that I am a 'Japanese-American.' I actually simply thought of myself as a person of Japanese ancestry from Hawai'i. The Hawai'i connection was much more important than the Japanese part or the American part." Growing up in Hawai'i, Craig simply saw himself as a person of Japanese ancestry, and this did not conflict with being from Hawai'i, so he never felt the need to label himself a "Japanese American."

This attitude reflects the prominent social representation of ethnic Japanese in Hawai'i, in contrast to the underrepresentation of ethnic Japanese on the US continent which causes gaps between how they see themselves and how others see them. Before going to Japan, Craig was simply a local in Hawai'i. However, in Japan, he has learned to see himself as a "Japanese American" because his Japanese ancestry has become more salient to people in Japan. Through categorization as "Japanese" when he blends in and through conversations about his ancestry, Craig has become more aware of his combination of characteristics—being an American citizen of Japanese ancestry.

Differences from continental people are also expressed in cultural terms, such as lifestyle, food, and values. Though he has Japanese and other foreign friends and acquaintances, Jimmy feels most comfortable around other Hawai'i people, explaining, "There is a natural bond there . . . lots of common topics like what school you went to and your favorite places to go . . ." Talking with people from the continent, he distinguishes: "It's easy to make small talk but harder to have meaningful conversations." Shared local histories and communities in Hawai'i—not to mention two to three degrees of separation at the most—make for a wealth of conversation topics and reflect similar lifestyles and attitudes. Though he lived on the continent for several years, Jimmy still feels more of an affinity and level of comfort with Hawai'i people, similar to most of my Hawai'i interviewees.[16] This reflects the strong cultural dimension of a "local" identity (Edles 2004).

---

Acceptance as Representatives of Hawai'i. The general acceptance in Japan of Hawai'i Japanese Americans as representatives of Hawai'i can be attributed to several factors: the familiarity of Hawai'i to most Japanese, either through advertising, the media, or actual visits; the distinction of Hawai'i from the US continent; and a positive image of Hawai'i. Since the 1960s, Hawai'i has become increasingly familiar to people in Japan. Yujin Yaguchi and Mari Yoshihara have observed that, "Hawai'i has become the most popular and familiar foreign tourist destination for the Japanese. Today, images of the islands abound in magazines, television programs, and other media. The number of tourists who visit Hawai'i has increased by almost twenty times in the last forty years, and today nearly two million Japanese vacation in the islands every year" (2004: 82). The numbers may have decreased slightly with the Japanese recession in 2008, but with 1.24 million Japanese visitors to Hawai'i in 2010—more than 50 percent of whom were repeat visitors—the number is still very significant (Hawai'i Tourism Authority 2011: 2).[17]

Familiarity with Hawai'i also means familiarity with its population. Whether through the aforementioned encounters with people in Hawai'i or contemporary media images, most Japanese know that there are ethnic Japanese among the peoples of Hawai'i.[18] While constructions of Hawai'i in the Japanese imagination have shifted over time, especially due to the changing economic relationship between Japan and Hawai'i, broadly speaking, ethnic Japanese have long been a part of these images (see Yaguchi and Yoshihara 2004). More recently, in 2002, NHK (*Nihon Housou Kyoukai* or Japan Public Broadcasting Corporation) produced a morning drama series called *Sakura*, about a perky Japanese American yonsei woman from Hawai'i (see Fukushima 2002, Yano 2008). The regular incorporation of Japanese Americans in representations of Hawai'i has resulted in an image in Japan of Hawai'i as including ethnic Japanese.

The image in Japan of people in Hawai'i is distinct from that of people in the continental United States. Reflective of this difference, a Japanese woman I spoke with said, "For me, Hawai'i doesn't seem American. The image is different. The image of Hawai'i doesn't mesh with the image of America. Japanese Hawaiians? [she was unsure of the term] are almost completely different from Japanese Americans. When I go to Hawai'i I don't think [of it as America] because Hawai'i is so close to us." She added that there are a lot of Japanese in Hawai'i, then paused and said, "In Japan, if you go to Idaho, you say you're going to America. But if you go to Hawai'i you won't say you're going to America." This woman is pointing out several factors here: the geographic proximity of Hawai'i to Japan, the large number of ethnic Japanese in Hawai'i, and the way in which this leads Japanese to feel closer to Hawai'i than to the continental United States. While she did not know exactly what to call them ("Japanese Hawaiians"), it was clear that this woman distinguished between Japanese Americans from Hawai'i and Japanese Americans from the continental United States, reflecting a common view among Japanese I spoke with formally and informally who knew Japanese Americans from both places.

One reason for the distinction between "America" and "Hawai'i" became apparent to me while commuting to the center of Tokyo on a regular basis. At every major train station at least one travel agency prominently displays tourist brochures for pedestrians to notice as they pass by. Touristic marketing divides "America" and "Hawai'i" as different destinations. "America" refers to the US continent, with brochures depicting major cities and attractions such as the Statue of Liberty, the Hollywood sign, and the Grand Canyon. Meanwhile, "Hawai'i" information is typically grouped with other island getaways in the South Pacific with images of sandy beaches, blue skies, and palm trees. On an everyday level, people in Japan are exposed to these types of representations that both reflect and reinforce the differentiation between Hawai'i and the rest of the United States.

The Hawai'i/continental differentiation also includes a racial dimension. While the image of "America" is racialized white, Hawai'i is associated with people of Asian and Pacific Islander heritages—Japanese as well as others. These representations in Japan reflect the racial and ethnic demographics of each place. As a result, when Japanese-looking people say they are from Hawai'i, discussion turns to Hawai'i itself rather than trying to figure them out—which is similar to the experiences of my white American interviewees from the US continent who were not questioned about their racial or ethnic backgrounds. This is illustrated by the succinct quote from Michelle noted at the beginning of the chapter: "In Japan, people are more likely to ask about Hawai'i than about being Japanese American."[19] In other words, being of Japanese ancestry does not conflict with most *nihonjin* views of people from Hawai'i. Thus, there is no need to probe what it means to be Japanese American and from Hawai'i, since the two go together. This effectively reinforces their acceptance as being "from Hawai'i" and leads to the salience of this identity for most Hawai'i Japanese Americans.

Everyone from Hawai'i made positive comments about how *nihonjin* respond to them once their Hawai'i backgrounds become known. Michelle was illustrative of this when saying that because Japanese people she meets are always interested in Hawai'i, she is always having conversations about Hawai'i. Kyle was straightforward in describing how he has learned to see being from Hawai'i as beneficial: "When I first came I did try to blend in. But you can't get away with that for long if you don't speak the language properly. I immediately learned how to say '*Hawai'i no nikkei desu* [I am a Nikkei (descendent of Japanese emigrants) from Hawai'i].' It's like your get out of jail free card." Typical of my interviewees, Stewart recalls that when he says he is from Hawai'i, the response is usually, "Oh, I just went there." He adds that "no one hates Hawai'i." A Japanese man I interviewed said, "When Japanese go to Hawai'i it's just vacation. For Japanese people, Hawai'i means Honolulu, shopping, beautiful beaches . . ." The positive responses received by Hawai'i Japanese Americans encourages them to describe themselves in this way to receive positive feedback.[20] None of my interviewees seemed critical of this attention or of the portrayal of Hawai'i as a comfortable, friendly place to visit, perhaps because they agree with this image or perhaps because they just enjoy the cultural capital it brings them.

Most significant here is that Hawai'i Japanese Americans are rarely questioned about their ancestry once they divulge that they are from Hawai'i. This is noticeably different from the experience of most continental Japanese Americans, who are often questioned for more details once they say they are from the United States. In other words, *nihonjin* can accept ethnic Japanese as being from (and representing) Hawai'i but not from "the United States," i.e., the continent.

## Conclusion

Japanese American identity formation in Tokyo for those who can visually blend illuminates how the intertwined processes of Japanese categorization of Japanese Americans and subsequent Japanese American identity assertions construct and reconstruct symbolic and social boundaries. When *nihonjin* presumptions about Japanese Americans are initially based on phenotype alone, Japanese Americans are viewed as part of the majority Japanese population. But with social interaction, when linguistic ability and social and cultural knowledge are also considered, *nihonjin* redraw the boundary around "Japanese" to exclude Japanese Americans. This prompts Japanese Americans to assert identities that clarify their backgrounds, specifically why they phenotypically resemble the Japanese majority yet lack knowledge of the Japanese language and social norms. As Japanese Americans become more aware of Japanese categorizations and social expectations, they find ways to describe themselves that provide them with the best possible social positioning. In other words, once they notice how racial and social boundaries in Japan are affected by linguistic and cultural boundaries, Japanese Americans strategically reposition themselves.

The identities that Japanese Americans assert and the ways they are interpreted in Japan are shaped by a combination of how Japanese Americans previously identified in the United States as well as their adjustment to mainstream Japanese categorizations of them. This is reflected in the different ways that Japanese Americans from the US continent and Hawai'i learn to identify in Japan.

On one hand, when Japanese Americans who visually blend assert American national identities, they are typically questioned further about their ethnic backgrounds due to the conflation of nation, ethnicity, and phenotype in Japan, where Americans are expected to look "white" and Japanese are expected to look "Japanese." As a result, Japanese Americans from the US continent typically reconstruct identities in Japan as not simply "Americans," but "Japanese Americans."

On the other hand, when a Japanese American asserts a "Hawai'i" identity, despite it not being a national identity, this identity is widely acknowledged among Japanese people, leading to its salience as a possibility for social acceptance in Japan. Identifying as being "from Hawai'i" becomes a source of cultural capital and elicits positive responses. People who fit the category of "local Japanese" in Hawai'i translate to fitting the category of "from Hawai'i" in Japan. This effectively reinforces their identification with Hawai'i and their ability to represent Hawai'i as ethnic Japanese.

The different experiences and identity formations of Japanese Americans from Hawai'i and the US continent in Japan reveal how people in the ancestral homeland can view the branches of a global ancestral group very differently. Yasunori Fukuoka points out that although "Most Japanese have the feeling that [*nikkeijin*] are basically Japanese," this feeling "tends to last only until they actually meet one" (Fukuoka 2000: xxxiii). My findings further suggest that through contact, *nihonjin* perceive and treat *nikkeijin* differently depending on where they say they are from—even when they are from the same country. For Japanese Americans, the larger societal contexts and demographics of each branch, including racial images of them, affect how they are perceived and treated in the ancestral homeland. In international contexts, national distinctions are often most salient, but the reconstructions of other kinds of sub-national identities abroad also need to be considered in an increasingly globalizing world.

The strategies and identity constructions of Japanese Americans in this chapter have centered on those who phenotypically blend in Japan and grapple with how to inform strangers that they are not *nihonjin*. But what about Japanese Americans of mixed ancestry? The next chapter explores how mixed Japanese Americans develop different strategies due to the opposite challenge of letting strangers know that they are of Japanese ancestry.

CHAPTER 3

# From *Hapa* to *Hāfu*

## MIXED JAPANESE AMERICAN IDENTITIES IN JAPAN

Since the population of people of Japanese ancestry in the United States is increasingly multiethnic and multiracial, "mixed" Japanese Americans are also part of the Japanese American population in Japan.[1] As people of Japanese ancestry who are often more phenotypically ambiguous, mixed Japanese Americans are not always initially categorized as Japanese, unlike the Japanese Americans discussed in the previous chapter who are phenotypically similar to most Japanese. Thus, rather than just grappling with the two main social categories of *nihonjin* (Japanese) and *gaijin* (foreigner) in Japan, mixed Japanese Americans also commonly encounter the category of *hāfu* (half Japanese) as they attempt to describe themselves in ways that are intelligible in Japan. What does it mean to identify as *hāfu* in Japan? How are the connotations different from identifying as *hapa* in the United States? Why or why not might a mixed Japanese American choose to identify as *hāfu*?[2]

The ways in which mixed Japanese Americans negotiate categorization as *hāfu* reflect a combination of how Japanese categorize them as well as how they see themselves and respond to this categorization (Cornell and Hartmann, 1998, 2007). Significant factors shaping both categorization and identity assertion include phenotype, generational distance from Japan, and knowledge of Japanese language and society. Focusing on mixed Japanese Americans enables a comparative discussion of "monoracial" and "multiracial" Japanese American identity formations in Japan, as well as US and Japanese conceptions of "mixed" people and how they relate to the issues of citizenship, phenotype, and emigration history.[3]

## Hāfu As a Social Category in Japan

Commonly heard in the Japanese media and in everyday language in Japan, *hāfu* literally means "half" in Japanese (taken from the English word). In Japan, this refers to someone with biological parents of two different nationalities or races. For example, President Barack Obama would be described as "kokujin to hakujin no *hāfu*," or "black (person) and white (person) *hāfu*." In the absence of qualifying descriptions (e.g., "black and white"), *hāfu* refers to the child of a "Japanese" parent and a "foreign" parent.[4] While "foreign" refers to anyone not "Japanese," mixed Japaneseness has always had connotations related to class and phenotype that have shifted depending on the historical context. Both the terminology itself and the mainstream connotation attached to being of mixed ancestry in Japan have changed drastically since the immediate postwar period. As discussed below, new terms are beginning to emerge as more politically correct substitutes for *hāfu*, although none have yet been used widely.

Japanese national identity has racial connotations such that the term "Japanese" (*nihonjin*) implicitly refers not only to those possessing Japanese citizenship, but also to being of "pure Japanese blood" and speaking and acting Japanese (Sugimoto 2003, Yoshino 1992). These assumptions, combined with the persistent myth of Japanese homogeneity, have led to a mainstream discourse in which there are, on the one hand, unquestionably Japanese people and, on the other hand, everyone else. The myth of Japanese homogeneity "leads to the view that Japanese who do not fit with this narrow image must be foreigners so that the existence of those who are different is either glossed over or relegated to the status of outsiders. Some of these individuals are those of multiethnic ancestry" (Murphy-Shigematsu 2000: 210). In other words, so long as the mainstream, homogenous view of "Japanese" as being ancestry-based and "pure-blooded" continues to dominate, then people of Japanese ancestry who are also of other ancestries are excluded from claiming a "true" Japanese identity.[5]

The mixed Japanese population and images of its members in the immediate postwar period were shaped by the presence of white and black Americans among US military personnel, especially in Okinawa, which continues to host the bulk of US armed forces in Japan.[6] Mixed Japanese in the immediate postwar period were predominantly the children of US military men and Japanese women. Discrimination against these mixed-Japanese children arose not only from narrow views of Japanese as a monoethnic people that did not include them, but also from the residual animosity toward the US military, which had recently dropped atomic bombs on Hiroshima and Nagasaki. Moreover, mixed children with "black" features experienced more social discrimination than those with "white" features.[7] According to a 1967 *New York Times* article, a professional social worker in Japan bluntly summarized, "Japanese assume that the black baby's mother was a prostitute," whereas the white baby is assumed to have been the product of a love match, even if the parents did not marry (Trumbull 1967). Many mixed children were abandoned and raised as orphans, especially in Okinawa.[8] In 1953, the Ministry of Welfare in Japan reported almost 4,000 children left without one or both parents (Trumbull 1967).

Since the 1980s, within a larger context of Japan's internationalization and globalization (McConnell 2000), mainstream Japanese images of *hāfu* have been highlighting attractiveness and a whiter phenotypical appearance.[9] *Hāfu* are no longer related to the military, single mothers, and poverty (Murphy-Shigematsu 2001: 212), instead they are associated with glamorous images of mixed Japanese/white models and celebrities,[10] and are commonly found in popular fashion magazines such as *Non-no*, *Can Can* or *Vivi* (equivalent to *Teen Vogue* or *Elle*).[11] One study found that more than 80 percent of models in *ViVi* were mixed white and Asian (Sato 2009).[12] On television, mixed white Japanese celebrities are also becoming more prominent, such as Becky, a half-British woman, born and raised in Japan, who speaks only Japanese. As the creators of the 2013 documentary, *Hafu* (Perez-Takagi and Nishikura 2013), explain on their website, "In modern Japan, the Hafu image projects an ideal; English ability, international cultural experience, western physical features—tall with long legs, small head/face, yet often looking Japanese enough for the majority to feel comfortable with" (see also, Murphy-Shigematsu 2001).[13] Exposed to these images, many young people in Japan perceive mixed people as cool and trendy.

This public portrayal of mixed Japanese in a positive light suggests that future conceptions of Japaneseness and the boundaries around it may be changing in Japan. Moreover, the crowning of the 2015 Miss Universe Japan, Ariana Miyamoto, the daughter of an African-American man and a Japanese woman, provides hope that mainstream Japanese society is embracing and normalizing mixed Japanese people and backgrounds—and not just white Japanese mixes. Ariana Miyamoto seems to be willingly leading the way toward a broader notion of Japaneseness in Japan by saying, "I want to challenge the definition of being Japanese" (Fackler 2015). This statement signals possibilities for a racialized image of Japanese national identity that acknowledges the range of skin colors and ancestries among "Japanese" people in Japan.

In everyday usage, *hāfu* references physiological traits (e.g., skin color, eye shape, hair color) that are different from the majority of people in Japanese society (Murphy-Shigematsu 2000), but depending on the context *hāfu* may also reference less visible traits such as ancestry, language ability, and cultural knowledge. In other words, *hāfu* can also be of other Asian ancestries, e.g., Japanese and Korean, Japanese and Thai.

Whether their connection to "foreigners" and other countries is seen as negatively or positively marginal, mixed Japanese are still considered marginal in Japan. Murphy-Shigematsu (2000: 213) summarizes, "Whether denigrating or worshipping, the person labeled as [*hāfu*] is vulnerable to depiction as different, making it difficult for them to be treated as individuals or as ordinary Japanese." Indeed, though their class image may have changed, *hāfu* are still depicted in stereotypical ways and differentiated from the "regular" Japanese population.

Due to the connotations of both phenotypical difference and mixed ancestries, *hāfu* is also different from *nikkeijin* (the descendants of Japanese emigrants). Technically, the two categories could overlap, with *nikkeijin* subsuming *hāfu*, since the former refers to people of Japanese ancestry and does not specifically imply blood quantum. But practically speaking, Japanese I spoke with in Japan have heard and used *nikkeijin* to refer to people who are phenotypically similar to most Japanese but lack other Japanese traits. In contrast, *hāfu* refers to people who are phenotypically foreign (or at least not clearly Japanese) but Japanese in other ways.[14] The best example is that the child of a "monoracial" Japanese American and a Japanese would be nikkeijin, not *hāfu*, despite being the child of an international marriage.

*Hāfu* is currently the most frequently used term in Japan, though other terms (e.g., *ainoko, konketsuji*) have previously been more common, with newer terms continuing to be introduced.[15] Opinions differ on the nuances and connotations of each expression, which clearly change with social and political context and are also dependent on the user. The term *kokusaiji* was promoted in 1979, the International Year of the Child, as "an attempt to redefine multiethnic people in a positive way by emphasizing the international quality of their parentage and cultural backgrounds" (Murphy-Shigematsu 2001: 213). "Double/*daburu*" is a more recent expression that encourages a paradigm shift for understanding people of mixed ancestries (see Life 1995).[16] In addition, "quarter/*kuoutā*" can be heard from time to time to imply that a person is one-fourth foreign, with one grandparent who is not *nihonjin*.[17]

*Hāfu* is different from the category of "foreigner" because it acknowledges a connection to Japan through Japanese ancestry and cultural knowledge. *Hāfu* can look foreign but have knowledge about Japanese society and culture, differentiating them from complete foreigners, assumed to have no knowledge of or connections to Japan.

On the other hand, since mainstream Japanese are defined according to traits such as citizenship, ancestry, language competence, place of birth, current residence, and cultural knowledge (Sugimoto 2003: 186–187), with foreigners constructed as possessing none of these traits, people with any combination of these characteristics are often grouped together as *hāfu*. This includes Americans of only Japanese ancestry who lack basic Japanese social and cultural knowledge (Yamashiro 2011), as well as foreign-looking people who speak Japanese fluently (see Burgess 2012). Many foreign-looking, foreign nationals of foreign ancestry who are fluent in Japanese that I interviewed said that they are commonly asked if they are *hāfu* once their language abilities and cultural knowledge become apparent.

With the increase in international and interracial marriages in Japan, the population of people referred to as *hāfu* is also on the rise. For example, about 5 percent of marriages in Japan are international. In addition, the number of marriages between two Japanese nationals has been decreasing over the past forty years, while the number of marriages between a Japanese national and a foreign national has been steadily increasing (Lise 2011). Most of these marriages do not involve military personnel (Murphy-Shigematsu 2001: 213). Beyond Japan, increasing cultural, ethnic, and racial blending is leading to "an increasing social acceptance of mixed cultural identities (both individual and collective) across the world" (King-O'Riain, Small, Mahtani, Song, and Spickard 2014: xi). As local and global demographic and discursive shifts occur, it will be interesting to see how the growth of this population might possibly open up a third social category in Japan.

Since *hāfu* is a Japan-specific category, connotations are based on historical context in Japan rather than in the United States. In this regard, *hāfu* is different from identifying as "Japanese American," which typically alludes to a history of incarceration in the United States. Several of my interviewees also pointed out how "Japanese American" suggests generational distance from Japan. Thus, those who have postwar Japanese immigrant parents and do not identify with prewar Japanese American history and experiences, do not necessarily identify as "Japanese American."

Finally, *hāfu* is different from *hapa* because the latter category is not widely recognized in Japan. The word *hapa* suggests "mixed Asian American" within US national and continental racial and ethnic categories, but it means something slightly different in Hawai'i, where it originated. Before turning to individual narratives that show how people find creative ways to relate to the category of *hāfu* in Japan, it will be helpful to discuss its mixed-category counterpart, *hapa*, as used and understood in the United States.

## *Hapa*: Mixed Japaneseness and Asianness in the United States

*Hapa* is an increasingly common term in the United States used to refer not only to mixed Japanese Americans but also to other mixed-heritage Asian Americans. Examples of famous people who would be considered *hapa* include Apolo Ohno, who is mixed Japanese and European American, as well as Tiger Woods, who is mixed African American, European American, Thai, Chinese, and Native American. Due to the racial structure in the United States, where Japaneseness is subsumed into the larger panethnic "Asian" racial group, it is difficult to discuss mixed Japaneseness without also linking it to mixed Asianness more generally. To my knowledge, no term refers specifically to only mixed Japaneseness in the US context.

Similar to the overall population of Japanese Americans, mixed Japanese Americans in the United States are diverse in terms of Japanese linguistic ability and cultural knowledge, due in large part to whether their families are part of the prewar or postwar migration wave from Japan. In addition, mixed Japanese Americans are diverse in terms of phenotypical characteristics and names, with a wide range of hair and skin color, as well as first and last names, that sometimes reflect their Japanese ancestry and other times do not.

Mixed-heritage Japanese Americans have been and continue to be an important part of the Japanese American community.[18] According to the 2010 US Census, of all Asian groups, people claiming Japanese ancestry had the highest proportion reporting multiple heritages—41 percent of the Japanese American population claimed two or more races or ethnic groups (Hoeffel, Rastogi, Kim, and Shahid 2012). If the mixed-race and mixed-ethnic Japanese American population continues to grow at this rate, demographers predict that by the year 2020, the majority of Japanese Americans will identify as being of mixed heritage. Among mixed Japanese Americans, the most common combination is "white" and "Japanese" (Shinagawa et al. 2011). This is reflective of the larger trend among "Asians," where the biggest and fastest growing group claiming multiple races is represented by those who are "Asian" and "white" (Hoeffel et al. 2012).

Focusing on mixed white/Japanese Americans, Williams has identified two main sources of contact leading to the continued growth of this population: "U.S. military, government, and business involvement in Japan" and "the significant numbers of intermarriage between Japanese Americans and European Americans" (Williams 1997: 35). In other words, multiracial Japanese Americans in the United States are the product of interracial relationships begun both in Japan and in the United States. These interracial relationships are considered international when they include Japanese in and from Japan, but they are considered domestic when they are between later-generation Japanese Americans and other Americans in the United States.

As Wei Ming Dariotis points out, mixed Japanese American experiences are diverse, including being imprisoned in World War II incarceration camps in the United States and growing up on US military bases in Japan (and elsewhere) during the postwar period. At least 700 Japanese Americans of mixed heritage and about 1,400 Japanese immigrants married to non-Japanese (and some of their non-Japanese spouses) were incarcerated during World War II, along with the rest of the Japanese American community (Dariotis 2003: 117). In addition, some mixed-heritage Japanese who grew up in Japan, or were raised in both Japan and the United States, move to the United States and become part of local Japanese American communities.

On the US continent, many people in the Japanese American and larger Asian American communities have adopted the term *hapa* to refer to mixed Asian Americans, i.e., an American of mixed Asian ancestries not including Japanese (Dariotis 2003).[19] Since "Asian American" was already an established panethnic racial category, with "Japanese American" an ethnic group within it, the leap from *hapa* as referring to mixed-heritage Japanese Americans to more broadly including mixed-heritage Asian Americans was not a difficult one to make. Taniguchi and Heidenreich (2005: 136) have pointed out that "[mixed-race] individuals navigate within a monoracial Asian American/Asian/Pacific Islander/Pacific Islander American (APA) framework to create a place for themselves." Thus, *hapa* needs to be understood as a category constructed in relation to the existing racial classifications in the United States, specifically as constructed against "Asian American," a monoracial designation on the US continent.

Etymologically, the term *hapa* emerged out of Native Hawaiian contact with white foreigners, but subsequent mixtures, including other groups in Hawai'i and on the continent, have resulted in broadened usage, which is contentious for those who promote adherence to the original meaning (see Yamashiro 2017). The term *hapa haole* was widely used to describe Hawaiians with European ancestry as early as 1849 (Kauanui 2008: 56). In this context, *hapa* is defined as "part" in the Hawaiian language and *haole* refers to foreigners, most of whom were distinguished by their whiter skin.[20]

Over time, as migrants from Asia, Europe, and other parts of the world settled in Hawai'i, *hapa* was adopted as a way to describe other kinds of mixtures, sometimes not including Native Hawaiians at all. In Hawai'i in the 2000s, *hapa* is used in everyday language to describe people of mixed ancestry, such as Chinese and Hawaiian, Filipino and English, and Japanese and "white" (Folen and Ng 2007). According to Jonathan Okamura, locals who live in Hawai'i use the term primarily to refer to people who are mixed "white" and "Asian American" (Folen and Ng 2007). It is believed that ethnic Japanese who had adopted the term in Hawai'i brought it with them when they migrated to California in the postwar period, resulting in the spread of the term's usage to the West Coast.

Mixed Japanese Americans do not always have phenotypical traits that mark them as ethnically Japanese. In the United States, factors considered in racialization (association with a race or races) are usually phenotypical: skin, hair, and eye color, as well as eye shape. The racialization of mixed Japanese Americans is no exception, often depending on physical cues. Since multiracial individuals range widely in phenotypical appearance, racialization of them also varies greatly (see Hall and Turner 2001, Spickard 1997, Williams 1997).

Another way in which Japaneseness is expressed is through names. However, multiracial and multiethnic people often have names that do not "match" their physical appearance or mannerisms and do not accurately reflect their race, ethnicity, or identity (Nakashima 2001: 114).[21] Nakashima explains that to more clearly express their ethnic backgrounds, people of mixed heritages "will sometimes employ a middle name or a mother's maiden name to make visible a part of their background that would have otherwise remained hidden behind conventional usage of one's first name and patrilineal surname" (Nakashima 2001: 116). The ways in which they use their names to express their ethnic backgrounds reflect the belief that multiracial and multiethnic people have some agency in directing how they are racially and ethnically categorized (Nakashima 2001: 119).

Within the United States, both where and how the term *hapa* is used has changed over time. Similar to the usage of the term *hāfu*, when people describe others or identify with the term *hapa*, they are referencing mixedness. But this mixedness is located within very different racial formations; it is a mix of different categories, with different boundaries and meanings. While *hāfu* denotes a mix of Japaneseness and foreignness, *hapa* refers to a mix of Asianness and other "races" in the United States, or Hawaiianness and foreignness, depending on the perspective. These disjunctures are important to note because ways of categorizing people and identifying are always understood within specific societal contexts and are not interchangeable—and this includes mixedness because it is based on the premise that specific categories exist into which mixed people do not fit.

Even within a single national or societal context, mixedness can be labeled and interpreted in multiple ways, so as people migrate internationally, both how to describe themselves and the idea of mixedness become more varied.

G. Reginald Daniel, Laura Kina, Wei Ming Dariotis, and Camilla Fojas point out that "The terms used to describe someone of mixed heritage . . . have different meanings depending on the country or place of origin" (Daniel, Kina, Dariotis, and Fojas 2014: 26). As people migrate between the United States and Japan, their histories, their bodies, and their ways of speaking and acting are viewed through different lenses, with different boundaries marking criteria for inclusion and exclusion. Through the physical experience of internationally migrating from the United States to Japan, mixed Japanese Americans move from a context where mixed Japaneseness is described as *hapa* to another context where it is conveyed through the term *hāfu*. Ways of identifying and categorizing people are always shaped by historical circumstances and located within systems of power. Thus, examining the transnational reconstruction of mixedness for Japanese Americans in Japan is a way to understand both the boundaries around the category of *hāfu*, a term that sometimes includes and sometimes excludes them, and how mixed Japanese Americans see themselves in relation to Japanese people and struggle to have their Japaneseness acknowledged by people in Japan.

## Five Individual Negotiations

It should be clear from the previous two sections that ways of thinking about mixed Japaneseness in the United States and Japan are different, even sometimes contradictory, due to the different demographics, history, and social categories in the two countries. As mixed Japanese Americans move from the United States to Japan, they encounter new terms for describing their own mixed Japaneseness. In what ways do mixed Japanese Americans identify as *hāfu* in Japan, and in what ways do they not? When do Japanese people seem to accept them as *hāfu*, and when and why do they not? What do Japanese Americans gain from identifying as *hāfu*?

As international migrants, Japanese Americans grapple with how to describe themselves in Japan and specifically negotiate *hāfu* as a mixed-Japanese category. How they choose to do this highlights gaps between taken-for-granted definitions and individual perceptions of categorical boundaries and meanings in Japan. Some mixed Japanese Americans adhere to US-based labels (e.g., *hapa*) for mixedness even when living in Japan. Others attempt to use Japan-based labels (e.g., *hāfu*) with varying levels of success and satisfaction.

In contrast to mixed Japanese raised in Japan who grew up exposed to the concept of *hāfu*, making it harder to consider other identity options, mixed Japanese Americans from the United States encounter a new social categorization system and must adjust to new vocabulary to be understood in Japan. Examining their choices illuminates three issues: when and why Japanese Americans choose to identify as *hāfu*, the array of other identity options for them, and limitations to their identity assertions.

### *Jordan:* Hapa, *not* Hāfu

Jordan says that sometimes people can see that he has some Asian ancestry, but at other times they have trouble believing that he is Japanese American. He speaks very little Japanese and has learned to see himself as a foreigner in Japan, but he also wants people to recognize his Japanese background. In both the United States and Japan, Jordan describes himself as *hapa* and gets frustrated when people in Japan do not respond to him in the ways that he is accustomed to in the United States. Years after I spoke with Jordan, I heard that he had eventually returned to the United States and currently lives in California.

When I interviewed him in 2006, Jordan was a thirty-five-year-old, self-described hapa sansei from the San Francisco Bay Area who had been teaching English at a private elementary school in the Tokyo area for two years. This was his second trip to Japan; the first had been as a tourist when he was thirty. Before going to Japan, Jordan spoke limited Japanese; growing up, he only learned a few food words and phrases, which was typical of my sansei interviewees. At home, his family had some Japanese art and books and ate some Japanese food. Specifically, he remembers eating teriyaki chicken, rice, miso soup, *sukiyaki*, sushi/*onigiri*, *sashimi*, special New Year's food, and *daikon* (white radish). But when asked to describe Japanese customs practiced in his home, Jordan replied, "Customs—that's hard to define I think for some or many Japanese American sansei like me." As a youth, Jordan was involved in the local Japanese American community through the Little League baseball program. Both from Southern California, Jordan's mother is second-generation Japanese American (nisei), and his father is fourth- and fifth-generation Italian, Polish, German, and Scottish-Irish American. His mother's parents were from Fukushima and Kagoshima. Twice a year, he would visit his maternal grandparents in Southern California and remembers their house containing "Japanese things like newspapers, art, food, and other Japanese cultural . . . items."

Jordan strongly identified with the US-based, mixed-heritage term *hapa*, even while he was living in Japan—and even though Japanese people seemed unfamiliar with the term. When asked how he would describe his ethnicity to someone in the United States, he responded: "I describe myself as Hapa.

Furthermore I might explain that I am of mixed ancestry, part Italian/Polish and part Japanese and 100 percent [his hometown]." Unprompted, he continued on to explain that although it is common in the San Francisco Bay Area to be asked about your ethnic background "and have meaningful conversations about such," Japanese rarely ask him about his heritage. His explanation for these conversations not occurring in Japan was that most Japanese seem "extremely ignorant about cultural diversity and issues related to diversity such as personal identity formation and experiences."

Though I asked him a question about how he identifies in the United States, Jordan answered regarding his experiences in both the United States and Japan, suggesting that he does not clearly differentiate between them. In fact, he expects to have conversations about his ethnic background in Japan similar to those he has had in the United States (or is at least disappointed when such conversations do not occur). Since Jordan takes pride in his mixed ancestry, he misses conversations about his background that were common in the US context of multiculturalism. He has noticed that attitudes about diversity in Japan are different from in the United States, but he seems unaware of the hegemonic discourse of Japanese homogeneity, where most people in Japan are assumed to be either Japanese or foreign, rather than a combination of both.

When asked if Japanese people usually know what *hapa* means, Jordan replied, "Usually not. There are a few people who have heard of it, but not Japanese ... and most Americans, too. The few people who have heard of it are from California, maybe." So although he seems aware that *hapa* is not a common term in Japan (and has limited usage even in the United States), he prefers to keep self-identifying this way in Japan. Unfortunately, this choice appears to guarantee that he will feel some level of frustration in Japan, where the term, as well as discussions about one's ethnic background, are much less common. Thus, "meaningful conversations" may not be unfolding for him in Japan partly because the term *hapa* is not familiar to Japanese.

Additionally, Japanese people may see Jordan as a white foreigner and not ask about his ethnic background since he does not exhibit any markers of Japaneseness. He does not look similar to most Japanese, does not use Japanese names, and does not describe himself using Japanese terms for being mixed Japanese. Jordan's resistance to the term *hāfu*, as discussed below, as well as his insistence on identifying as *hapa* in Japan, appears to reflect his lack of understanding of Japanese language and society. He seems to be using a US-based term simply because he is unaware of other, more common terms in Japan. But when asked about the term *hāfu*, another explanation becomes apparent.

Though aware of the term, Jordan does not identify as *hāfu* because it does not include later-generation mixed Japanese like him whose ties to Japan are quite removed. When asked if he has heard people use the term, he answered, "Yeah, I think that's a stupid-ass name, personally. To be honest, I don't know because I don't consider myself *hāfu*. In my understanding, that's usually used to describe someone who's half Japanese and half something else. Usually American or European. And I don't consider myself as that." In other words, Jordan sees *hāfu* as inaccurate in describing his background because of his generational distance from *nihonjin*. He continued to explain that while he recognizes that *hāfu* is used to describe "someone half Japanese and half something else," it is a "stupid" way to refer to people: "You're half what, half Japanese, or half foreigner, what?" While he resents the idea of not being seen holistically, this does not mean that he completely rejects the term as a category to describe people. Although he does not know who developed the term or where it came from, Jordan does recognize that "there are a lot of *hāfu* people here and I would think in general their experience would be a lot different from mine."

By pointing out that *hāfu* people probably have different experiences from himself, Jordan is making two claims. First, he is asserting that *hāfu* describes a group of people—people who have one parent from Japan and one parent from another country. In contrast, Jordan's parents are both from the United States. Jordan's assertion of this ontological difference suggests that the term *hāfu* does not capture his biography and experiences in the United States, while the term *hapa* does. That is, Jordan's comments and resistance to using *hāfu* to describe himself in Japan imply that US-based and Japan-based terms are not only not compatible, but also that they describe different groups of people and experiences.

Second, when he says that *hāfu* refers to "half Japanese and half something else," a group that does not include him, Jordan is referring to Japaneseness not as ethnicity but as citizenship. In Japan-based conceptions of Japaneseness, ethnicity and citizenship are conflated. The children of international marriages between Japanese citizens of Japanese ancestry ("Japanese") and foreign nationals not of Japanese ancestry ("foreigners") do not challenge this conflation, but someone like Jordan does because he is mixed Japanese in terms of ancestry but not in terms of citizenship. Born to parents who are both US citizens, Jordan identifies as being of mixed-Japanese heritage, but not as the child of a Japanese national or of an international marriage. Thus, according to this logic, he cannot be *hāfu*.

As much as Jordan enjoys living in Japan, he is frustrated that his Japaneseness is not recognized by most Japanese people. Within bifurcated

Japanese social categories, Jordan understands that most people consider him to be a "foreigner," rather than a "Japanese," despite his Japanese ancestry.[22] In fact, Jordan, too, sees himself as a foreigner. At the same time, however, he wants the historical family connection he feels to Japan to be acknowledged by *nihonjin*. Jordan usually informs Japanese people of his shared ancestry because most do not think he looks Japanese. He added, "Many people don't believe me, in the States as well, as if I have to prove it to them—ain't that some shit. And sometimes I do—I [break] out the family pics and they're all amazed." Jordan feels frustrated that others do not see him how he sees himself. Even when he asserts a Japanese ethnic identity, his phenotypical difference (as well as lack of other traits such as Japanese language fluency or a Japanese name), make it hard for *nihonjin* to recognize his Japaneseness.

As a multiracial foreign national of Japanese ancestry, Jordan has mixed emotions about the way he is treated in Japan. "Yo, being [a foreigner] in Japan is a trip. I get mixed feelings often but overall enjoy being here. I feel fortunate to be Hapa in Japan because in a sense I feel at an advantage over other foreigners in the sense that I am more knowledgeable and comfortable in certain cultural situations having Japanese culture in my blood and in my upbringing. But I get mad upset when I feel like I'm being discriminated against in Japan—mad angry. Pisses me off like I've never really felt in Cali." Jordan describes his Japaneseness not only as juxtaposed against foreignness, but also in terms of familiarity with Japanese culture and in biological terms. In other words, he makes the common conflation of ancestry and culture—that culture is in your "blood." Though he is of Japanese ancestry and has been raised in a Japanese American community, this is different from being raised in Japanese society, where Japaneseness takes on different meaning.

To Jordan, being seen as as *hakujin* ("white") and as a foreigner by Japanese people means experiencing discrimination because of the way he looks, which he resents. He explains, "I notice people not wanting to sit next to me on the train. I tell Japanese people about it and they deny it." He says they contend, "We're not discriminatory—we don't know so how can we discriminate?" Jordan differentiates between ignorance and malice, wanting to believe that most *nihonjin* are just ignorant and without negative intentions. But these types of actions can be considered microaggressions. While we may never know what *nihonjin* are thinking when they see Jordan on the train, Jordan's point is well-taken: racist and discriminatory acts may be unconscious or unintentional.

In the context of Japanese society, Jordan's whiteness can be interpreted in two main ways. On the one hand, whiteness is associated with a minority positioning in Japan, in terms of both the numerical population and representation in mainstream society. Since racism is about systematic privilege and power based on perceived notions of race, in Japan everyone not "Japanese" experiences racism, including people perceived to be "white."

On the other hand, within Japanese society, as well as globally, people benefit from being racialized "white." It is well-known that being racialized white affords various privileges in the United States (Lipsitz 2006, López 1996, McIntosh 2007, Rothenberg 2008); Jordan was well-aware of his white privilege in the United States. But in Japan as well, white Westerners occupy a privileged position; whiteness has been associated with measures of progress and standards of beauty dating back to the Meiji era (Creighton 1997).

Moreover, the privileged status of people deemed "white" extends beyond Japan, reflecting larger global trends and the fact that some constructions of race transcend nation-states and circulate globally. For example, on a worldwide basis, it has long been held that whiteness is associated with power (Bonnett 2004, Mills 2008) and that the ideology of whiteness as superior to all other races has long been key to the global subjugation and domination of peoples of color (Mills 2008: 98). In contrast, globally, blackness is associated with a lack of power (Bashi 2004, Minter 2005). Specifically, the low global position of blacks can be explained by "centuries of slavery, conquest, and colonial rule" (Minter 2005: 452), as well as a history of anti-black sentiment in Western immigration policy (Bashi 2004: 585).[23] It is important to keep these local and global constructions of whiteness and blackness in mind when examining constructions of race beyond a single nation-state.

In an attempt to convey his feeling of racial exclusion in Japan, Jordan compared his experiences with those of blacks in the United States and said that he identifies as a "person of color." I have often heard white Americans casually make this comparison between their experiences in Japan and black experiences in the United States. This statement is typically made by people who are not thinking critically about structures of power and inequality or the inhumane treatment that blacks have received in the United States—dating back to their forced migration as slaves. But Jordan, who had been an ethnic studies major in college, was aware of his white privilege in the United States (and his American privilege in Japan—to easily find a well-paying job teaching English). As soon as he suggested parallels between his experiences in Japan and black experiences in the United States, he clarified, "I don't know what it's like to be black in the US . . . and don't equate those experiences, but I do identify with the experience of being treated as different because of your skin color." Jordan was hesitant to make this comparison, but it was the easiest way for him to describe his visual salience and different treatment in Japan, in contrast to his blending in back in the United States. This points to the lack of a term to describe the position of whites as both a minority in a particular society, yet also associated with power globally.

While "person of color" is a US-based term that conjures up specific histories of genocide and racism and may seem inappropriate to apply to the position of whites in Japan, Jordan is consistent in using US-based terms to interpret his experiences in Japan, despite the different racial formation. The labels one uses reflect forms of identification, in this case indicating which society is the point of reference. With both limited Japanese language ability and limited knowledge of contemporary Japanese culture and society, it makes sense that Jordan continues to describe himself in US terms such as hapa while living in Japan. It also helps to explain the tension between how Jordan sees himself as connected to people in Japan based on ancestry alone and how Japanese people see him as foreign because he lacks the other social and cultural characteristics expected of Japanese people in Japan.

From a US-based perspective, in which most later-generation Japanese Americans do not speak Japanese or know anything about Japanese society, what does make them "Japanese" compared to other Americans is their ancestral ties to Japan. Ironically, however, by describing himself as *hapa* in Japan to claim a mixed identity that acknowledges his Japanese ancestry and differentiates him from other foreigners, Jordan is using a non-Japanese term that appears to confuse Japanese people and actually highlights his foreignness and unfamiliarity with Japanese society. While Jordan wants his Japaneseness to be recognized and validated in Japan, he is also clear that he does not feel connected because of a Japanese national identity or because of close ties to a Japanese citizen. For these reasons, Jordan identifies as being of mixed ancestry, but he does not identify as *hāfu* due to its inference of international parentage. Despite the possibility that identifying as *hāfu* might be more intelligible to Japanese people and might provide the recognition of his Japaneseness that he desires, Jordan dislikes the term and avoids using it. But what happens when a later-generation, mixed Japanese from the United States does identify as *hāfu* in Japan? The next example explores this scenario.

### *John:* Hāfu *as More Easily Understandable Than Nikkei Yonsei*

Through trial and error, by the second time John was living in Japan, he had found that Japanese people understood him better as *hāfu* than as *nikkei yonsei* (of Japanese descent, fourth generation). While nikkei explains his generational distance from Japan and why he lacks social and cultural knowledge, it does not directly reference his mixed ancestral background. The term is typically used in Japan to describe people who look Japanese but are culturally different (e.g., *nikkei* Brazilians). At the same time, *hāfu* is also limited in its explanatory power to acknowledge mixedness in that it only describes the child of a Japanese national. In contrast to Jordan, who continued to use US-based terms to describe himself in Japan, John had the linguistic, social, and cultural knowledge to cast himself in Japan-based terms. However, John's experiences reveal how Japanese terms focus on either generational distance from Japan or mixedness. With no term in Japanese to recognize Japanese of mixed-ancestry who are also later-generation, people have found that explanations are almost always necessary.

When I first interviewed John in 2005, he was a twenty-nine-year-old law school student who had taken a year off to study Japanese in Japan.[24] Born in the Southwest to parents who were from and had met in Hawai'i, on a regular basis John spent summers in Hawai'i visiting his paternal grandparents—until they moved to the continent to live with his family when he was a teenager. John's exposure to Japanese language and culture was primarily through his paternal grandparents, whether visiting them in Hawai'i or spending time together on the continent. John's father is sansei from Hawai'i, while his mother is a "European mix," including German, Native American (Blackfoot Indian), and Scottish. He sometimes wonders if his mother notices that he has not taken much interest in "her side," but he explains that "since she's mixed, it's harder to choose one to identify with . . . if she were only Italian maybe I'd identify with that or take more of an interest in it."

Partly due to the demographic makeup of his schools (that included few Asians) while growing up and partly due to the fact that John never felt connected to Asian people simply because of their shared backgrounds, John says that through college he never spent much time around predominantly Asian students. Rather, he chose to spend time with more racially diverse groups. While attending college in Arizona, he identified as "Japanese American," but there was no club focused on Japanese Americans because they were so few in number. He joined an Asian American student association, but he remembers not feeling very accepted because "there weren't many other people of half backgrounds." Later he had a girlfriend who was very involved with the club and was subsequently more accepted, but this just showed John how cliquish the people were. The Japan club (different from a "Japanese American" club) focusing on the society and culture of Japan would have interested John, if it had not primarily consisted of "Asiophiles [who were] into anime [Japanese animation] or Japanese women." So John spent his time working as a counselor to help diverse students of color and economically disadvantaged students transition to college life with the aim of increasing retention rates. He also started a fraternity with a friend, which ended up being culturally diverse and coincidentally included a membership of about half Asians.

In the United States, John ethnically identifies as "Japanese-American" more than with terms that reference multiraciality.[25] He explains that in the United States, "I primarily would say that I am Japanese-American. If pressed further I would say that my father's side is Japanese and my mother's side is European." One reason for this might be the kinds of Japanese Americans around whom John has spent time. When asked how being around Japanese Americans from Hawai'i and the continent compare, he replied that when he meets people from Hawai'i, they tend not to discuss his background, race, or ethnicity. He has not spent much time with Japanese Americans from the continent—perhaps because his connection to Japanese Americans is through his father from Hawai'i.

A lack of questioning and conversations about racial and ethnic background from Japanese Americans in Hawai'i may be due to the large proportion of ethnic Japanese and Asian people in Hawai'i, including those who are multiracial. Another reason might be because when John spends time in Hawai'i and around Japanese Americans from Hawai'i, it is time spent with his own family and friends, people already familiar with his family background. It is possible that if John spent more time around other Japanese Americans or Asian Americans from the continent, he would be asked more about his mixed heritage.

When I spoke with John, it was his second time living in Japan so he had already developed identification strategies based on trial and error experiences. After finishing college in the United States, John spent two years on the JET (Japan Exchange and Teaching) Program living in the Japanese countryside. He said that in Japan, he has not received the same attention as "white" people and can blend into a crowd, though in a one-on-one situation, people do notice that he is a foreigner.[26] In the United States, John never described himself as *nikkei*, perhaps because both of his parents were from Hawai'i or because he was brought up in the Southwest. But when he first lived in Japan, nikkei yonsei seemed like an appropriate way to describe his background to Japanese people. As with my other interviewees of Japanese descent, *nikkei* was a term used to acknowledge their ancestral connections to Japan, while also recognizing that they themselves were not raised in Japan.

For Japanese Americans who are phenotypically similar to most Japanese, *nikkei* is an unproblematic term in Japan to describe them. But for Japanese Americans who are phenotypically ambiguous or look different from most Japanese, *nikkei* as a descriptor by itself does not explain phenotypical differences. John found that describing himself as *nikkei* did not clarify his background for Japanese people; he has since learned to say that he is *hāfu*. While John did not go into detail about this process of switching terms, the change itself suggests that phenotype and ancestry were important characteristics in choosing the labels that he used.

While *nikkei* and *hāfu* both describe people of Japanese ancestry who may lack cultural knowledge of Japanese society, *hāfu* are typically assumed to be phenotypically differentiable from most Japanese, as mentioned earlier. So despite both terms referring to people of Japanese ancestry, the same person, in Japanese terms, would never be referred to as both *nikkei* and *hāfu* because of the different traits that each term embodies. John added that *hāfu* is readily comprehensible to Japanese people and is also trendy; he also mentioned that its usage seemed to have the additional benefit of being more popular with women. A friend of John's, who also self-describes as *hāfu*, introduced him to the term.

In the three years since John last lived in Japan, he related that the popularity of the term *hāfu* has increased, which has affected the ways in which he can identify and be understood by Japanese people. Regarding how he identifies in Japan now, John reflected "Although I feel as though I am connected somewhat to Japan and the Japanese people, I have never truly felt Japanese. The emphasis on citizenship in Japan and my interactions with people from a wide variety of countries here in Japan makes me feel more American than in the U.S. The recent popularization of 'half' and 'hapa' has seemed to create a new category I have been able to fit into as well." After spending two years in Japan, John identifies as not "Japanese." His experiences teaching English, meeting people from all over the world, and representing the United States may all help to explain his sense of feeling more American in Japan than in the United States. Despite his feeling "more American," rather than just feeling like another "foreigner," John asserts a multiracial identity in Japan, even though he tended to identify as "Japanese American" in the US context more than in terms of his mixedness. (It is unclear if he is aware that *hapa* is a US-based term; he seemed to be introduced to both terms from mixed Japanese American friends also living in Japan.)

The increasing recognition of *hāfu* as a social category does not necessarily mean that someone with John's particular background is readily understood. As someone who is of Japanese and "foreign" ancestry but does not have a parent from Japan, John still has trouble explaining his background in Japanese terms. He explains the flow of conversation, even when he begins by telling people that he is *hāfu*, "First, I say that I am 'half.' Then, I usually qualify the statement by saying that my father is 3rd generation Japanese-American, sometimes in response to puzzled looks or to the question, 'which one of you[r] parents are Japanese?' I am usually corrected and told that I am not half, but a quarter. I also often tell people that my great-grandparents left Japan and went to Hawaii during the early 1900s." The confusion generated by John's use of *hāfu* to describe himself reflects the tension between generational assumptions regarding mixedness in Japan and in the United States. In Japan, the term *hāfu* implies that one parent is *nihonjin* from Japan. In contrast to John, Jordan seemed to sense this tension because he conscientiously avoided using the term *hāfu*.

When John asserts that he is *hāfu*, he focuses on Japaneseness in terms of ancestry and disregards the connotation of citizenship. In the United States, people of Japanese ancestry are generally lumped together as "Japanese"— both by others and by themselves. According to US racial categories, "multiracial Japanese Americans" can include both the children of international marriages and later-generation Japanese Americans. But as John's experiences demonstrate, the lines are drawn differently in Japan because Japaneseness is conceptualized in a way that also includes citizenship, thus excluding later-generation Japanese Americans.

Phenotype, language ability, and other traits affect how conversations about mixed backgrounds occur. As described earlier, Jordan claimed that he was not given the same opportunity in Japan as in the United States to explain his Japanese ancestry. This was probably because he looked, sounded, and acted foreign. On the other hand, since John looked more phenotypically ambiguous (and also had a higher level of Japanese fluency and a Japanese last name), his assertion of a *hāfu* identity was initially unproblematic. John's conversations with Japanese suggest that his "nonwhite" phenotype and his Japanese language ability enabled him to have conversations about his Japaneseness.

Whether or not people accept John as *hāfu* reflects how they define "Japanese"—as based on ancestry or citizenship. As the child of two American citizens of different ancestries, John is certainly not the product of an international marriage. When Japanese refers simply to ancestry, as is common in the United States, then John fits the meaning of *hāfu* as a mixed-ancestry identifier. This is actually closer to the US-based term *hapa*, but since that term is not common in Japan, *hāfu* is the most recognizable term for Americans to describe their being of mixed ancestries.

However, when Japaneseness conflates ancestry and citizenship, as is common in Japanese society, then John is clearly not *hāfu*. Thus, most Japanese are confused when John explains his generational distance from Japan in addition to his mixed heritage, causing different math calculations about how to describe his Japaneseness. Bringing together the concepts of *nikkei* and *hāfu* to describe the same person—or in John's case, the concept of *hāfu* with later-generation Japaneseness (even if the term *nikkei* isn't necessarily used)—causes confusion in Japan because *hāfu* already implies a specific parentage (and generation) as well as an ethnic percentage. The confusion as to whether John is half, quarter, or an eighth Japanese derives from these multiple axes of Japaneseness that are implicit in everyday conceptions in Japan.

### *Emma:* Hāfu *as not 100 Percent Foreign*

Emma identifies as "mixed" in both the United States and in Japan and over time learned to describe herself as *hāfu* in Japan. As a university exchange student, she was studying Japanese language and culture when I met her. In fact, she learned most of what she knew about Japan from school even though her mother was an immigrant from Japan. Unlike Jordan and John, Emma felt a special connection to and curiosity about Japan because her mother was born and raised there. In discovering that *hāfu* was the easiest way to describe her mixed background to Japanese people, she also found that it was a way to distinguish herself from foreigners not of Japanese ancestry. After her year of study abroad in Tokyo, Emma has said that she has no plans to live in Japan again.

Emma was born and raised in Southern California to a mother from Japan and a father from the Midwest who is half Italian and half American of English and Scottish descent. Growing up, meals at home consisted mostly of Japanese food, perhaps reflective of her mother doing most of the cooking. Around the house Emma remembers seeing mystery novels in Japanese, the *Asahi Shimbun* newspaper, Japanese magazines, and other printed materials in Japanese that her mother would read. Emma had always wondered about her mother's background, which seemed mysterious because it entailed a language and place unfamiliar to her.

So at age twenty-one, Emma went to Tokyo as an exchange student during her junior year of college. "Before coming I was interested in Japan, in finding out about it and if it was relevant to me." She imagined that learning about Japan might help her learn more about a hidden side of her mother. However, after going to Japan, she concluded, "Mom is just mom—there's nothing hidden there. The language part had mystified me." Emma's questions about her mother's background are reminiscent of Maxine Hong Kingston's famous query about the difficulty of separating what is due to culture and ethnicity, what is specific to a person or a family, and what is attributable to other demographic factors (Kingston 1976: 5–6).

I spoke with Emma two times in 2006—first, in January, six months after she had arrived in Tokyo, and again in June just before she completed her year-long stay. These talks revealed details about her socialization in the United States and resocialization in Japan. In the first interview in January, when asked about how she identified in Japan, Emma said, "Since I appear mostly white, I don't readily identify as an Asian American since people generally don't treat me as one—which unfortunately has a lot to do with my racial identity. Over the years I guess my strongest identification is of a mixed ancestry. Maybe the second strongest would be Japanese American, third, hapa, fourth, Asian American. In Japan I feel more American than I do at home." Though I had asked about her identification in Japan, Emma began her response by describing how she identified in the United States, using the categories of "white," "Asian American," "Japanese American," and *hapa*. Similar to Jordan's response, this type of answer reveals her desire to continue identifying herself in US terms, even outside of the United States, perhaps because even though Emma had studied Japanese society and culture, our first interview was only six months after she had moved to Tokyo. At that time, she had not yet had enough interactions in Japan to think about herself in Japanese terms. Also, similar to Jordan, Emma identifies most strongly as someone "mixed" who "appear[s] mostly white."

However, in contrast to Jordan, Emma's positioning as the child of a Japanese emigrant, as we will see below, led to shifts over time in how she thought about and described herself within Japanese society. It helped that she engaged Japanese people in conversation and learned to see herself in Japanese terms. In a separate question, when asked how she describes her ethnic background in the United States, Emma responded, "Mixed first. If they ask further I say half Japanese, and further one quarter Italian and one quarter American." In addition to these US-based ways of identifying, after six months in Tokyo, Emma's national identity also became salient. When asked specifically about how she describes her background to people in Japan, Emma explained: "I usually say ha-fu (though I don't like it) since it is the easiest to understand term for Japanese. They are usually surprised since I don't look like a typical half."[27] Japanese girls in Emma's dorm have told her that they have a hard time distinguishing between "whites" and *hāfu*.

In the United States, relates Emma, people can usually tell she is not completely white. Sometimes she's seen as a Latina but "usually other halfs can tell." She expressed a clear disdain for the term *hāfu* because it implies that one is only half (and not whole). However, she explained, since people in Japan do not understand the concept of *hapa*, she uses *hāfu* instead. In contrast to Jordan, who had never studied Japanese before going to Japan, Emma had taken Japanese classes in college and continued to take them as an exchange student in Tokyo. Once she realized that Japanese people were not familiar with the term *hapa,* her cultural resources enabled her to shift to a Japanese term, even one she disliked.

Six months later in June, Emma's views on *hāfu* and her categorization in Japan had become a bit more complicated. At the end of her year as an exchange student, Emma felt more "white," though she would sometimes describe herself as *hāfu* to acknowledge that she did have some ties to Japan. Much of her experience was shaped by her phenotype, though her non-Japanese last name, lack of fluency in the Japanese language, and ignorance about Japanese culture were certainly also significant factors in how her Japaneseness was perceived.[28] Reflecting on how she is perceived in the United States versus Japan, Emma asserted, "before coming . . . in retrospect at home people ask me what I am so I guess I stick out, but in Japan I stick out and have no chance of being Japanese."

In other words, in the United States sometimes others will notice that she is not only white (but also Japanese), but in Japan she is more consistently seen as just white. People are surprised when she tells them she is of Japanese ancestry: "Without explaining myself I'm gaijin [a foreigner]. I don't explain my ethnic background to everyone I meet so I just deal with it." This tone suggests that being a foreigner is something to tolerate, not how she would prefer to be seen. Ideally, Emma wants people to know her background and to see her as connected to Japan and its people. She identifies with Japanese people, but they do not identify with her in the same way since they perceive her to be a "foreigner."

Emma described the two main ways she asserts her connection to Japan when she speaks with Japanese people. Both of these methods reflect her strategy of identification in Japan as a mixed Japanese American who is the child of a Japanese immigrant. When asked where she is from, she adds information about her mother to assert her connection to Japan, which may not otherwise be apparent. One pattern is: Where are you from? I'm *hāfu*—my mom's from Hokkaido. Another is: Where are you from? Los Angeles, but my mother is from Sapporo. Emma explains that she shares this information in an attempt to relate to Japanese: "I use it to identify with them on some level." She clarifies that she only adds her mother's information if it appears that she will be talking to someone for a longer length of time. For example, if it seems like it will be a short conversation with someone in a store, she simply says that she is from America.

This type of background simplification was common among all of my Japanese American interviewees. That is, determining how much background information to provide was based on how far the conversation was anticipated to go. Though the omitted information varies, most of my Japanese

American interviewees preferred to use the strategy of keeping things simple for short conversations with strangers.

Though earlier in her stay in Japan, Emma did not like the term *hāfu*, over time she specifically began adopting it to describe herself because of the positive responses she received as well as the connection it gave her to Japanese people. She explained, "When I say [hāfu] I usually get positive responses. It's a way to bridge the Japanese gaijin [foreigner] gap." It's like saying "oh, I'm not totally a foreigner, even though I feel 100 percent like a foreigner . . . culturally I'm no more Japanese than someone who's 100 percent Australian and comes to Japan. My mom being Japanese has no cultural effect. . . . But other people see it differently . . . I don't look half enough so there's not as big [of] an effect . . ." To Emma, who does not speak, act, or look very Japanese, asserting a *hāfu* identity is a way to feel closer to Japanese people. As the child of an international marriage, unlike Jordan or John, Emma fits the generational image of *hāfu*. Since by her own admission she does not see herself as any more culturally Japanese than other foreigners, describing herself as *hāfu* is claiming a part-Japanese identity based on ancestry. She further explains what *hāfu* means to her: "It's not that I'm from Japan but that I know someone from Japan and have close relations with someone from Japan . . . not that I have roots in Japan . . . I'm not Japanese but I'm related to a Japanese person."

In other words, Emma identifies not as Japanese, but as someone who is related to a Japanese person. *Hāfu* is a category that refers to people who are both Japanese and foreign, but it is clear from Emma's explanation that her own definition is more removed from Japan, simply implying a connection to a Japanese person. When asked if previously she thought that a *hāfu* identity meant that she was Japanese, she responded: "At the beginning maybe I felt it meant that I could be but now I know I'm not." Thus, through her experiences in Japan, Emma has learned to disidentify with being Japanese, despite continuing to use the same descriptor.

Emma's racialization as a white foreigner has reinforced an identity that is not Japanese. In fact, after her year-long stay, she feels less Japanese and more "white" and "American." Interestingly, this racialization experience is diametrically opposed to that of Japanese Americans who are racially categorized as Japanese and start to feel more Japanese, even being able to pass as Japanese in certain situations. Despite being opposite experiences, these two types of racialization are two sides of the same coin. Both reflect the racialization of Americans as "white." In the previous chapter, I showed how when Japanese Americans assert an American identity but do not look white, they consequently reconstruct racial minority identities as Japanese Americans. In the same situation, when Japanese Americans do look white, responses by Japanese reinforce a national identity where they match the racialized image of Americans. Thus, it is not surprising that after living in Japan for a year, Emma concludes, "I'm feeling more white," adding that she means both racially and culturally.

### Sara: Hāfu, *not Japanese American*

Sara was raised near a Japanese community in the Midwest portion of the United States and grew up self-identifying as *hāfu*. She continues to identify in this way. For her, the adaptation to Japanese societal categories was not too difficult since she had already been exposed to them in the United States through her immigrant mother. Though born and raised in the United States, Sara does not identify as "Japanese American." This is because to her, that label assumes a distance from Japan that she does not have as the child of an immigrant. After finishing her language program, Sara married her longtime Japanese fiancé and found a job in an office in Tokyo.

Sara visited Japan several times as a child and also several times as an adult. Just after she was born, she spent four months there while her mother cared for her own mother until she passed away. Then Sara spent almost two months attending a Japanese kindergarten during the summer. At that time, her Japanese language skills were minimal because they were predominately from exposure to Japanese children's songs her mother played for her. Sara's next trip was when she was a sixth grader. All of these were family trips to her mother's hometown in Yamaguchi prefecture. When she was fifteen years old, Sara babysat for a family that she had met in the United States who lived in a suburb of Tokyo. Her most recent trip prior to this 2005 interview took place when she was an exchange student during college.

Every Saturday, from the age of six through high school, Sara attended Japanese school in the large Midwestern town where she grew up. It was mostly "half-Japanese kids like [her]." At home, her mother spoke to her in English and Japanese, to which she likewise responded in a mix of the two languages. In college, her Japanese was too advanced for undergraduate language courses, so instead she took a reading course, where they read Japanese novels in Japanese. However, even after the class, Sara still felt as though her *kanji* needed improvement. So while studying abroad in Japan, she took a *kanji* course. In 2003, the summer before she finished her master's thesis, Sara spent a month at a language school in Tokyo. "Identity-wise," she says, "I always had to struggle because since I was partly Japanese, I felt like I should have a certain level of Japanese I didn't feel that I had achieved." Similar to many children of immigrants whom I met, guilt motivated Sara to improve her language skills. By the time I interviewed Sara in 2005, she was a full-time language student becoming quite fluent and comfortable expressing herself in Japanese.

Sara does not identify as "Japanese American." To her, "Japanese American" suggests an historical, rather than contemporary, relationship to Japan. Sara joined the Japanese American Citizens League (JACL) in the United States but says, "I never identified as Japanese American." She won a JACL scholarship and even visited a former incarceration camp but was still not able to identify with the "Japanese American" community because of what it represented and how it was constructed. "They talk about Japan like it's a class or something—it's not a lived experience for them." This is different from her own connection to Japan, as someone with an immigrant parent and having visited and lived in Japan as a child and as an adult.

Sara sees herself as "an American citizen, half Japanese ethnically with a half Japanese [cultural] identity." On the other hand, "Japanese Americans" have lost their Japanese language skills and customs and see themselves as Americans and not as "Japanese." "I think of Japanese American as an ethnicity, the same as being Irish or German American. There is that history and background, but you're always American first." To Sara, "Japanese American" identity is firmly grounded in the United States and claims a history there—a history of incarceration and generations of experience in the United States. In that way, Sara's identification with both the United States and Japan excludes her from being "Japanese American."

Since Sara knows John, I asked how he would be described in Japan. She replied, John "says he's *hāfu* but for me you're not *hāfu* if you're Japanese American and white because Japanese Americans—other than ethnically—are not Japanese." She sees him as *hapa* and added, "*Hāfu* to me means one parent is from Japan and one parent is not." So to her, John is Japanese American, not *hāfu*.

Sara's identification as *hāfu* organically emerged from her growing up thinking of herself as *hāfu* around friends who identified in the same way. It was a positive and asserted shared identity. In the United States, Sara and her *hāfu* classmates would distinguish between *hāfu* (the children of one Japanese parent and one American parent), the children of two Japanese parents, and "Japanese Americans." To her, *hāfu* is not a racial identity. Rather, it connotes cultural forms such as mannerisms and food. However, in Japan, Sara explains that people often ask her, "Why is your Japanese so good?" to which she replies, "Because I'm *hāfu*." Responses to her, which differ by generation, include "*bijin* (beautiful), *kakkou ii* (cool in a trendy way), and *urayamashii* (envious)." She says younger people associate *hāfu* with an image of being "trendy" or "cool," with everyone saying "it must be nice to be brought up with two cultures." When asked if describing herself as *hāfu* ever leads to follow-up questions or causes confusion, Sara responded, "In Japan people get *hāfu* right away. In the United States I say I'm half Japanese. If I elaborate I say my dad's side is Irish and French Canadian."

The connotations of this category changed for Sara when she lived in Japan as an adult. During the summer of her sophomore year of college, Sara encountered the image of *hāfu* people as "stars" for the first time. Before that, *hāfu* was just a term she and her Japanese school friends had used to describe themselves. But after exposure to this new image, she felt objectified: "I got a lot of attention, both male and female. Females usually said, 'you're so pretty . . . *hāfu*.'" Though being asked where she was from did not bother her because she recognizes that people are curious, this experience made her feel self-conscious and objectified. These feelings reveal the difference between asserting an identity and being categorized and associated with stereotypes.

The connotations changed from how Sara and her friends wanted to see themselves to how people used the term to construct Sara as different from them. Sara has learned to be more forgiving and to not take the objectification personally, since she now sees it as part of the typical obsession with the West in Japanese society. It was after this experience that Sara began to see *hāfu* as a separate category. Previously, when she and her friends asserted this identity together, she did not see it this way.

Sara views herself as *hāfu*, not double, because she feels as though she is in the middle with everything, that she is half of everything. This may have to do with the fact that she has used two names for most of her life: an English first name with English-speaking Americans and a Japanese middle name for Japanese school and around Japanese people.[29] Literally, she felt like she was in two worlds. As she has spent more time around mixed crowds, her usage of the names has become more blurred. Eventually she stopped using her Japanese middle name, but when she did, she felt like "part of me had died, just from a name." However, some Japanese school friends and her Japanese husband still call her by her Japanese name.

Sara's physical appearance is interpreted differently in the United States and in Japan. In both places, some people can tell she is "mixed Asian and white," while others cannot. In the United States, she has been asked if she is English or French and has also been told that she has an "Irish chin." Regarding her racial identity, Sara says, "I never really identified with racial issues. Part of that is because where race is an issue I pass as white." In Japan, she sees how the racial formation is different. There is "a gaijin block and within that there are differences between Chinese, Korean, Southeast Asians, etc."

Sara says she does not quite fit into that categorization either. In terms of physical blending, Sara says "Appearance-wise I can always catch people staring or glancing. But I try not to make assumptions about why they're looking at me. In the United States if people look at me I wonder if my fly is unzipped or if I have something on my face. But in Japan I wonder if people are looking at me because I'm *gaijin*. It would be nice to be able to blend in." On the upside, she comments, "In Japan, if you pass as white you get an elevated status." For example, some of her white-looking friends, when stared at, just imagine that they are receiving attention because they are "stars." In other words, while foreignness is generally associated with negative connotations, whiteness, more specifically, is associated with higher status and privilege (Prieler 2010).

### *Ying: Asian American*

In contrast to Jordan, John, Emma, and Sara, Ying is a Japanese American of mixed heritage who is phenotypically similar to most Japanese in Japan. He is of Japanese ancestry on his father's side and Chinese/Taiwanese ancestry on his mother's side.[30] Ying identifies most strongly with the US-based racial label of "Asian American," which makes him similar to Jordan, in terms of Ying's inability to find a Japan-based term that fits the way he sees himself. Ying does identify with other Japanese Americans, but in both the United States and Japan, Japanese Americans have told him that he is only "half Japanese," thus making "Asian American" seem like a better way to recognize his mixedness. However, in Japan, Asian American is an unintelligible term so Ying struggles with finding a place for himself as someone who is of Japanese ancestry and phenotypically blends but is also of "foreign" ancestry and thus not fully accepted by other Japanese Americans or by Japanese people.

Ying and I met in 2006, about six months after he had moved to Tokyo for a year of study abroad. As we sat and talked in the university's cafeteria on a chilly January afternoon, he told me about how he remembered growing up in Northern California and being teased in elementary school because of his "bowl cut" and his *onigiri* (rice ball) lunches. He further recounted that he was also teased because of his last name, which is not "American" but also "does not sound typically Japanese" so "other Japanese American kids didn't know what it was." He added that only people from Japan seem to recognize that his last name is Japanese. As he gave examples of things for which he was made fun of, Ying also remembered Japanese American kids telling him that he was Chinese, to which a "pretty good friend who was Chinese," said, without any animosity or apparent malicious intent, "No, he's Japanese."

The memories that Ying shared suggest a childhood filled with experiences of feeling different, like an outsider, due to cultural differences on both sides. He was seen as not American because of his name, food, and hairstyle. In addition, his narrative included being "othered" by fellow Asian Americans, with Japanese American and Chinese American kids both pointing out ways he was different from them. At the same time, Ying related that in high school, where his friends were all Asian American, he "started having pride in being Asian American," demonstrating the multiple, contradictory, and fluid nature of identities.

In addition to the ways in which Ying sometimes felt different from his Japanese American peers in terms of ethnicity, in college he also began noticing generational distinctions. Ying related that it was not until attending college (where the majority of students had Asian ethnic backgrounds) that he thought about his mixed background: "I realized I was half and half. Or started thinking of myself as half and half." But here he is not simply referencing being of Chinese and Japanese ancestries. Rather, the conversation that led up to this statement began with him recounting how it was in college that he first realized there were two different kinds of Japanese Americans: those from the prewar wave and those that came after in the postwar wave.

Though he believes it changes from year to year, Ying described his college Japanese American club as having activities "centered around the old Japanese Americans" such as "stuff commemorating internment," a basketball tournament, and ties to the Japanese American Citizens League (JACL). He also mentioned "food like Spam musubi" as being associated with the prewar wave of Japanese Americans. In contrast, the "new Japanese Americans," according to Ying, all read manga, watch anime (he noted that these days everyone watches anime but new Japanese Americans do so more than others), listen to "J-pop" or Japanese pop music, and speak Japanese to each other. Since the "old Japanese Americans" (from the prewar wave) may not speak Japanese as much, he suggested that this excludes them from these conversations and causes them to disengage.

In noticing these two different groups of Japanese Americans, Ying pointed out the unclear positioning of his family background: having a nisei/sansei father whose mother immigrated from Japan in 1908 and a mother from Taiwan raised in Japan. Ying's background "never became an issue until, well, here [Japan]." Occasionally in the United States "another Japanese American kid would be like 'well, you're half,'" to which Ying would respond that he speaks Japanese and has been to Japan while his interlocutor had not. Ying's response to this later-generation Japanese American, who has less familiarity with contemporary Japanese society and language, reflects the problematic assumptions of essentializing and attempting to measure Japaneseness.

When someone claims to be "more Japanese" than someone else, how is this quantified, measured, or compared? Rebecca Chiyoko King-O'Riain has pointed out how mixed-race Japanese American beauty pageant contestants "compensate for having less race by having more culture" (King-O'Riain 2006: 114). Ying seemed to be attempting the same strategy with his rebuttal about his Japaneseness in terms of cultural and social knowledge. He concluded that "most of the time in the United States I just think of myself as Asian American." This strategy has seemed to work for him in the United States, especially in California, where because there are enough Asian Americans, it has become a recognizable identifier.

As we spoke, it became apparent that the problem for Ying in Japan was that "Asian American" is not an intelligible category. "Most people [in Japan] don't know what [Asian Americans] are and think I'm the only Asian kid in America. They still ask white kids about America." He attributed this to the lack of representation of Asian Americans in the media and in mainstream culture. Ying also pointed out how your identity is reaffirmed by people around you and concluded "You can't just choose Asian American or Japanese American here because there's not enough people to reaffirm that identity. With that said, you have two options: you can become Japanese or become American. Naturally, everyone wants to fit in. So this is why I'm assuming so many Japanese Americans go the Japanese route and try to treat everyone else like they're stupid. Because you're not so comfortable with how Japanese you are. And it is a natural human reaction . . . so I try not to hold it against people when they do it to me, but it's still really annoying." Ying's comments relay his sense that other Japanese Americans in Japan excluded him because he did not have the same cultural knowledge that they did, even as he recognized that they themselves were struggling with their own Japaneseness in the new context of Japan.

Ying's assertion of an Asian American identity in Japan was shaped partly by his expectations before migrating to Japan and partly by his returning to California over the winter break, just before we met for the interview. He reflected "I appreciate California more now because I'm able to maintain an Asian American identity there . . . I tried to prepare myself. I'd heard that many times Japanese Americans don't get accepted and Japanese people don't welcome them as one of them . . . so I said, okay, I'm not going to be Japanese, I'm going to be Asian American. But I come here and there's no Asian Americans here or there are a couple but . . ." Since he had gone to

Japan expecting to identify as Asian American, it was disappointing when that strategy failed because that identity was not validated by Japanese people. Ying had also gone to Japan thinking that his Japaneseness made him special and was frustrated when "you come here and everyone is either more Japanese or wants to study about Japanese culture . . . other than your name and your relatives . . . [becoming Japanese is] easily obtainable."

The linguistic and cultural knowledge that he had previously displayed as a way to pride himself about being Japanese (as when comparing himself to the later-generation Japanese American who did not speak Japanese or visit Japan) became obtainable by any foreigner in Japan. In other words, in the United States, Ying was made to feel "not Japanese enough" in terms of ancestry, encouraging him to identify as "more Japanese" by focusing on his cultural and social closeness with Japan, where he had close relatives. However, in Japan this strategy backfired, because any foreigner could become knowledgeable about Japanese language and culture.

Ying's visit home to California over the winter break gave him some perspective on his Japan experiences by reminding him of how US-based racial categories better fit how he sees himself. Since he had been frustrated with not fitting into Japan-based categories, it was reassuring for him to be recognized as an Asian American by people in California:

> Since coming to Japan, I went back to America and then that's when I stopped caring so much because before that I was like all . . . I realized how realistically you don't need the language if you live in America. I mean I know they always say you can use it for business or whatever but realistically, all you need is the native language of the country you're living in. Even at the Japanese market everything is written in English anyway. Everyone speaks English. It's not like there's special places you can go if you speak Japanese. Nobody cares if you speak Japanese. You know? When I went back, I realized how ridiculous I was being about who's more Japanese and this and that. That's when I reaffirmed the Asian American thing because that's one thing I can hold on to.

After living in Japan, Ying not only reaffirmed his identity as an Asian American but also reconstructed his Japaneseness by deemphasizing Japanese language ability as an integral part of his identity.

Interestingly, in both the United States and Japan, Ying described feeling excluded from both Japanese and Japanese American identities, yet he never claimed a "mixed" identity in either place. That is, Ying would not be considered "mixed race" in the United States, where "Asian" is a race. He would be considered "mixed ethnicity" in the US context, which mattered when he was with other Japanese Americans, who enforced that boundary by telling him he was "half." However, he would be considered "mixed race" in the context of Japan, where Japanese and Chinese are considered different races (i.e., different "blood"). In this sense, he shares the experience of not being "pure-blooded" Japanese with my other mixed Japanese American interviewees, even though he is of Japanese and Chinese ancestry and the others mentioned in this chapter are of Japanese and European ancestry.

Yet, due to his experiences in the United States as being part of a racial minority, even in Japan, Ying strongly identified as being different from whites due to phenotypical traits. This differentiation made by Ying is reflected in his thoughtful response when asked if he could ever become Japanese in Japan. While he recognized that he himself might never "be Japanese," Ying imagined: "I think having this appearance if I learn Japanese and become really fluent in it, and decide I want to live and work here, I could have like a normal everyday life and not worry about standing out." He compared his situation with whites, who he says could never fit in, regardless of the amount of language or culture they learned. In contrast, if he dedicated himself to learning the culture, Ying believes that if he had a Japanese wife and children raised in Japan, "they'd have the blood and if I did the citizenship thing . . . you know, as long as you never met their dad, you wouldn't know he's not from Japan because they have the name and they have the blood and they have the registry and that's all that really matters."

He concluded that within two generations, "it would just be back to normal," with his children becoming mainstream Japanese. Ying's perspective on the potential for his children to fit into Japanese society takes into consideration not only race and phenotype but also names and citizenship, probably because he is aware of these issues from the assimilation of his maternal family in Japan. Ying's mother is originally from Taiwan and immigrated to Japan as a teenager, then went to the United States in her twenties or thirties (he was not sure of the exact timing). Ying said his mother's family went to Japan during the colonial period and "tried to assimilate," changing to Japanese names and obtaining Japanese citizenship. He said that all of his uncles in Japan married Japanese women, had children, and speak only Japanese—none of them speak Taiwanese.

He pointed out that they celebrate Japanese holidays, not Taiwanese ones. In fact, "as a kid," Ying "didn't know I had Taiwanese blood in me . . . my mom is actually more Japanese than my [nisei/sansei] dad because she's the one who speaks it and does the Japanese business." In this statement, Ying is comparing his mother's Japaneseness with his father's in terms of her growing up in Japan, speaking fluent Japanese, and having Japanese citizenship—versus his only being of Japanese ancestry and having a Japanese name. Ironically, while Ying is of Japanese ancestry on his father's side, his relationship to Japan and Japanese culture is more distant through his father than through his mother, who is ethnically Taiwanese but raised in Japan. So Ying's dream of a future where he could "become Japanese" derives not only from his background as an Asian American, or Japanese American, but is also inspired by the story of his mother's family's assimilation into Japanese society during the colonial period.

## Conclusion

As a mixed-race Japanese American scholar once observed, "Whether it is cultural or racial, distance is distance. Neither Japanese Americans nor Japanese *Amerasians* are Japanese. Both of us are American and Japanese. Both us of are *between two cultures*" (Houston 1997: 152, emphasis in original). Indeed, this chapter has demonstrated how mixed Japanese Americans, similar to the Japanese Americans who can phenotypically blend in Japan discussed in Chapter Two, struggle to be recognized for their Japaneseness and foreignness in Japan, both of which are necessary to validate how they see themselves.

My Japanese American interviewees of mixed heritage related to the Japanese category of *hāfu* in a variety of ways, from not identifying with this label to claiming it as an identity even as the meaning shifted from the United States to Japan. Jordan and Ying both used US-based terms (i.e., hapa, Asian American) to describe themselves in Japan, even once they realized that these terms were not intelligible to people in Japan. This was partly due to their limited Japanese linguistic and cultural knowledge, i.e., limited integration into Japanese society and its social categories and partly due to their strong identification with being of mixed heritage. John and Emma both described themselves as *hāfu* primarily because it seemed to make it easier for Japanese people to relate to them. Finally, although Sara was comfortable describing herself as *hāfu* because it had been an asserted group identity while growing up with other *hāfu* in the United States; in Japan she disliked the stereotypes associated with *hāfu* that Japanese people externally imposed on her.

This chapter has shown how mixed Japanese American experiences are diverse due to phenotypical differences; knowledge of Japanese language, culture, and society; and generations removed from Japan. In response to commonly being racialized white in Japan due to a lack of noticeable markers of Japaneseness, Jordan and Emma both developed the strategy of claiming a multiracial identity in Japan as a way to differentiate themselves from foreigners not of Japanese ancestry, a differentiation that seemed less important for my mixed Japanese interviewees who were more phenotypically ambiguous, had stronger Japanese language skills, and had Japanese names. At the same time, Ying, who was mixed but phenotypically blended in Japan, noticed the white privilege that marginalized him in both the United States and Japan. Research on mixed black Japanese Americans offers yet another mixed Japanese experience as racial minorities who are phenotypically salient in both the United States and Japan. Though Jordan and John tried different strategies (asserting hapa and *hāfu* identities), they both caused confusion for *nihonjin* as Japanese Americans who were mixed as well as later-generation (not the children of international marriages), revealing the lack of a single term in Japanese to conceptualize and describe this type of background. The strategic ways of identifying that mixed Japanese Americans develop in Japan demonstrate how individuals can creatively assert identities but are limited by preexisting conceptions of Japaneseness mediated through various categories and their connotations.

The narratives discussed in this chapter also suggest an analytical difference between being the child of a Japanese person from Japan and being the child of a US-born and/or raised Japanese American. Interestingly, Ying's experiences highlighted this tension as his Japaneseness on the one side (his father) stemmed from ancestry and a Japanese last name, while his Japaneseness on the other side (his Taiwanese mother) referenced learned culture, language, and experiences after migrating to Japan. He discovered that the Japanese traits he was so proud of in the United States became less unique in Japan, thus altering the way he saw his Japaneseness in the United States after living in Japan. From this it is clear that Japaneseness is relative and contextual, making it difficult to smoothly transfer so-called markers for Japaneseness from one context to another.

In addition to migrating between different constructions of "Japanese" in the United States and Japan, Americans of Japanese ancestry are also migrating between mixed-race categories. Multiracial experiences reveal racial formation processes because they illuminate how people make decisions about the categorization of individuals who are not easily categorizable (Cornell and Hartmann 2007, Omi and Winant 1994). At the same time, these experiences show the diversity in how individuals respond to their categorization. Just as constructions of race and ethnicity differ on the US continent, in Hawai'i, and in Japan, so do constructions of what it means to be multiracial. Thus, transnational racial and ethnic identity formations include multiracial identity formations as well.

While Sara was exposed to Japanese language, culture, and social norms while growing up in the United States, most Japanese Americans have not had the same level of engagement with contemporary Japanese society before moving there as adults. Most Japanese Americans I interviewed learned to significantly alter their behavior and ways of identifying only through sustained interactions with Japanese people in Japan. The next chapter explores how residency and language acquisition in Japan affect how Japanese Americans perceive their position as Americans of Japanese ancestry in Japan and develop strategies using language to help Japanese people understand them in the best way possible.

CHAPTER 4

# Language and Names in Shifting Assertions of Japaneseness

I will never forget Cindy Spencer. When I was an exchange student from 1992 to 1993 at International Christian University (ICU) in Mitaka City in Tokyo, I lived in one of the women's dormitories on campus. Cindy was a dormmate and a regular four-year student (not an exchange student). What I perceived to be Cindy's bilingualism and biculturalism intrigued me, since my Japanese was still only conversational. (For my first six months in Japan, I carried around a Japanese-English dictionary—"just in case"—due to my limited vocabulary.) Whenever I conversed with Cindy in English, she sounded like a native speaker from the United States, so it was hard to believe that she was born and raised in the Philippines and Japan, not in the United States.

The child of a man from the Philippines and a woman from Japan, Cindy had attended international schools in both countries. So when she spoke in Japanese with native Japanese speakers, as far as I could tell, she sounded the same as them, even changing her tone of voice (more high-pitched in Japanese) and facial expressions according to the cultural context. Cindy also had dual citizenship, with different legal names for each national identity. For one passport, she was the English-speaking Cindy Spencer. But for the other passport, she was the Japanese-speaking Miki Nishimura. Her language abilities appeared to reflect her two names and sets of cultural knowledge. So it surprised me when she recounted stories from studying abroad the year before at UCLA, hanging out with her fellow students but not understanding some references to popular culture. She said the UCLA students expressed disbelief about her not being from the United States because of her fluent English and seemed confused when she lacked knowledge of American popular culture from her childhood era. In my mind, I imagined Cindy speaking like a native English speaker, yet unable to keep up with US-based references such as watching *The Brady Bunch* on television as a child. It was the first time that I thought about how language ability is different from cultural and social knowledge.

Most Japanese Americans I met are not as bilingual as Cindy, but her story raises issues about language and culture in Japan that all of my interviewees faced. For those not fluent in Japanese, it was common to assume that linguistic proficiency equals assimilation and the possibility of eventual full social acceptance. However, after improving their Japanese, residing in Japan for several years, and learning more about mainstream thinking in Japan, my Japanese American interviewees realized that although linguistic ability is connected to social and cultural knowledge, becoming fluent in Japanese does not necessarily mean that one also becomes culturally informed or socially proficient. In Cindy's case, as someone fluent in English, in the US context, she was also expected to be knowledgeable about American popular culture. Her experiences growing up internationally were unintelligible to Americans who were unfamiliar with "third culture kids" (Pollock and Van Reken 2009). In other words, being able to speak a language overlaps with but is different from having cultural and social knowledge. If Cindy had been speaking accented or stilted English in the United States, I am certain that most Americans would have believed that she had not been raised in the United States and would not have expected her to be familiar with US popular culture from her childhood era.

Cindy's situation also differed from that of most of my Japanese American interviewees in Japan due to social interpretation and categorization processes in the United States and Japan. People born and raised in the United States come from diverse backgrounds. So while racism and xenophobia certainly persist, in large US urban areas most people are familiar with the premise that Americans (i.e., US citizens) can be of different ethnic or racial backgrounds. In contrast, in Japan, the hegemonic discourse of Japanese homogeneity associates "Japanese blood" with Japanese language, culture, and social knowledge. So when someone who looks phenotypically similar to most Japanese, speaks fluent Japanese or has a Japanese name, this person is typically also expected to be familiar with Japanese social etiquette and norms.

This chapter discusses how linguistic and cultural knowledge inform shifting presentations of self as Japanese Americans manage Japanese expectations of them and assert identities as insiders or outsiders in Japanese society depending on the context. While managing role expectations (Goffman 1959) can be understood as a universal phenomenon, in Japan the framework of *uchi/soto* (inside/outside) contextualizes this role management in specific ways. Bachnik points out how "the *universally defined* orientations for inside/outside are linked with *culturally defined* perspectives for self, society, and language in Japan" (1994: 7, italics in original). When do Japanese Americans assert identities as insiders in Japan? When is it to their benefit to distinguish themselves as outsiders?

Depending on their Japanese language fluency, immersion in Japanese society, and length of residence in Japan, Japanese Americans selectively use Japanese and English in a variety of ways. As Japanese Americans increase their language fluency and increasingly interact with Japanese in Japan, they discover the benefits and drawbacks of asserting their Japaneseness or foreignness, depending on the context. The strategies that they develop to navigate Japanese society as people who have both Japanese and foreign characteristics illustrate prevalent assumptions in Japan about the relationship of language to race, nationality, culture, and identity.

## Japanese American Language Abilities

The Japanese language ability of Japanese Americans in the United States varies greatly, often in relation to generational distance from Japanese immigrants, as well as the United States' World War II experience with Japan. The children of *issei* (first-generation immigrants), *kibei nisei* (US-born, second generation, partly raised in Japan), and *shin-issei* (postwar, first-generation immigrants) are all often exposed to Japanese language in the household, whether their parents speak Japanese to them or in front of them. In contrast, the children of *nisei* (second generation), *sansei* (third generation), as well as later generations, are exposed to very little Japanese from their parents, so if they speak Japanese, it is usually learned from grandparents, attending Japanese school, or taking courses in high school or college. Scholars have attributed this lack of linguistic continuity among later-generation Japanese Americans not only to more universal generational factors related to "assimilation" and "language shift," but also to the particularities of Japanese American history, namely their World War II incarceration in the United States, causing conscious distancing from Japanese culture and language (Takamori 2010: 220), both of which were associated with the enemy.[1]

An important distinction to make is between native and nonnative speakers because "a heritage language speaker will never be . . . a native speaker" (Takamori 2010: 227). In the US context, this distinction may be less important, but in Japan, where the majority of the population are native speakers of Japanese, those who speak nonnative Japanese stand out, especially if they are phenotypically similar to most Japanese. Over time, these Japanese

Americans realize that rather than helping them blend in, speaking Japanese may instead serve to accent their foreignness. Moreover, Japanese Americans with high levels of Japanese skills learn to be selective in when and where they choose to use Japanese or English.

## Japanese Language, Alphabet, and Name Representation in Historical Context

As with any language, the structure and history of the Japanese language shape its contemporary usage and meaning. The demarcation between Japaneseness and foreignness is often based on language ability, since the strictest definition of Japaneseness is marked by native fluency in the Japanese language. Since Japanese people use multiple alphabets, each serving a slightly different purpose and having varying connotations, a person's Japaneseness can be assessed based on which alphabet(s) one is familiar with and capable of using. Moreover, the politics of name representation in Japan is shaped by these multiple alphabets and how one chooses to express one's name in writing. The political construction of Japaneseness through language and name representation can be traced back to Imperial Japan's system of assimilation, which included forced Japanese language adoption, as well as policies concerning name representation in *koseki* (family registries) and other official government documents. (In Japan, they do not have individual birth certificates. One's legal citizenship and birth record are part of larger registries by household.)

Since the Japanese language uses four different writing systems—*romaji, kanji, hiragana,* and *katakana*—Japanese Americans have options regarding how to represent their names. *Romaji* is the Roman alphabet applied to Japanese, so it is mainly "for the sake of foreign people" who cannot read any Japanese alphabets (Sakamoto 1976). It also masks the differences in the three other systems more commonly used in Japan by Japanese people. *Kanji* are characters originally from China, though their usage in Japan incorporates different readings and some different meanings, including the characters used for typical Japanese names.

*Hiragana* and *katakana* are monosyllabic phonic symbols that lack individual meaning, but they are easy to learn because in each system, the pronunciation of the forty-six basic symbols remains consistent. Since the syllables represented in *hiragana* and *katakana* are the same, their usage is determined by context. Specifically, *hiragana* is used with *kanji* in the majority of Japanese writing, while *katakana* is used to denote words borrowed from other languages. Kindaichi explains the symbolism of using *katakana* in this way: "The writing of foreign words in stiff katakana to distinguish them from other words as if they were objects of our enmity, is an expression [that distinctions should be made between Japanese and foreign things]" (Kindaichi 1988). Thus, when names are written in *katakana*, they are also generally read as "foreign," rather than as "Japanese," including Japanese names.[2] Once Japanese Americans learn this distinction, when they have one or more Japanese names, they can choose whether to accent their Japaneseness or foreignness depending on which alphabet they use.

Japanese American language usage in Japan is understood within the larger social context of shifting boundaries between "Japanese" and "foreigners," that are partially constructed through language use. Historically, the boundaries around who has spoken Japanese have changed because of Japan's nation-building policies, including linguistic assimilation policies that were required of colonized populations. For instance, before the Meiji era, Japanese officials perceived Ainu people to be "non-Japanese" and forbade them to speak or write Japanese. But once Japan asserted that in fact Ainu were Japanese (in order to claim Hokkaido as Japanese territory), they were suddenly no longer allowed to use their own language, in addition to which their children were to be educated only in Japanese (Gottlieb 2005: 18–19, Walker 1999).

Moreover, even among Japanese language users, subgroup distinctions reflect yet more categorizations in Japan. For example, in Japanese, there are two terms for the Japanese language: *kokugo* (literally, country's language) refers to the Japanese language when it is taught to Japanese people, while *nihongo* (literally, Japan's language) refers to when it is taught to foreigners (Gottlieb 2005). This distinction reflects the Japanese attitude that "Japanese and foreign things" need to be differentiated (Kindaichi 1988), "clearly designating the insider-outsider tenets of the Nihonjinron stance on language" (Gottlieb 2005: 15). That is, who officially speaks Japanese and how this is described reflect assumptions about who is considered Japanese.

The usage of Japanese names in Japan also reflects the unstable boundaries between Japaneseness and foreignness that have been shaped by colonial history. As part of Japan's colonial assimilation policies, often referred to as the "Japanization" process, many Okinawan names were pronounced with Japanese readings. For example, "today's Tamashiro was Tamagusuku or Tamagushiku in premodern times" (Smits 1999: 11). Similarly, in 1940, as part of the colonization of Taiwan and Korea, the Japanese government instituted a policy called the Japanization of Personal Names, according to which colonial subjects were required to assume Japanese names (Hsu 2014). It is worth noting that even with Japanese names, colonial subjects were not considered equal to Japanese citizens, suggesting that historically there have been layers and hierarchical positionings regarding Japaneseness which continue to this day. For Japanese Americans as well, having Japanese names is only one measure of Japaneseness and does not ensure their full inclusion into Japanese society.

On the other hand, people of Japanese ancestry do not always have Japanese names.[3] In both Japan and the United States, the system of name representation is patrilineal, meaning that if a woman of Japanese ancestry (with a Japanese last name) marries a man not of Japanese ancestry (without a Japanese last name), the child, even with Japanese ancestry, typically lacks a Japanese last name because s/he takes on the father's name. As discussed below, sometimes mixed-heritage Japanese Americans without Japanese last names have Japanese first names or will use Japanese middle names or their mothers' maiden names to express their Japaneseness. In addition, children who have different ethnic backgrounds from their adoptive parents have last names that do not reflect their ancestry. So marriage, adoption, and having multiple ancestries can lead people to have last names that do not match their phenotype or ancestry (see Nakashima 2001).

Different legal systems shape the importance and meaning of last names in expressing identity. In the United States, women are not legally required to change their last names when they marry men, and couples (of any gender) can have different last names. In Japan, however, married couples are legally required to use the same last name in official matters (Osaki 2015), so having a Japanese last name is a clear marker of Japanese identity.

Finally, choosing to use Japanese or foreign names is a way to publicly express identification. For later-generation, Japan-born and raised *zainichi* (residing in Japan) Koreans who speak only Japanese, Korean names may be the only public marker of their foreignness. "Regardless of nationality, [*zainichi*] can control the extent of their visibility by employing certain names in everyday use" (Lim 2009: 89). Japanese Americans use Japanese names while living in Japan—sometimes even asserting Japanese names not usually used by them in the United States—to create meaning, both for themselves and for Japanese people in Japan.

## Two Main Japanese American Usages of Japanese Language and Name Representation

When Japanese Americans speak Japanese in Japan, the meaning attached to that usage is different from that of most other foreigners because of the former's ancestral connections to Japan. Ayako Takamori has examined these meanings through the lens of Japanese as a heritage language for Japanese

Americans, pointing out the importance of national context, as she asks, "What happens . . . when a heritage language is a dominant language . . . when heritage language learners actually 'return' to the place, or nation, of heritage?" (Takamori 2010: 218). To answer this question, she contrasts the hegemonic discourse of multiculturalism in the United States with the ideology of Japanese blood and cultural homogeneity in Japan, both of which underpin assumptions about Japanese American language abilities.

Contrary to what one might expect within the US context, in Japan, "competency in their heritage language . . . sometimes serves counterintuitively to further distinguish and separate Japanese Americans from Japanese beyond other forms of cultural and social alienation, rather than creating a bridge to their Japanese heritage" (Takamori 2010: 225). That is, while Japanese language abilities might be read as cultural symbols in the United States (Gans 1979), the practical usage of Japanese in Japan makes clear that just having the ability to speak some Japanese is different from native-level fluency with which one speaks. Furthermore, when Japanese Americans speak fluent Japanese, according to the mainstream conflation of race, nation, and culture in Japan, it is expected that they also be familiar with Japanese social norms and exhibit proper behavior. When they do not have this knowledge and act inappropriately, as often occurs, problems tend to arise. Although my Japanese American interviewees began residing in Japan with optimism about their abilities to increasingly assimilate into Japanese society as their language abilities increased, the opposite often happened—the more competent they became in Japanese, the more they became skeptical about the possibility of ever being fully accepted in Japan. While I believe that this change in outlook reflects a shift from US-based to Japan-based views of what it means for a Japanese American to speak Japanese, it also supports Takamori's conclusion that "the idea that Japanese Americans should learn Japanese as a way to maintain ethnic affiliation (in U.S. multiculturalist discourse) paradoxically plays into Japanese nationalist language ideologies even as those ideologies serve to exclude heritage language learners" (Takamori 2010: 237).

In other words, the assumption that people of Japanese ancestry should speak Japanese is basically an essentialist notion that supports both the US multiculturalist ideology of having ethnic pride as well as the Japanese nationalistic belief that true Japanese are native speakers. Since Japanese Americans born and raised in the United States are typically not native speakers of Japanese, this assumption, although it may enhance their claims to a Japanese ethnic identity in the United States, ironically excludes them from claiming a Japanese identity (that includes linguistic ability) in Japan.

The Japanese language abilities and name representations of most Japanese Americans I met can be divided into two main groupings: 1) those with lower levels of Japanese language ability and less immersion in Japanese society and 2) those with higher levels of Japanese language ability who have more interaction with Japanese people. In 2013 in Washington, D.C., I interviewed Glen Fukushima, a Japanese American who has had a career in Japan-related fields for more than fifty years and has intermittently resided in Japan for over twenty years.[4] In that conversation, he described correlations he has observed between how Japanese Americans use the Japanese language and how they write their names. On the one hand, there are "Japanese Americans who have the least knowledge or the least exposure to Japan," who "are more likely to want to use *kanji* [Chinese characters] and the more likely to want to use Japanese" because they think that people in Japan will appreciate their closeness to Japanese culture and feel more comfortable.

On the other hand, Japanese Americans "who are more experienced with Japan are more likely to use *katakana* [a simpler Japanese alphabet used to identify foreign words], and more likely to be selective in their using Japanese." This is because they are able to more consciously consider the appropriateness of using Japanese or English in a particular situation. My research supports Fukushima's observation that the majority of Japanese Americans living in Japan fit into these two groups (though they can also move from one group to the other over time).[5]

Interviews I conducted reveal that Japanese American ways of identifying in Japan change over time in relation to language ability and knowledge of Japanese culture and society, influencing the use of languages in which they choose to express themselves. Moreover, the alphabets they use to write their Japanese names reflect the identities that Japanese Americans want to assert: *kanji* is used to express Japaneseness, while *katakana* is used to express foreignness.

Similar to Cindy, who when using her Japanese names (and *kanji*), asserted her positioning as Japanese, some of my interviewees chose to write their Japanese names in *kanji* as reflections of their similarities with Japanese people in Japan. However, unlike Cindy, some of my interviewees were not familiar enough with Japanese society to understand the drawbacks of taking on roles as Japanese.

Thus, in addition, I found that as Japanese Americans became more immersed in Japanese society and improved their Japanese language ability, they discovered the benefits of asserting their foreignness and tended to move from the first group to the second group. The rest of the chapter examines the two groups of Japanese Americans in terms of language ability, then focuses on how the two groups write their names in Japanese.

## JAPANESE AMERICANS WITH LOWER LEVELS OF JAPANESE LANGUAGE ABILITY AND LESS IMMERSION IN JAPANESE SOCIETY

When their lack of Japanese fluency was the most noticeable difference separating them from Japanese people in Japan, Japanese Americans tended to believe that once they attained a higher level of language ability, they would be able to fit in and be more comfortable in Japan. To a certain extent, this is a commonsensical assumption, and certainly the case for international migrants, who over time tend to increase their ability to communicate in the local language. But most Japanese American assumptions about the possibility of social acceptance in Japan tended to specifically reference their experiences as a racial minority in the United States, contrasting it with the idealization of someday being able to fit in as a full-fledged member of Japanese society if they already fit the racial, and more specifically, phenotypical criteria.[6]

### *Imagining Social Acceptance with Fluency in Japanese*

It was common for the Japanese Americans I met to contrast and compare their experience as a racial minority in the United States with their experience in Japan of not speaking much Japanese. This comparison idealized the potential of their becoming part of mainstream Japanese society once they improved their linguistic and cultural competency. Since language and culture can be learned, they appear to be smaller obstacles than phenotypical traits used to racially categorize that do not typically change over time. Gary, a sansei (third generation) Japanese American, was in the US military and stationed in the Tokyo area when we spoke. In addition to comparing his own experiences in Japan and the United States, Gary also juxtaposed his experiences in Japan with those of his wife, an American of Irish descent:

> I feel very comfortable here in Japan and I know my wife doesn't and I think the reason why is because I look like everyone else in Japan and I think like most everyone else here but I don't speak the language. So it's that discomfort because I think like I'm in the United States but we're living in Japan. That's kind of like the opposite, in a sense, discomfort. It's not like the whole not looking like everyone else discomfort or discrimination or racism that you get in the United States. But it's the whole . . . it's the language. I think if I spoke Japanese I'd feel comfortable living here all my life.

To Gary, being uncomfortable due to his looks and language ability is what makes his US and Japan experiences different. He grew up as one of the only Asian families in a suburb of Chicago and says he joined the military partly out of an interest in flying and partly because growing up as a minority, he wanted to find a place where he could "fit in better." That is, he saw joining the military as "a signal of your being American and loyalty and patriotism." Indeed, historically, Japanese Americans and other people of color have been motivated to serve in the armed forces as a demonstration of their loyalty and Americanness.[7] Gary described being a racial minority not only in Chicago, but in other places as well: "I have always lived in places where there were few Asians. In the military there are not a lot of Asian officers—you stick out on a base."

With two parents of only Japanese ancestry, Gary says he can blend in quite easily in Japan as long as he keeps his mouth shut. "So I feel very comfortable here, in some respects more than in the United States." He adds that since he likes the "discipline, the regimen and the detail [mindedness]" he thinks that his "thought process and personality fit . . . in better in Japan." Many of my interviewees made similar comments about personality fit in Japan due to neatness, meticulousness, and cleanliness. Gary acknowledges the discomfort he still feels as an outsider and as someone who is more outspoken, but he points out that his phenotypical similarities to most people in Japan represent a source of comfort, in contrast to the experiences of his Irish American wife, who is made uncomfortable by her phenotypical salience in Japan.

Indeed, Gary's point is well taken: expectations of him are different from those of other Americans, whether black or white. Gary recalled a story about how once, when he was drinking at a social function, the main translator, a Japanese person, "referred to me as a banana. I was offended. I told them that." He took offense to this comment because it "reinforces the fact that you're an outsider here." It should be noted that "banana" is a derogatory word for an Asian American who is "yellow" on the outside and "white" on the inside, inferring that people who "look" Asian should "act" Asian (Castillo 2015). Because this term is relatively common slang in the United States, I would presume that Gary's translator had spent time and learned this concept in the United States. Based on the racialized implications of the comment, the translator probably did not expect Gary's non-Japanese American coworkers to have the same Japanese language ability or social and cultural knowledge of Japan.

At the same time, perhaps unconsciously, Gary and many other Japanese Americans themselves seemed to support the idea that phenotype should match cultural and linguistic knowledge when asserting the belief (sometimes expressed through guilt) that they, as people of Japanese ancestry, should speak Japanese (or feel badly because they do not).

### *Surviving in Tokyo without Speaking Japanese*

Gary was one of a number of Japanese Americans I met who had lived in Japan for several years but had limited Japanese language skills because their work and home environments did not require fluency in Japanese. Gary's job had him working mostly with Japanese civilians, meeting and arranging training for different branches of the US military. But he always used a translator for work, so he had not been forced to improve his Japanese to adequately conduct his work. Gary told me that he wanted to improve his Japanese but had not yet had the chance. Since his wife was also from the United States, he was able to live his daily life with her and their four children and have his basic needs met mostly using English.

In a similar vein, several Japanese American lawyers and businesspeople I interviewed had bilingual Japanese spouses who enabled a comfortable lifestyle by managing an English-speaking household. For example, Jim spoke enough Japanese to shop, order in restaurants, and speak with taxi drivers, but he is able to live most of his life in Tokyo using English. His bilingual Japanese wife handles most household responsibilities that require Japanese skills. In addition, his children attend international school so that Jim can speak to them (and to his wife) at home in English. The children began speaking Japanese at home with Jim's wife, but when Jim's son was three years old and Jim could not understand the Japanese his son spoke to him, Jim and his wife "decided that it would be a good idea for [the children] to go to international school." In addition, Jim's work transactions in international law are conducted in English, while his bilingual office staff manages Japanese-language communications for him.

Bob, a sansei lawyer, similarly described how he "had a [Japanese] secretary who could speak English, so if there was anything I needed done, like banking or anything like that she would take care of it." Regarding people who go to Japan on an "expat" package—an international compensation package that includes "base salary, goods and services allowance, housing allowance, tax equalizations, premiums, benefits and perquisites, and relocation allowance" (Overman 1992), Grant said that they are "not really living a Japanese lifestyle" because they do not have a small home, do not have the same commute, and are "sort of sheltered." He had lived in Tokyo for about fourteen years spread across three stints when I interviewed him in 2007.

Grant's experience working at a *gaishikei* (foreign corporation) in Tokyo meant that all of his emails were in English. Moreover, since he was not in sales, he did not have much contact with people outside of the company (e.g., customers). Reflecting on his experience adjusting to life in Tokyo, Grant said, "Once you can figure out how to live—ordering at a restaurant, going shopping, what you need for your work—once you get over that, unless you just want to study . . . you don't have the need to improve your Japanese." He also pointed out how working at a foreign company was different from working for a Japanese company.[8]

The ability of Japanese Americans to work comfortably in Japan for years without needing to improve their Japanese is related to the prominence of English as a global language and to Tokyo's status as a global city.[9] International migrants often have trouble learning the language of the new society to which they move. Especially when their native language is a minority language in the new society, not speaking the majority language may cost them the ability to function, find good jobs, and thrive. Native-English speakers living in Tokyo do not have this problem because of the cultural capital afforded to them as native speakers who can find jobs teaching English, if not using other skills to do work in English.[10] Ian, a sansei from California, moved to Tokyo to pursue a career in dancing and supported his lifestyle by teaching English—an option not available to all international migrants to Japan, many of whom instead take on unskilled labor to support their lifestyles. In this respect, Japanese American migration to Japan is different from Japanese Brazilian migration to Japan due to the cultural (as well as social and economic) capital associated with English versus Portuguese (Yamashiro and Quero 2012).

The literature on English linguistic imperialism is too large to review here, but it is worth pointing out that "English has become the language of global intellectual discourse and the dominant language of intellectual communities involved in the production, reproduction and circulation of knowledge" (Short 2001). English is taught in all Japanese schools and is the most common language needed for international business in Japan. In this regard, Tokyo's status as a global city is significant because many international businesspeople and lawyers are able to find work, either transferred between offices of their multinational firms or hired by the Tokyo office (either locally or as "expats"). Many of my Japanese American interviewees specializing in international business or law had previously lived in places such as New York and London and viewed their residence in Tokyo as part of these global networks. In this way, working and living in English-supported environments was enabled by the infrastructure of Tokyo, which has businesses, institutions, and neighborhoods that rural areas do not.

## Challenges of a Japanese American Couple

An English-supported work environment makes living in Tokyo easier, but having a bilingual spouse at home also matters. Joel, a Japanese American working for an American multinational corporation had a Japanese American wife who moved with him. I informally met with Joel and his wife repeatedly over the two years they resided in Japan. When I first met them, within a month of their move to Japan, their attitude was typical of new Japanese American arrivals whom I encountered. Both were sansei from California who grew up speaking only a few phrases in Japanese (although Joel spoke a bit more because he had taken some Japanese classes in college). They were both clearly excited and optimistic about the three years or longer that they planned to live in Japan. Joel was working for a US-based company (technically as a "local hire," not an "expat," since he applied for the Japan-based position) and functioned primarily in English. His wife was now a full-time housewife and mother who had left behind a job in the United States so that she could care for their one-year-old on a full-time basis in Japan. When we sat down to dinner, during which I learned more about their plans in Japan, both expressed how they expected their Japanese to improve over time, which would ease their transition, thinking that they could probably live in Japan indefinitely if they improved their Japanese skills enough.

About a year later, I met Joel and his wife at their home and found out that they were still having trouble performing daily tasks. For example, they could not read the directions on their washing machine or dryer and did not use the functions on their *ofuro* (bathtub) because they did not know how. I ended up ordering a pizza for us because I was able to read the menu and place the phone order in Japanese. Joel's wife seemed understandably frustrated at this point, expressing an interest in returning home to the United States to put her daughter in regular public school. She commented that in Japan they could put her in international schools but that it was expensive, costing approximately $12,000 per year.[11] Moreover, she explained that Japanese schools were not an option because she was not able to communicate with the teachers. Joel's wife was responsible for overseeing the home and childcare, doing her best, but with her limited Japanese it was a difficult task. This would not have been the case if Joel had had a Japanese wife.

In contrast, Joel was still happy to be living in Japan. This attitude was probably due to the fact that his daily life comprised mostly of working in an office, where he conducted business in English and had many bilingual Japanese coworkers who were handling his Japanese-language administrative needs. While Joel's Japanese was slightly more developed than his wife's, the satisfaction gap between them surely had to do with her lacking the linguistic support system that Joel had through his work situation.

When I interviewed Joel in 2015 after he and his family had moved back to California, he reflected that things might have turned out differently if his wife's situation had been easier. He noted how many of his American colleagues in Japan had Japanese wives and that if his own wife had had more of a support system in Japan to help her manage childcare, she might have been interested in staying in Japan longer. He recognized that in addition to not speaking Japanese fluently, it had been hard for his wife to not have her mother or other family members close by, as she did in the United States.

Among my Japanese American interviewees, those less immersed in Japanese society, including those who had recently arrived, tended to be more focused on their similarities to Japanese people and the possibility of eventually fitting into Japanese society as their Japanese language ability increased. However, as the subsequent section shows, having Japanese language skills and knowing when to use them are two different abilities. Japanese Americans with advanced language fluency became aware that in addition to language skills, social and cultural knowledge were as important in becoming socially accepted in Japan, as Cindy learned through her experiences migrating to the United States.

### Japanese Americans with Higher Levels of Japanese Language Ability and More Interaction with Japanese People

As Japanese Americans acclimate to Japanese society, they become more knowledgeable about how to present themselves. Those with higher levels of Japanese language ability and more contact with Japanese people become strategic about when to use their Japanese and when to speak English. Ironically, some develop enough fluency to reach a point where they become demotivated to become more fluent. In contrast to foreign-looking foreigners who may be encouraged to speak Japanese as one way to demonstrate their knowledge and understanding of Japanese society and culture, Japanese Americans who phenotypically blend in Japan generally appear the most Japanese when they are not speaking or interacting with Japanese people. After studying Japanese and gaining a certain level of fluency, a number of my interviewees identified a point where they became demotivated to improve their Japanese because this ability became less useful to them in navigating Japanese society.

### Japanese Language Ability and the Law of Diminishing Returns

Advanced Japanese fluency combined with visually blending in Japan can lead Japanese Americans to become demotivated to improve their Japanese because it becomes less valuable as they increasingly assert their foreignness. Masato, a shin-nisei, says that he never strove to make his Japanese good enough to "blend in and be a spy or anything like that." Rather, he has a theory about why his Japanese language skills have not continued to develop as he has lived in Japan (for almost a decade at the time of the interview in Tokyo):

> I have one theory . . . subconsciously, I think I might have stopped my development of my Japanese skill because I wanted to . . . identify as a foreigner. That I don't want to be seen completely as Japanese because I would be handicapped because I find that being completely Japanese from a business perspective, or even socially is a disadvantage for Japanese Americans because you don't know exactly how to act in given situations or you can't act at the same sophistication level you can in your native tongue. You know, so whether it's the use of humor or understanding subtleties or conveying subtleties. You can't do it if it's not your native language. So, I definitely, like for example on my business card I write my name in katakana. That was actually, that was [Glen Fukushima's] advice.

In addition, as mentioned earlier, for Japanese Americans working in international offices in Tokyo where English is commonly spoken, becoming fluent in Japanese is not necessary to be able to function well at work.

When I interviewed Steve, a sansei/yonsei banker, we met at his home, where his bilingual Japanese wife Naomi joined us. Steve said he knows about seventy long-term resident Japanese Americans who are not very fluent in Japanese and about seventy white Americans who are all very fluent in Japanese. He and Naomi further commented on how a Japanese American background, combined with skills needed for working as a professional in Tokyo, leads to "diminishing returns" regarding Japanese language improvement:

> STEVE: "I think that has to do with being Japanese American."
> NAOMI: "Here they want to be more American so they don't study Japanese so much. Haoles [whites] get more into being Japanese."
> STEVE: "You hit a point . . . then it's a steady decline."
> NAOMI: "At first [Steve] was taking Japanese lessons twice a week. Then it got to a point of diminishing returns."
> STEVE: "It's not part of my job. If I had to interact with Japanese-speaking

people a lot, it would be different. But professionals—in law, accounting, finance—it's all in English. There's lots of technical detail in contracts and documents.

NAOMI: "You do start trying to fit in, but then you hit a wall. The extra effort that it takes to refine the language doesn't pay off as much."

STEVE: "I no longer feel that there's a need or a benefit [to improving my Japanese]."

NAOMI: "If you don't need a language then you don't become fluent . . . there are a lot of Japanese Americans who have lived here a long time but don't speak it much."

Although Steve had been studying Japanese for years (his first trip to Japan was as a college exchange student) and continued to have an interest in learning Japanese, his work situation was such that continuing to improve his Japanese was not a priority. In addition, though Steve did not comment on his family situation, having a Japanese wife who speaks fluent English also made it much less necessary for him to become more proficient in Japanese.

### *Gendered Demotivation*

The demotivation to improve Japanese language skills is also gendered. Carrie explains how, as a Japanese-looking foreign woman, she has found strategies for navigating Japanese society given her particular set of characteristics. To let people know that she is not Japanese, Carrie uses this strategy:

I only speak English. I've lived in Japan for fourteen years but still I don't speak Japanese well. There's no incentive as an executive woman. If a blonde babe says 'konnichiwa' they'll say 'oh my god, your Japanese is so good!' but if I speak Japanese, if they're not paying attention, they will think I'm Japanese and think I'm an idiot before they eventually figure it out. So I always start not speaking Japanese then if I use it I purposely exaggerate my accent. For example, in talking to the train guy, at first I would say 'ginza ni doko desuka' [using the wrong particle] and he would explain in English. Then I learned how to say it in a nicer way but that [just got her into trouble because they'd respond in a way she didn't understand] . . . I purposely dumb down my Japanese if I do use it, to make sure that I tip them off . . . I give them like six sentences before I ask my question, so they can answer in a way I'll understand.

After I pointed out that this was an example from everyday life, not one taken from a business setting, Carrie added that in a business sense Japanese women lawyers also have their challenges. They try to speak in a gender neutral way, dropping their *keigo* (formal language) and using *desu/masu* (polite forms of everyday language). "They don't say '*go annai shimasu*'—just '*annai shimasu*.'" (In Japanese, "*go*" is often added to express an extra level of formality.) Then she referenced Deborah Tannen's *You Just Don't Understand* (1990) and said, "In any country, if a woman is overly masculine in her speech, people will punish you." Carrie continued:

> I can say I don't speak Japanese. But for women [*nihonjin*] bengoshi [lawyers] it's harder. If you say '*yoroshii desuka*' [an example of formal language] they treat you as a woman first, then as a partner. But you can't talk like a partner because they'll think you're a freak. I don't have that problem because I'm a foreigner. It's a huge communication style advantage to be a foreigner. If you're a woman, it's a huge advantage to be a foreigner because you can break the rules. They won't hold you to the same standards. I can do a lot of things that a man can't do, that a Japanese can't do.

Carrie gave the example of a young associate wanting to be promoted to manager. She believes she could joke about why his incompetence made him unqualified to be a manager, but she says that a man could not say the same thing to another man because it would be taken more competitively and because the second man would feel threatened.

Regarding the situation of Japanese American women in Japan, Carrie observes, "The only way to be successful is to take your unique qualities and turn them into something else that no one else can offer.... That's why I don't use Japanese. I do speak it pretty well but I always downplay it. That way I can catch stuff and they don't realize I've caught it." She continues, "I think that's one reason why professional women eventually return [to the United States]. If you don't pick up on your qualities as a competitive advantage, you're just fighting against the grain and it's hard. You could be the pioneer, but life is too short and I'd rather be the one behind the pioneer." While Carrie seems to have learned how to turn her set of characteristics into a strength for navigating Japanese society, she also points out that many professional foreign women do not remain in Japan long term. Indeed, research shows that a lack of gender equality is one reason highly skilled migrant women are discouraged from working for Japanese corporations (Oishi 2012).

## Japanese American Name Representation in Japanese Alphabets

Language usage in Japan includes how one writes one's name, due to the slightly different connotations of each alphabet in Japanese. Writing names is a daily occurrence: filling out forms, signing up for rewards cards, dropping off dry cleaning. How one presents oneself on *meishi* (business cards) is also important. Thus, how one writes one's name is frequently a clue to how Japanese Americans present and construct themselves through interactions with Japanese people. Writing about multiracial and multiethnic Asian Americans, Daniel Nakashima pointed out that names are one of the ways we perform classification (Nakashima 2001). As a group of people who challenge binary, mutually exclusive categorization, Japanese Americans in Japan choose particular alphabets to write their names in Japanese to indicate their positioning in relation to the "Japanese" and "foreigner" categories. The choices they make are affected by other traits that signal their Japaneseness, such as phenotype and language ability, as well as the depth of their awareness and understanding of contemporary Japanese culture and social norms in Japan.

As they become more immersed in Japanese society and more knowledgeable about the benefits and drawbacks of being seen as Japanese or as foreigners, Japanese Americans discover how to articulate Japanese and foreign identities through name representations in *kanji* as insiders or *katakana* as outsiders to manage Japanese expectations of them. The majority of Japanese Americans I met had a non-Japanese first name and a Japanese last name (e.g., Sherman Abe), while almost all others had either two Japanese names (e.g., Kiyomi Mizuhara) or two non-Japanese names (e.g., Martin Artz).[12] In addition to alphabet choice, whether or not Japanese Americans choose to use their Japanese names and/or middle names (which most Japanese people do not have) reflects the negotiation of bifurcated categories to construct complex identities that assert both their Japanese and foreign aspects.

### Using Kanji *and Middle Names*

The Japanese Americans I met who were newer to Japan spoke limited Japanese, or had limited interactions with Japanese, tending to fit the profile of the first group described by Glen Fukushima. These Japanese Americans wrote their Japanese names in *kanji* and believed that this expressed their connectedness to Japanese people and culture. These less-immersed Japanese Americans liked to denote their Japanese names in *kanji* as assertions of their Japanese ancestry and ties to Japan. Expressly because they had a limited understanding of the Japanese language, culture, and society, their ancestral ties to Japan were the best way for them to assert their connection to Japan. Moreover, having these ties also served to differentiate them from the general foreign population. In other words, the reference point for comparison for these Japanese Americans was typically other foreigners, not *nihonjin*. So, by writing their Japanese names in *kanji*, they were asserting their position as being more Japanese than the foreigners who did not have Japanese names and had to write their names in *katakana* or *romaji*.

Bob, a fifty-one-year-old sansei lawyer from Hawaiʻi, was typical of the majority of my Japanese American interviewees because he had a non-Japanese first name and Japanese middle and last names—and was typical of those who used *kanji* because he said it was to express his Japaneseness. Born on the US continent and raised in Hawaiʻi, Bob had been taking Japanese classes intermittently from first grade through attending college at UCLA, even hiring a Japanese tutor in recent years. He recounted that through living in Japan, "I maybe doubled the level of proficiency I had coming here," ostensibly referring to the gap between classroom learning and immersion in a country where the language is spoken every day and all around you.

When I interviewed Bob in 2006, he had been living in Tokyo for about two years but was just beginning to feel like his Japanese had improved to the point where he could interact with Japanese and "blend in even after I open my mouth." He said that he usually spoke Japanese as much as possible "to avoid awkward situations" and further implied that since his Japanese was still only able to get him through simple situations ("nothing too complicated"), he wanted to prove to himself that he could survive in Japan. "I want to be able to speak Japanese. I mean, it's kind [of] my own sense of pride that I am living here. I mean . . . this is a very simple situation, trying to find out where the bar is, and that's why I'm taking all this language study because I should be able to do that."

As discussed earlier in this chapter, since his work environment was primarily English-based, the opportunity for Bob to improve his Japanese was limited to time outside of work. In Bob's attempts to fit in and adapt to Japanese society, he preferred to write his Japanese last name in *kanji*, also including his Japanese middle name, on his business cards—an unusual occurrence in Japan since typically *nihonjin* do not have middle names. He relates:

> I only use my middle initial in the United States, and the only time I write my middle name in the United States is for formal documents where I'm supposed to have it there, and on a lot of formal documents you don't need to have your middle name, your middle initial is sufficient, so, but here maybe I tend to do it more, if you want to show that you're Japanese. It's, if anything, it's a good conversation thing, when I pull out my *meishi* [business card] then the Japanese start asking me about my middle name. So it makes for something to talk about.

While Bob already had a Japanese last name that he could express in *kanji*, he also consciously used his Japanese middle name, partly out of an interest in asserting his connections to Japan and partly out of practical concerns because its usage became a topic of conversation.

Other Japanese Americans in business and law also commented that having a Japanese name or middle initial on their *meishi* made them memorable to people with whom they met. This usage made them memorable because it both accentuated their shared Japanese background to establish a connection between them and their Japanese clients, yet also differentiated them as foreigners because, as mentioned, of the rare occurrence in Japan of having a middle name. So having both a middle name (or initial), as well as a Japanese name, was a way to assert similarity to and difference from Japanese in Japan at the same time.

Ironically, some Japanese Americans did not use their Japanese middle names because the connotations of those names marked them as too different from their peers in contemporary Japan. Jay was a twenty-five-year-old sansei/yonsei who had been living in Japan for about two years when I interviewed him in 2005. He had previously spent a year as a college exchange student at International Christian University (ICU) and was now working as a coordinator of international relations in the Japan Exchange and Teaching (JET) Program, based in a government office where he used Japanese on a regular basis. Jay learned to interpret his antiquated Japanese middle name and more common last name differently as he became more familiar with contemporary Japanese society.

When Jay took a Japanese language class, his Japanese professor told him that he should use *kanji* to write his name, while the textbook said that all Japanese who live abroad should use *katakana*. At first he followed the textbook suggestion and used *katakana*, but then his professor told him he could use *kanji*, even though Jay pointed out that he was a *nikkeijin* (the descendant of Japanese emigrants) and living abroad. Jay concluded, "I like writing in kanji because it's cool to have kanji. It makes me feel more Japanese because I have kanji for my last name. Sometimes it's easier . . . to pass . . . I'm glad I have a Japanese last name."

However, Jay added that even though he has a Japanese middle name, he does not use it because "it's *dasai* [lame], like the name of a fifty-year-old guy." He previously "thought it was a cool name, but after coming to Japan I figured it out. It almost never came up but then if it did, it was [the name of] a fifty-year-old guy." So learning about the usage and connotations of his Japanese middle name in contemporary Japan changed how Jay saw it—he had previously seen it as "cool" and a more general marker of Japaneseness within the

US context. While he used his Japanese last name and even wrote it in *kanji*, Jay had enough knowledge of contemporary Japanese society to know that in order to blend in, it was better not to use his antiquated Japanese middle name, more common among older Japanese men, because that would have made him stand out as being different from most Japanese his age.

### *Using Parents' Japanese Last Names to Publicly Assert Japaneseness*

For people of Japanese ancestry without Japanese first or last names, consciously using their Japanese middle names or taking on their parents' Japanese last names was a way for them to publicly assert their Japaneseness and prevent misunderstandings about their heritage. Martin is an example of someone who has three legal names—Martin Yamane Artz, of which he uses his Japanese middle name as his last name in Japan. In Martin's case, his legal middle name was actually his Japanese father's last name before Martin's father was legally adopted as an adult by a European American family in the United States.[13] In Japan and in the United States, Martin uses all three of his names on official, legal documents such as immigration or tax forms. He said that in the United States, in more informal situations, he would typically use just his (non-Japanese) first and last names because for people in the United States, his Japanese name was "awkward . . . and they misspell it." In Japan, in more informal situations dealing with Japanese people such as making reservations at restaurants or hotels, Martin typically uses only two names, but they are his first and middle names so that he has a Japanese last name. He explained, "When I use a Japanese [last] name, [Japanese service people] are less likely to freeze up and be like 'Oh my god, this guy isn't going to know what I'm saying.' It makes everyday life a little bit easier." He added that he is thinking about legally changing his last name to his Japanese middle name because "it's a better reflection of who I am." Martin believes that his English first name, Martin, and Japanese last name, Yamane, represent his identity well, as he sees himself as *hāfu*—the child of a Japanese father and a foreign mother.[14]

Martin discussed how other people have advised him on how to represent his names. When Martin was younger, growing up in Boston, he did not use his Japanese middle name very much. Then from junior high school, Martin's Japanese immigrant father suggested that Martin use his full name to demonstrate his mixed ancestry. By the time Martin attended high school in Tokyo, he was using his Japanese middle name more than his legal last name as a last name. In addition, Martin said that when his father was in Japan, despite the legal last name change, in interactions with Japanese people he would always use Yamane—his father's mailbox in Tokyo even has the Japanese last name on it. After describing how in Japan he and his father both use his father's former Japanese last name, Martin reflected that he learned it from observing his father: "I'm just doing what [my father] does in Japan." When I spoke with Martin in 2005, halfway through his one-year, intensive, Japanese language immersion program, he explained: "I prefer the Japanese . . . I think it's cool." Though he thinks the mix of foreign and Japanese names fits him well, he says that when he asks Japanese people about it, they say the American last name is a better fit. By expressing this opinion, it is clear that they see him more as a foreigner. In this context, Martin's assertion of his Japanese name indicates his interest in having his Japaneseness be publicly recognized in Japan so that others will see his combination of backgrounds and validate his mixed-Japanese identity, rather than reducing him to simply being another foreigner.

Martin's strategy of using a parent's Asian surname to express ethnic connections is a common practice in the United States, where multiracial and multiethnic Asian Americans without an Asian-sounding first name or family name often use their mothers' maiden names or middle names to express their Asianness (see Murphy-Shigematsu 2012: 178). Daniel Nakashima explains how this prevents misunderstandings and makes "visible a part of their background that would have otherwise remained hidden behind conventional usage of one's first name and patrilineal surname" (Nakashima 2001: 116).

## *Japanese First and Last Names*

Regardless of phenotype, those with Japanese first and last names who use *kanji* see it as natural choice in Japan to express their Japaneseness and differentiate themselves from other foreign nationals without Japanese names. Takamori was a fifty-year-old lawyer from New York with Japanese first and last names and two *nihonjin* parents. He enjoyed using *kanji* for both of his names, commenting that writing his name in *kanji* invites questions, in particular about his first name because it is so unusual (his first name sounds generally older and is no longer very common). Several times during our conversation, he commented on how unusual his being bilingual and bicultural was, suggesting that he enjoys being seen as unique in Japan. He added that other foreigners in prominent positions are all white and that there are no Japanese-speaking Japanese Americans in these kinds of high-profile appointments. However, as discussed later in this section, as someone who is phenotypically similar to most Japanese and has above-average Japanese language abilities, by writing his two Japanese names in *kanji*, Takamori encountered some problems.

In contrast, Hiroshi was an example of a mixed-heritage Japanese American with limited Japanese language abilities whose use of *kanji* for his first and last names did not put him at risk of being mistaken for a mainstream Japanese person. When I met Hiroshi, the child of a sansei father and a second-generation Irish American mother, he had been in Tokyo for four months as a college exchange student and was happily using *kanji* for both his Japanese first and last names. He did not use his Western middle name in Japan unless it was necessary. His desire to feel close to Japanese people and distinguish himself from other exchange students was apparent as he explained that he "gets treated better" than other students because he has a Japanese name. As one example, he cited a Japanese shopkeeper who told him and Leo, a yonsei (fourth generation) friend of his with a Japanese last name, that they "have good hearts but others from your school don't." Further, the shopkeeper asked them to talk to the other students about how he felt, suggesting that he viewed Hiroshi and Leo as intermediaries.

Hiroshi said that this conversation only came about after they revealed their names while signing up for a card. He also added that having a Japanese name helps in getting job interviews—their (Japanese) names get them moved up to the top of the list. Friends and relatives have also told him he is lucky to have Japanese first and last names. He said that many people he knows switch to their Japanese middle names while in Japan. Responding to this statement, his friend Leo, who had a Western first name and Japanese last name, added that if he had a Japanese middle name, he would have been using it. At the time, Leo had also been residing in Tokyo for four months and was using *katakana* for his first name and *kanji* for his last name.

Japanese Americans of varying phenotypes and language abilities may use *kanji* for their first and last names, but when they are visually similar to most Japanese and very fluent in Japanese, Japanese people get confused. Takamori continued to happily write his names in *kanji*, but he seemed aware that there were drawbacks to positioning himself as Japanese in Japan. In contrast to Hiroshi, who was still focused on the positive aspects of asserting his Japaneseness and using *kanji* for his names, Takamori was aware that strategies for Japanese Americans to reap the benefits of being a foreigner might exist, but he was unsure what they were.

While Takamori has lived in Japan off and on for a number of years in multiple cities and considers his Japanese to be fairly good, it was also clear that his immersion in Japanese society and interactions with new people were limited. He explained, "Practically all of my interaction outside of work is with Japanese people whom I know, either directly or through my [Japanese] wife. I have not met that many new people (Japanese or non-Japanese) outside of work, as my non-work social life is fairly limited." As a result, Takamori has not needed to adjust the ways he presents himself outside of his work environment and has not yet figured out how to switch back and forth to his benefit between asserting Japanese and foreign characteristics. When asked, "When is it beneficial to be seen as Japanese? When is it beneficial to be seen as foreign?" he replied, "Obviously, the ideal situation is to be seen as Japanese or as *gaijin* when it is to one's advantage and to be seen as the other when it is to one's disadvantage. I don't know whether it's possible to manipulate one's Japanese or *gaijin* characteristics depending on which would be more advantageous under a particular set of circumstances." Takamori commented that in Japan, because he looks Japanese and speaks Japanese "fairly well, I am assumed to be Japanese, which can be an advantage but can also be burdensome, since I am not always knowledgeable about (and sometimes am uncomfortable with, even if I know) the behavior that is expected of me in certain situations." He said that he is "generally comfortable in day-to-day life, although there are situations where my Japanese is not good enough and/or I am in circumstances where I am not sure how to behave, and people think I am Japanese and thus are not aware of my discomfort in certain situations." In other words, although Takamori enjoyed blending in, he also found it to be a burden because of expectations placed on him regarding social norms and behavior. As someone who visually blended in Japan, spoke relatively fluent Japanese, and had two Japanese names, there was very little to initially warn people in Japan that he was not Japanese.

### Using Katakana *to Express Foreignness*

One way for Japanese Americans to indicate that they are not *nihonjin* (mainstream Japanese) is by writing their Japanese names in *katakana*. Japanese Americans who wrote their Japanese names in *katakana* tended to have more knowledge of Japanese language, culture, and society and were usually trying to signal that they were not Japanese from Japan in order to elicit the appropriate expectations of them as people not raised in Japan. In contrast to people such as Takamori, who used *kanji* and was unsure of how to manage and redirect expectations in Japan, those who were aware enough of social norms in Japan either did not want to conform to them or knew that their knowledge was partial—so even if they wanted to, they would not have been able to behave appropriately. Japanese Americans I met who visually blended in Japan and were relatively fluent in Japanese were the clearest about letting people know that they were not Japanese by writing their Japanese names in *katakana*.

The switch from *kanji* to *katakana* usually came about as Japanese Americans realized that the confusion they caused might be mitigated by asserting their foreignness. Glen Fukushima recounted that in his early years spending time in Japan as an adult, he switched from using *kanji* to using *katakana* as he realized that it was a clearer way to express his combination of characteristics. In 1969, he spent two months in Japan as a college student through the Keio-Stanford summer exchange program and had *meishi* with his last name in *kanji* "because I thought that was the thing to do. But I quickly discovered that it could be confusing. So from 1971 when I went for the one year, at that time I decided that it's better to use katakana."

Glen's comments suggest that using *kanji* for his Japanese last name at first seemed like a standard convention but caused unexpected confusion, ostensibly because he spoke Japanese relatively well and was phenotypically similar to most Japanese. As a result, he switched to using *katakana*; he now advises Japanese Americans who visit Japan to write their names in *katakana* to avoid confusion.[15] Indeed, some of the Japanese Americans that I interviewed who knew Glen said that they were following his advice by writing their names in *katakana*. Takamori also received this advice from his Japanese teacher, who suggested that he use *katakana* to let people know that he is foreign (though he disregarded the advice and was still writing his name in *kanji*).

Confirming Glen's observations, the Japanese Americans I met who expressed both their English and Japanese names in *katakana* were trying to let Japanese people know that they lack the linguistic, cultural, and social knowledge of a Japanese person. Grant, who speaks Japanese quite well, writes his Japanese last name in *katakana* to inform Japanese people that he is a foreigner. Similar to the majority of my Japanese American interviewees who visually blend in Japan, he said, "as long as I don't speak, they think I'm Japanese." Then he continued, "In work situations, I want [it] known [that I'm not Japanese] because I don't want them to think I'm stupid." So he writes his name in *katakana* on his *meishi* so that people he encounters through work clearly know that his knowledge base is US- and English-based, rather than Japan- and Japanese-based.

Japanese American navigation of name representation in Japan is also shaped by phenotype and being of mixed ancestry. Multiracial and multiethnic Japanese Americans with Japanese last names sometimes switch from using *kanji* to using *katakana* because Japanese people have told them that foreigners should not use *kanji*—in other words, emphasizing their foreignness (and differences from Japanese), rather than their Japaneseness. John is a yonsei with a sansei father and German, Native American, and Scottish-American mother. In Japan, he says he can visually blend into a crowd and does not get the same attention as white people. If people see John's Japanese last name, they can often guess that he has Japanese ancestry. When he first lived in Japan, similar to other Japanese Americans (mixed and not), John used *kanji* for his last name. But his reason for switching to *katakana* was slightly different from most Japanese Americans I met, who are more consistently racialized Japanese in Japan. John stopped using *kanji* once Japanese people told him that it was ridiculous for a foreigner to use *kanji*. This contrasts with my more phenotypically Japanese interviewees who said they stopped using *kanji* when they realized it confused people or when they learned to identify more as foreigners. Thus, deciding to make the switch from *kanji* to *katakana* is sometimes motivated by a desire to express their identities or avoid confusion and is sometimes instigated by others telling Japanese Americans the appropriate way to represent their name.

## Romaji *as Another Option*

In addition, a handful of Japanese American interviewees with very limited Japanese skills use a third alphabet, *romaji*, to express their foreignness—and seemed quite happy to reap the benefits of being seen as a foreigner. Oliver, a thirty-nine-year-old yonsei who had been living in Japan for nine years when I interviewed him in 2005, wrote his non-Japanese first name and Japanese middle and last names all in *katakana* on his *meishi*. However, when we talked, Oliver said that he usually writes his name in *romaji*, rather than *kanji*, so as to be able to better manage expectations: "I don't want to write my name in kanji because then I would be expected to be treated like a Japanese person." He does also use *katakana*, but "it's faster to write in romaji." If there is an official document that he needs to fill out, his Japanese wife helps him. This seems to reflect Oliver's satisfaction with his role as a foreigner in Japan, as well as his comfort with negotiating the Japanese and foreigner categories: "It's nice to have an Asian face . . . we can see a more 'true' Japan because they don't even notice us . . . we can just open our mouths and speak English and be a *gaijin* if we want to." Oliver's narrative was one of learning to see the advantages of being a foreigner in Japan, in both everyday life and special situations (such as dating).

When he first arrived in Japan, he had much more trouble "with my [Asian] face and just being 'duh' they must think I'm 'retarded' . . . then after a year I could say something back." Though he has not developed fluency in Japanese, he is now more comfortable. Oliver says, "[I] never felt like I'm Japanese American so I should speak Japanese." As a yonsei, he just explains to people in Japan that his parents do not speak Japanese and that he only learned it from a class he took in college. In Japan, although his Japanese has improved since he first arrived, as an English teacher with a bilingual Japanese wife, he can live comfortably without having to become fluent in Japanese.

## Conclusion

In Japan, language ability and cultural knowledge influence how Japanese Americans identify as well as claim in-group and out-group membership. The Japanese Americans I met who were less fluent in the Japanese language and less familiar with social norms and customs, as well as less immersed in Japanese society, emphasized their Japaneseness and were optimistic about their eventual inclusion in Japan. As they became more immersed in and knowledgeable about Japanese society—i.e., more competent in everyday Japanese activities, functions, and tasks—my Japanese American interviewees felt more of a need to distinguish themselves from Japanese people to manage expectations of them that exceeded their abilities. This demonstrates the strategic assertion of Japaneseness and foreignness within the larger context of intersecting abilities and knowledge bases. Those who had lived in Japan a long time and were most fluent and immersed seemed more focused on their differences from Japanese people. A significant factor was whether comparison to and differentiation from foreigners or Japanese was the reference point. This distinction depended on language and cultural knowledge which could change over time, but also on phenotype and names that signal one's Japanese heritage to others.

The management of others' expectations by Japanese Americans reflects the importance of positioning as either insiders (Japanese) or as outsiders (foreigners). This kind of strategic positioning occurs whenever people must negotiate boundaries that they cross over. When Japanese Americans speak fluent Japanese but are not familiar with the social norms that mainstream Japanese are expected to follow, rather than position themselves as inadequate or unknowledgeable Japanese, it is to their benefit to be seen as knowledgeable foreigners who exceed expectations. While social categories are always limiting, over time, most individuals find ways to navigate how they are positioned in these categories to their benefit. With that said, as this chapter has shown, time and proficiency alone were not enough to inform Japanese Americans of how to manage expectations of them; interactions with Japanese people and immersion in Japanese society were also important ways that they learned about social norms.

Finally, the linguistic experiences of Japanese Americans in Tokyo highlight the privileged position that English-speaking foreigner communities in Japan occupy, as well as the complicated relationship between language acquisition and necessity. Work and home environments in Japan both shape Japanese American attitudes about improving their Japanese skills. Some Japanese Americans speak limited Japanese but have English-supported work environments and are perpetually in a state of idealizing a future where they could speak Japanese fluently. Others study Japanese, develop basic fluency, then lose the motivation to keep improving because their work environments do not require them to hone their Japanese skills.

Either way, when a workplace does not encourage or necessitate improving Japanese skills, other things in life compete with a person's time and lower the priority of improving Japanese, even when individuals have an interest in doing so. Having home environments with English-speaking spouses and children also allows Japanese Americans to live in Japan comfortably without needing to improve their Japanese fluency. This situation is possible because the global currency of speaking English makes the Americanness of Japanese American experiences in Japan a more salient part of their choices.

Though some Japanese Americans develop comfortable lifestyles in Tokyo due to combinations of work, home, and social environments, the majority of my interviewees eventually returned to the United States. The next chapter examines how Japanese Americans look back at their Japan experiences once they readjust to life in the United States and rethink what living in Japan has shown them about what it means to be "Japanese" and "Japanese American."

CHAPTER 5

# Back in the United States

## JAPANESE AMERICAN INTERPRETATIONS OF THEIR EXPERIENCES IN JAPAN

How do Japanese Americans make sense of their Japan experiences after they return to the United States?[1] To answer this question, Japanese American experiences in Japan must be recontextualized back into the US context and related constructions of Japaneseness there. In other words, once they are back in the United States what it means to be "Japanese" or "Japanese American" in the United States shapes how Japanese Americans interpret the experiences they had in Japan.

Changes in what it means to be Japanese American are reflected in the large historical Japanese communities in the United States. While at one time there were more than forty enclaves known as "Japantowns" across the United States, in 2016, only four remain: San Francisco's "Nihonmachi," San Jose's "Nihonmachi," and Los Angeles's "Little Tokyo" and "Little Osaka" (see Pease 2008). As contemporary urban centers for Japanese American communities, these areas have long served as focal points for a variety of cultural and social activities, including Japanese American churches, temples, Boy Scout troops, and sports leagues. In addition to these urban ethnic centers on the US continent, there is a large Japanese American or "local Japanese" population in Honolulu (and other parts of Hawai'i). All of these Japanese American communities take pride in tracing their history of immigrant settlement back to the late 1800s and early 1900s. On the West Coast, despite forced mass evacuation and incarceration during World War II, Japanese Americans, although in smaller numbers, reestablished communities in these areas during the postwar period (see, for example, Inada 2000,

Kashima 2003). In Hawai'i, the majority of Japanese Americans were not incarcerated during World War II but demographic and generational shifts among the population have caused their own set of challenges regarding how to build and maintain the Japanese American community.

For Japanese Americans who grew up in areas like these with large concentrations of Japanese Americans, ethnic identities may have centered around belonging to particular types of organizations (e.g., Japanese American churches or temples) and participating in certain ethnic community activities (e.g., playing in the Japanese American basketball leagues in California). In Hawai'i as well as on the US continent, Japanese American community festivals reflect the long history of Japanese Americans in the United States, including changes over time (see King-O'Riain 2006, Kurashige 2002, Yano 2006). These festivals, organizations, and activities have been an important part of what it means to be "Japanese American."

Yet, ethnic Japanese experiences in the United States are not monolithic. They include experiences of more recent postwar migrants from Japan, collectively described as *shin-issei*, "new first generation" immigrants and their US-born *shin-nisei* children (Fujita 2009, see Befu 2002, Hyodo 2013, Kurotani 2005, Spickard 2009: 164–165), who do not have family histories of incarceration in the United States during World War II. In addition, many later-generation Japanese Americans have not grown up enmeshed in Japanese American communities. Since identities—ethnic and otherwise—are shaped by social environments, the multiple ways that ethnic Japanese in the United States identify complicate mainstream, previously established notions of who Japanese Americans are and what makes up their experiences.

The diversity of Japanese Americans is reflected in interpretations of the experiences they have had in Japan. That is, this chapter demonstrates different ways in which Japanese Americans have come to understand these experiences. Whether or not Japanese Americans have a parent who was raised in Japan shapes the meaning they attach to living in Japan. Moreover, as the lion's share of the chapter explains, the Japanese Americans I interviewed exhibit three ontological views of the relationship between Japanese Americans and Japan.

By focusing on Japanese Americans who have returned to the United States after having resided in Japan, this chapter addresses how the construction of Japaneseness in the United States (i.e., Japanese Americanness) is related to—and affected by—the construction of Japaneseness in Japan. Perhaps ironically, Japanese Americans who have lived in Japan learn to challenge notions of cultural authenticity stemming from the homeland. While Japanese Americans go to Japan and learn the language and culture, interactions with Japanese people in Japan also reveal how they are culturally different from their counterparts who were raised in Japan. After living in Japan, my Japanese American interviewees articulated these differences in a variety of ways. For many, experiences in Japan resulted in ontological shifts in how they perceived Japanese Americanness.

## Reasons for Returning to the United States

Before turning to what Japanese Americans think about their experiences in Japan as they look back from the United States, it will be helpful to review the motivations and reasons for deciding to return to the United States. As scholars have noted, factors in different phases of one's life course shape the priorities and decisions of migrants (Jain 2012, Levitt 2002). When I asked Japanese Americans why they left Japan, answers differed between younger and older interviewees related to factors such as career development and family. In addition, public health safety concerns and gendered experiences and perceived opportunities also shaped the decision to leave Japan.

Younger, single Japanese Americans, including college students and Japan Exchange and Teaching (JET) Program participants in their twenties, tended to respond that they left Japan because they wanted to get back to their "real lives" in the United States.[2] This included continuing their education and careers, as well as reuniting with US-based family and friends. Since studying abroad and participating in the JET Program are initially one-year commitments, most pointed out that they knew beforehand that the experience in Japan would be a limited one.[3] For example, typical of most former JETs, Erin said, "My one-year JET contract was up, and I was starting to feel like I needed to get home in order to start living my 'real' life. Something about living in Japan on the JET Program almost felt like vacation, even though I was working. It always felt temporary—and of course I knew it was." In a similar vein, Isabella said she left Japan to attend graduate school. She stayed on as a JET for two years (renewing her one-year contract once) and considered remaining for a third year, but her parents asked her to return to the United States. They saw the assistant language teaching position as a "dead-end job" and told her, "You need to get on with your life." So she took their advice and came back to the United States to attend law school.

On the other hand, older Japanese Americans who were mostly married, with full-time jobs, and often had children, said that concerns about family and careers were central to their decisions to leave Japan.[4] Educational opportunities and language and socialization environments for children, as well as a lack of career advancement in Japan, especially for women, were factors that this group considered. Since Alvin lived in Japan over a span of time, first as a JET, then as a lawyer, his story demonstrates different reasons for leaving each time: "I left Japan after the JET program to go to law school. I left Japan in 2006 because we had our third child and decided that it was time to move back to the States, as commuting around Tokyo with three little kids would be difficult. Also, since we were moving to Hawaiʻi, we wanted to make sure our oldest, who was four at the time, would start kindergarten in Hawaiʻi, so that she could culturally acclimate." Alvin left Japan the first time after finishing his JET contract so that he could continue his education in the United States. Then he lived in Japan a second time as a working professional. Concerns about raising his family in Tokyo prompted Alvin and his family to leave. The timing of having his children start school in the United States and having time to socially and culturally adjust to that educational environment were additional factors—factors that parents often consider when their children are at the age to start school.

After the March 11, 2011, earthquake, tsunami, and nuclear disaster in the Tohoku area of Japan, an additional consideration concerning the health and welfare of their children was the radiation scare, which some interviewees cited as a motivating factor to leave Japan. Masato illustrates this perspective when he explains how he and his family decided to leave Tokyo approximately one year after the triple disaster:

> These big decisions, there's always like multiple factors, but I guess one catalyst was the earthquake, which happened a year before [I left Tokyo]. Right after the earthquake there were a lot of concerns about radiation getting into the food supply and it was really immediately after the earthquake when it suddenly kind of struck me that maybe this was a good time to leave Japan . . . at that point I was in Japan eight and a half years. . . . And, you know, the government says it's safe but I don't trust what the Japanese government is saying . . . then I started thinking about other factors such as the fact that my daughter was just at the age when she'd be starting high school, if we were to move to the U.S. at that point. So we had already decided to have her go to the American School in Japan [ASIJ] from eighth grade . . . through high school. So this is a complete reversal of that plan that we had just constructed. So the catalyst was really the earthquake. And then it just seemed like that would be a good reason to leave and timing wise, if we did it right away we would be able to get our daughter right from freshman year to high school, which seemed like a good time to move, socially, etc. Even though we were planning on having her go to ASIJ, we were also planning on having her go to college in the United States. So she

either goes to college from ASIJ ... or apply after four years of high school in the United States. So you either make the decision to go now or you wait four or five years until she's done with high school. And the earthquake thing, I was really uncomfortable with it, more so than my wife, and that's what really got the ball rolling.

Masato's narrative illustrates how my Japanese American interviewees with children tended to prioritize their children's educational opportunities and socialization in considering where to live. Specifically, the 2011 triple disaster in Japan was the catalyst that pushed up the family's timeline for the trans-Pacific move, which coincided with his daughter being able to attend all four years of high school in the United States. In a similar vein, in my Tokyo-based interviews, practically all of the Japanese American male professionals married to Japanese women and raising young children described plans for their children to eventually attend college in the United States.

Women additionally mentioned gender roles and discrimination in Japan as factors that discouraged them from staying longer. Amy, for example, was a JET in Chiba for two years (from 1988 to 1990), then wanted to stay in Japan and broaden her horizons. She had no particular career goals, but knew she did not want to be teaching English anymore. So a Japanese friend of her father's from their undergraduate days at UC Berkeley found her a job working as an OL (office lady) at the headquarters of a steel manufacturing company in Tokyo. An "office lady" refers to "a female office worker engaged in simple, routine, clerical jobs usually without any expert knowledge or management responsibility" (Ogasawara 1998: 202). When asked if she ever considered staying in Japan long term, Amy responded:

> No ... I was at the steel company for three years. By then, it just started feeling like just regular work and just doing the daily things every year and the same thing. Just like any work—you just sort of get tired of doing the same thing. And I just thought, 'well, it's time to move on.' I guess I was in my mid-20s by then and I felt like, 'well, um, it was a nice experience working in a Japanese company but I know I'm not going to like grow in this company' ... just because the women in the steel company, they just don't get promoted. Some get to a certain point, I guess, but at that time, really, not much chance.

Similar to other young Japanese Americans in their twenties, Amy described moving back to the United States in terms of wanting to "move on." She later added, "I think I was around twenty-four at the time and I was one of the old women in the company because a lot of them graduated from high school and started working there, maybe at the most a junior college and then started working there and then they'd find someone to get married to and then they'd quit. But it was a really interesting experience." While she mentioned that she was happy to obtain another perspective on life in Japan by working there, especially doing something other than teaching English (the most accessible job to Americans at the time), Amy admitted that she did not end up learning much about business while working as an OL. She also described the job as "a little degrading," explaining that although Japan was "economically forward," women had very low status in that extremely conservative steel company (and in general).

Isabella also considered that gendered, racialized interpretations of her by others might affect her career prospects in Japan. She described how she pondered the challenges of being a Japanese American female lawyer in Tokyo:

> One of the things I definitely thought about is how difficult it is to be a professional lawyer in Japan, even in Tokyo because I had heard from women, especially when you're *Japanese* American that they still treat you the way they treat Japanese women, which is to say like a secretary or the tea lady and you're still expected, even if you're a lawyer going into a conference room with a bunch of other lawyers and you're American, you're still the one getting the tea—that kind of thing . . . the Japanese, especially when you're negotiating with Japanese lawyers, they still look at you like even if they on an intellectual level know that you're an American, and you're speaking in English or whatever, they still see you as a Japanese woman and so they don't treat you with the same level of respect. So yeah, I knew that that would be difficult and I didn't know how far I'd be able to go with that kind of attitude and how much I'd want to even deal with it.

Here Isabella notes how there may be a gap between someone's intellectual understanding of her and the interpretations of her phenotype and gender, evoking certain kinds of reactions that could illicit less respect than she would deserve as a colleague. She added that if she were white or a man, things might have been different: "What I heard is that it's an issue for Asian women in Japan . . . Asian foreigners working in Japan but not if you're white. If you're white, then they're like, oh, she's American and they treat you differently. . . . But maybe if I were a guy I would have made a different decision [about pursuing a law career in Tokyo]." So Isabella's hesitancy to pursue a law career in Japan was based on what she had experienced working as an assistant language teacher and what she heard from lawyer friends who had worked in Tokyo regarding how Japanese American female lawyers are not treated the same as male or white lawyers.

## Generational Differences

Among the Japanese Americans I interviewed in the United States, generational differences were a salient factor in how they interpreted their Japan experiences. The main difference was between the children of people who had been raised in Japan (i.e., the children of issei, kibei nisei, and shin-issei) and later generations who were more removed from people raised in Japan (i.e., most sansei, yonsei, and gosei). Although this may also appear to be a prewar/postwar migration wave difference, a handful of prewar-descendant nisei respondents made comments similar to postwar shin-nisei, suggesting that the salient factor was, in fact, the generational distance from people whose primary socialization was in Japan.

When I asked about identification with generational labels, answers typically reflected the relative closeness that shin-nisei feel to Japan versus the distance that sansei and yonsei feel. For example, one shin-nisei woman whose parents migrated from Japan in the postwar period said that she identifies as a nisei because her parents are issei, which meant that growing up they practiced Japanese customs and spoke Japanese in their household.[5] Of course, not all shin-nisei speak Japanese to their parents, and some have exclusively English-speaking households, but many of my interviewees focused on their maintenance of Japaneseness as the children of people from Japan when describing what it meant to identify as shin-nisei (another choice they could have made was to describe themselves as being not like their parents who are from Japan, pointing out the differences from the previous generation). In contrast, sansei and yonsei emphasized their distance from Japan. Stephanie's explanation of what it means to identify as yonsei illustrates this tendency: "At this point, it indicates how far removed I am from Japan."

In addition, there was a generational split regarding the perception of Japan as being a foreign, unfamiliar country—or not. Sansei and yonsei typically describe Japan, both before and after having lived there, as being like a "foreign country." Before living there, most remember feeling unfamiliar with the culture, customs, and language, all of which is partially reinforced through residing in Japan. Representative of my sansei and yonsei interviewees who felt distance at the same time that they felt a connection, Erin, a yonsei, commented that in some ways, going to Japan felt the same as going to Spain but with a safety net because she had family there.[6]

On the other hand, shin-nisei generally feel more familiar with Japan even before having lived there as adults. More than just affective ties because it was the country of their parents, the familiarity comes from having visited Japan as children, usually more than once to spend time with family during summer vacations and sometimes attending some school in Japan. Shin-nisei are part of what has been called the "new second generation" children of post-1965 immigrants from a variety of countries, who demonstrate various kinds of transnational ties to their parents' homelands (see Levitt and Waters 2002, Min 2002). Amy, the child of a shin-issei and a kibei nisei, remembers visiting Japan with her family as a child and feeling embarrassed about the remedial level of her Japanese—despite having attended Japanese school in the United States. She wished she could have communicated better with her relatives in Japan, and this eventually prompted her to study Japanese at UC Berkeley. She clarifies that these short summer visits made Japan feel familiar, though they were different from the depth of experience she gained through living in Japan on her own as an adult.[7]

The generational differences reflecting familiarity with Japan and expectations about language ability are illuminated by the case of Valerie, a sansei who studied abroad in Tokyo at the International Christian University (ICU). Though her parents were both nisei, their Japanese relatives were very wealthy and had the means to travel to the United States rather frequently, making Valerie feel a closer connection to Japan, compared to most sansei.[8] Before living there, more similar to how nisei feel, Valerie felt a strong affinity for and comfort with Japan.

However, spending time in Japan made Valerie feel like it was "a foreign country" where she did not "belong"—and the distance she felt began to resemble how her sansei peers generally feel. She explains how she considered staying in Japan long-term before she had ever actually lived there:

> I thought of Japan as possibly a home. I mean, it's because I had so many relatives coming back and forth I thought maybe I could go live with them or go have a life there. And so, um I didn't know. I knew that I would probably always want to be near my parents over here but I didn't know . . . but I was kind of open to the idea of being in Japan longer. And I left Japan thinking, 'I can't live here.' I'm not going to live here. I'm not going to become adept at Japanese, I am not going to be spending my life going back and forth because I was not going to become a Japan scholar. I wasn't going to pick up the language well enough. [My friend] made the choice very early on that she would become a Japan scholar, that she would do this and that's what she did. She picked up the language really well. She was a music major and had a very good ear for sound. I think I'm tone deaf.

Valerie comments on her lack of Japanese language ability and compares herself to her white American friend who "picked up the language really well" and intended to become a Japan scholar. On the other hand, Valerie, who went to Japan because she was interested in learning Japanese so she could communicate better with her grandmother, gave up on the goal of attaining a high level of fluency once she tested into the lowest Japanese class at ICU and was able to compare herself with her American peers. While she felt a familiarity with Japan through visits from her Japanese relatives while growing up in the United States, Valerie did not have strong enough Japanese language skills to enhance this affinity. As the next section describes, language ability and the motivation to improve it shape affective ties towards Japan.

## Developing a Better Understanding of Contemporary Japanese Society

While their experiences may be divergent across generations, geography, Japanese language ability, and motivations for going to Japan, after residing there, Japanese Americans all develop at least one thing in common: a better understanding of contemporary Japanese society. For some, this means a better understanding of their parents, whose primary socialization was in Japan. For others, this means a new way of differentiating between contemporary Japanese and Japanese American culture and society. Regardless of how familiar contemporary Japan felt before, residing there increases their knowledge of contemporary Japanese society and culture.

For Japanese Americans with limited Japanese language skills and whose parents were raised in Japan, living in Japan helps them to better understand their parents. June identifies as "nisei and a half" because her mother was issei and her father was kibei nisei. A 58-year-old, she says, "Most of my [age] peers are sansei, but as my parents are more Issei, I was raised as many Nisei were raised." One example of this is the use of language: while most nisei parents speak only English to each other and to their children in the home, June's parents spoke to each other in Japanese, plus her mother "never developed fluency in English. She spoke in a mix of English and Japanese." June recalls that she and her mother did not communicate well. Reflecting on her year of study abroad in Tokyo at ICU, June says, "Just being there surrounded by Japanese, speaking Japanese, spending time with family helped me understand my own family, my own parents better." When I asked her how that year has affected her since, June responded, "The primary way is that it gave me a better understanding of my family, my background, of where I came from."

Those with one issei and one later-generation Japanese American parent also learned to see their Japanese-speaking parent in a new light after their stay in Japan. Alvin, who is shin-nisei on his father's side and yonsei on his mother's side, said that before spending time in Japan, he lacked context for understanding how his father thought and acted. But "after my first year [of living in Japan], I came to understand my dad better. After being in Japan, I just realized, 'Oh, he's just being Japanese.'"

Similarly, Ryan, also a shin-nisei and yonsei, said that before living in Japan, he had never thought of his father as an immigrant. When he was younger, even up through college, he "just identified as yonsei." At first he identified as "fourth generation Japanese American" then as "yonsei Nikkei," switching to the latter term as he found "Japanese American" less acceptable and wanted to define himself using "my own language" (i.e., Japanese terms). He explained, "The identifying as shin-nisei part didn't come until recently."

Reflecting on how the Japan experience has helped him see his family in a different light, Ryan comments, "My dad is not as American as I thought he was. . . . Our family is not the same as other Japanese Americans because we have so many Japanese people in it. It wasn't Japanese Americans marrying other Japanese Americans—it was Japanese Americans marrying people from Japan. So I look at my family and at other Japanese American families and see that it's not the same." Living in Japan helped Ryan begin to see his father as a Japanese immigrant.[9] Despite spending many years of community activism around people of color and discussing immigrant issues, Ryan reflects, "I never thought of myself as the son of a immigrant [until going to Japan]. Saying 'shin-nisei' reclaims that." That is, my shin-nisei interviewees of mixed-generational backgrounds (e.g., father from Japan, sansei mother) learned to better understand their immigrant parents, whose cultural background was different from that of later-generation Japanese Americans.

While almost everyone with a parent raised in Japan described being able to understand their Japanese-speaking family members better, only a handful of later-generation Japanese Americans mentioned this to be the case for them. Todd is one of these exceptions, as a yonsei from California with a kibei nisei grandfather (raised in Japan from age 5 to age 20) in Hawai'i. Todd did not grow up speaking Japanese but has become a Japan specialist. In addition to being fluent in the language, he also teaches Japanese classes and conducts research in Japanese. He said that after living in Japan and learning Japanese, his grandfather seemed different to him, because he had a larger context from which to interpret him: "He's not strange anymore, he just doesn't fit the context of Hawai'i." His grandfather spoke in broken Hawai'i pidgin, but then he would mix in "this fluent Japanese . . . he's told me he feels more comfortable writing in Japanese. . . . He knew the language, the culture, how to behave in a Japanese sense."

This led Todd to having a breakthrough realization: "It's like wow, my grandfather, he's really really Japanese. . . . Sometimes he would be talking and he'd say '*ima* [now] ... (long pause, then he'd say it in English).' Now when I hear him do that, I know he's thinking in Japanese."

One reason why Todd's case is an exception is that in the 2000s, the sansei and yonsei who have become fluent in Japanese after living in Japan are not able to speak with their Japanese immigrant grandparents or great-grandparents because that generation has passed away. Instead, the way in which they view the relationship between Japan and Japanese Americans, generally not mediated through Japanese immigrants, gives them a different vantage point.

## "The Galapagos Effect": Japanese American Culture as Differently Evolved from Japanese Culture

Most later-generation Japanese Americans (with parents who were not raised in Japan) come from families who experienced World War II in the United States and fit the image of ethnic groups as increasingly assimilated and developing symbolic ethnic identities (Gans 1979) that are less and less relevant to their daily lives. As mentioned earlier, this includes not speaking Japanese or having gleaned much knowledge about contemporary Japan from their parents. Thus, the relationship of later-generation Japanese Americans to Japan is not like that of the transnational postwar flows of Japanese people and culture that have shaped shin-nisei ties and ethnic identities.

For later-generation Japanese Americans, it is common to find both differentiation, as well as conflation, of Japaneseness and Japanese Americanness. That is, on the one hand, Japanese Americans may know they are different from Japanese people in Japan. For example, several sansei and yonsei pointed out how Japanese were seen as "uncool" in the 1980s because of the way they dressed (compared to Americans) and their accented English (which did not challenge mainstream stereotypes in the United States of Asians as foreigners).

However, on the other hand, Japanese Americans who have not had much exposure to contemporary Japanese society tend not to know how different it is from the earlier forms of Japanese culture, such as Meiji culture from the late 1800s and early 1900s that prewar Japanese immigrants brought with them to the United States. Yonsei Isabella commented on how, before living in Japan, she did not differentiate between Japanese people in Japan and Japanese Americans. Through a US-based racial and ethnic lens, she viewed them as the same: "I was identifying with the racial aspect and didn't realize how big a difference there can be culturally." When I pointed out this contradiction to Todd, another yonsei, he agreed and commented, "When you see a Japanese tourist in the 1980s, you go I'm not that. But when you go to an *obon* festival [in the United States] you go 'I know Japanese culture.'" In other words, before spending significant time in Japan, later-generation Japanese Americans tend to equate US-based forms of Japaneseness and Japanese culture with Japaneseness and culture in contemporary Japan, both because they do not have the knowledge to be able to differentiate between them and because in the United States they are often conflated, especially when race or ethnicity is deemed more important than national differences.

The experience of residing in Japan causes this conflation to lessen. Prolonged exposure to contemporary Japanese society and culture leads sansei and yonsei from the US continent to develop a better awareness of contemporary Japanese society, enabling them to differentiate between the older forms of Japanese culture passed down to them through their families and the newer forms that exist in Japan today. Of course, one does not have to go to Japan to be aware that there are different forms of Japaneseness in Japan and the United States, but actually living in Japan and being able to observe firsthand highlights the distinctions and cultural gaps and makes them more concrete.

Thus, through living in Japan, later-generation Japanese Americans begin to realize that identifying with Japanese American culture is not the same as identifying with contemporary Japanese culture. Stephanie, a yonsei who has lived all over the continental United States, said, "After having lived in Japan, I . . . have a clearer understanding of what it means to be Japanese American. I used to think that being Japanese American was nearly synonymous to being Japanese . . . now I see a clear difference between the two." Brian, a sansei/yonsei from Central California, referred to this difference as the "Galapagos effect": how organisms that are physically separated evolve differently. Regarding Japanese and Japanese Americans, he explained, "I think they're distinct but come from a similar root."

Erin, a yonsei from the San Francisco Bay Area, also reflected on how she previously did not differentiate between Japanese and Japanese American cultures: "I thought that the things I knew from our Japanese American culture would help me understand Japanese people." In fact, like many of her generation, she used to see Japan as "the source" of Japaneseness. But living in Japan made her realize how the Japanese culture she had been exposed to in the United States was "antiquated" and was not changing in sync with developments in Japan—what Maira (2002) has referred to as "cultural fossilization." Erin puts it this way: "What I saw as the source of the things we do here doesn't exist anymore [in Japan]." Erin equated it to a time capsule. She had thought that "things just stay frozen over there" but "realized what a stupid assumption that was" when she lived in Japan. She explained, "If you don't live over there you don't think about it." Thus, what previously existed (i.e., her grandparents' Japan) has changed and essentially does not exist anymore. She concluded, "Knowing Japanese American culture does not mean I know Japanese culture. For us Nikkei, Japan has been conceptually frozen in time since our ancestors came to the United States. Meanwhile Japan has gone on evolving culturally and in every other way, and we haven't had much visibility into it beyond funny game shows and fashion trends that make their way over to the United States. I try much harder to think beyond my own stereotypes of Japan now that I have seen more of it in person." Andrea, another yonsei from the San Francisco Bay Area, distinguished between cultural forms in Japan and the United States by expressing that living in Japan she learned about being Japanese, while living in Los Angeles she learned about being Japanese American. Growing up in a predominantly white suburb, she had not learned much about either form of Japaneseness before moving to the two areas in question (Los Angeles and Japan).

Jay, a sansei/yonsei from the San Diego area, also summarizes how living in Japan has redefined his sense of what it means to be "Japanese American": "You can go to Japan and can understand your Japanese American background even better. I have a better idea of the point of diversion; I'm able to see what's common to both and can see why Japanese Americans are Japanese Americans. They took something and did it in a different way than Japanese did. Japanese Americans are different from Japanese. They start with the same ingredients like shoyu [soy sauce] and sugar. Then this group [i.e., Japanese Americans] goes crazy with the teriyaki and this group [i.e., Japanese] doesn't." Here Jay is alluding to the prevalence of teriyaki dishes as a symbol of Japanese food in the United States, whereas in Japan, it is much less common and not a major food genre.

Jay has reconstructed "Japanese American" against "Japanese" and can see similarities and differences. He alludes to a common ancestry and history when acknowledging the "point of diversion" but also recognizes that different cultural food traditions have evolved despite similar ingredients. He continues "I don't think Japanese and Japanese Americans are the same. They're different. They're different cultures. For example, it's hard for a Japanese to jump into a Japanese American festival or bazaar even if they spoke English. It's the same for Japanese Americans [in Japanese cultural contexts]. There are similar things in each but they're different. It's enough that it's not interchangeable. "This distinction based on "culture" can be understood as different "meaning-making processes" (Spillman 2002). The meaning associated with festivals and ways in which they are celebrated reflect traditions and practices (cultural activities or characteristics of a group) in the United States and Japan that, as Jay points out, are not interchangeable. On the surface, something called *obon* is celebrated in Japan and in the United States. But the way it is celebrated in each place differs. Generally speaking, *obon* is a major time of family gathering across Japan, more similar to Thanksgiving or Christmas in the United States, whereas in Japanese American communities, it is a summer festival that specifically includes *obon* dancing and does not have the same connotation of reuniting with family. The different meanings associated with *obon* reflect larger distinctions between "Japanese" and "Japanese American" cultures. That is, experiences in Japan have made it clearer to Jay that despite their shared ancestry, Japanese Americans think and perceive the world differently from their Japan counterparts.

At the same time, people who have not grown up around or identified with large, prewar-based Japanese American communities (such as in the San Francisco Bay Area or Los Angeles area) do not necessarily see Japanese American culture as having a separate existence. Masato, a shin-nisei who grew up on the East Coast, expressed this when he said that to him the difference between Japanese Americans and Japanese in Japan is that Japanese Americans think like Americans. He identifies as "Japanese American" but does not believe Japanese American culture is ontologically distinct as its own entity. When he goes to San Francisco Japantown, it feels like a "fake" or "watered down" Japan, rather than a separate cultural form of its own of which to be proud. It seemed surprising to him that people there might be aiming to create something Japan-like but intentionally different from contemporary Japan. His view can be explained by his having been raised on the East Coast and not having had much exposure to older, prewar, Japanese American communities and cultural forms.

Another shin-nisei who grew up in a rural area of California said that going to Japantowns (San Francisco or Los Angeles) felt like people were "trying to hold onto something." She also questioned the existence of a "Japanese American culture" and said that although she will attend Nisei Week in Los Angeles for the food and to see the parade, even after she goes, she will not feel "culturally enriched." To feel that, she says, she will need to travel to Japan.

Brian, a sansei/yonsei, also identifies himself as "Japanese American" but does not identify with Japanese American communities in the urban areas of California because he did not grow up around them. For him, being Japanese American means having a family history of incarceration in World War II (which he does), but he hesitates to speak about Japanese Americans as a whole because he is unfamiliar with those based in urban communities in California. He feels like he knows more about Japan than he does about

Japanese Americans. In fact, when he attends Japanese American obon festivals (which is not often) in the San Francisco area where he now lives, he feels they are "fake," compared to the Japanese festivals he has been to in Japan. He adds that having a Japanese wife and children who are dual citizens means that he can access Japan-based cultural activities, making him more oriented toward Japan-based cultural forms than toward US-based, Japanese American cultural activities.

To further illustrate that the difference in perspectives derives from familiarity with large Japanese American communities rather than from generation, the view of Saori, a shin-nisei, is telling. Saori was raised in San Francisco by shin-issei parents. She spoke Japanese and had spent a year in Japan on the JET Program when I interviewed her in 2014. When I told Saori about what Masato (and Brian) had said about Japantown feeling fake, though she understood because she has worked with many shin-nisei, she disagreed: "It's typical of a shin-nisei to think that way…They probably didn't grow up with those obons or with nisei aunties who have had internment experiences or had sansei uncles that would talk to you about how J-Town started and why this obon is located in this J-Town and why this super old JA culture tradition has been around for so many years. 'Cause I didn't have that growing up. I was shin-nisei. I only had my shin-issei parents. I just happened to be lucky enough to grow up in Japantown and go through all these JA programs that teach you about how J-Town started—it's not just a place for Japanese culture. It has so much historical meaning."[10] In explaining why one might see a Japanese American culture as existing or not, Saori is pointing to historical knowledge. She further explained the importance of knowing the struggles that small Japanese American businesses have faced from forced evacuation and incarceration during World War II to struggling to resettle and restart businesses in the postwar period, fighting to keep traditions (and recipes) alive. While she understands that a shin-nisei might compare Japantown to contemporary Japan and be disappointed, she commented that it makes her sad to hear that view knowing how hard the Japanese American community has worked to maintain a sense of culture and tradition.

In addition, Japanese Americans from Hawai'i have yet another perspective. They also both differentiate between and conflate Japaneseness in Japan and in the United States, but in a different way from people on the US continent. Hawai'i has a long history of a significantly large, ethnic Japanese population, but it has different dynamics from continental Japanese American communities.

Living in Japan encourages Japanese Americans from Hawai'i to differentiate between local Japanese and *nihonjin*.[11] In Tokyo, where I interviewed Kyle, a sansei lawyer from Hilo, he explained: "I now know the difference between *nihonjin* and *nikkeijin*. Before coming I thought they were closer than I do now. For example, Japanese in Hawai'i refer to themselves as *nihonjin*—I never hear the word *nikkei*. But in Japan it makes a difference—*nihonjin* means Japanese national. They make a distinction between people who are Japanese nationals and people who are not. We use [*nihonjn*] to mean ethnically Japanese. I have never heard the word *nikkei* before in Hawai'i."[12]

Interestingly, on the continent, Kyle was more likely to associate with a group of Hawai'i people than with a group of Asians, as was common for my interviewees from Hawai'i. He believes that culturally he has more in common with Hawai'i people and sees "Asian American" as a continental construction. "Asians on the mainland have had different experiences on the mainland. We were brought up as a majority. We never felt like we had to assert our Asianness or ethnicity. It's not something that needed to be proved." I asked what he would do if a Japanese American group were a third choice. Kyle said he would divide it into Hawai'i and continental people. So the ways in which Kyle draws boundaries around Japaneseness shift in Hawai'i (where all ethnic Japanese are described as *nihonjin*), in Japan (where *nihonjin* are different from *nikkeijin*), and on the US continent (where Hawai'i and continental ethnic Japanese are differentiated).

## The Ontology of Japanese Americans in Relation to Japan

As stated at the beginning of this chapter, Japanese Americans exhibit at least three ontological views of the relationship between Japanese Americans and Japan, conceptualizing how Japanese American culture exists in relation to Japanese culture in Japan. Understanding these different views helps to explain why the subpopulations of ethnic Japanese in the United States have different views of community, identity, and related activities—and raises the challenge of addressing this gap to see them as a single community. Moreover, it raises the question of where the cultural center is for Japanese Americans: Japan or the United States?

One view, espoused by people of various generations who have not grown up within large Japanese American communities, is that Japanese Americans are different from Japanese simply because they were raised in the United States, where they have internalized mainstream American values such as individuality. For shin-nisei in particular, the only difference between them and their Japanese cousins is that their Japanese parents raised them in the United States. That is, the only thing that differentiates them from their generational peers and relatives in Japan is where they were raised.[13] As their family history is one of recent migration, in thinking about the differences between Japanese and themselves, the experiences of shin-nisei are situated in the postwar period within a modern, global world. Specifically they are able to maintain ties to Japan in an uncontroversial way, as opposed to how issei and nisei needed to distance themselves from Japan in the prewar, wartime, and early postwar periods. In this view, Japan is the cultural center of Japaneseness, with Japanese Americans being bicultural because they understand Japanese culture from Japan at the same time that they understand mainstream American culture from the United States—the distinction is due to location rather than different cultural forms.

For shin-nisei, this perspective reflects adherence to a transnational, Japan-influenced view of the relationship between Japanese in Japan and Japanese Americans. Whether due to time spent visiting family in Japan as a child or to having lived in Japan as an adult, people with this view have been exposed to contemporary Japanese culture more than they have to older, US-based Japanese American communities. Thus, those with Japanese parents do not see a gap between forms of Japanese culture in Japan and the Japanese culture of their immigrant parents living in the United States.

A second view, embraced by people who have grown up within large Japanese American communities, is that Japanese American culture and identity in the United States are ontologically distinct from Japanese culture and identity in Japan.[14] To explain this difference, most on the continental United States will cite the World War II incarceration of Japanese Americans as a representation of both the psychological ("We're American, not Japanese") and physical (extremely limited migration back and forth between the two countries) separation that was induced by the wartime situation. As a result of this separation between Japanese Americans and Japanese in Japan, a distinct culture and ways of identifying "evolved" in the United States, in relative isolation from Japan.[15]

Moreover, it is important to note that in this conceptualization, "Japanese American culture" is also different from mainstream American identity and culture. That is, Japanese American culture is American but a subculture which overlaps with but is distinguishable from the majority society. For example, a Japanese American basketball league resembles mainstream American basketball leagues in terms of how the sport is played, but is different because of the way it both reflects and promotes ethnic community, through players sharing ethnic foods and participating in Japanese American community cultural events and activities (Chin 2012).

Within large Japanese American communities in California, different usages of space reflect the coexistence of people with these two different ontological views. In an essay titled, "The New Nikkei Movement?" Craig Ishii describes how the Orange County Buddhist Church in Southern California hosted weekly activities that served both populations—although he did not know this until he happened upon them on different days. As a yonsei, Craig was familiar with the Friday Boy Scout Troop meetings, the Saturday basketball practices and Junior Young Buddhist Association meetings, and the Sunday morning services. Then when he began spending more time at the church in order to earn a Boy Scout award, he noticed that on Thursday nights, he saw kendo practices, where he heard people speaking Japanese and realized that these were mostly shin-nisei. He further became aware of Japanese school taking place on Saturdays. The point he makes in his article is that "the Nikkei youth of today aren't a cohesive unit, they aren't sansei or yonsei, but instead a mix of different generations and different ethnicities" (Ishii, personal communication). In other words, the Japanese American community is comprised of multiple subgroups, whether this is known to its members or not.

A third view reflects the Hawai'i perspective that "local Japanese" have a distinct existence and worldview that separates them from both Japanese people in Japan and Japanese Americans on the US continent. This view parallels the previous view espoused by continental Japanese Americans in terms of not thinking that the cultural center of Japaneseness is Japan.[16] But it adds a nuanced perspective of Japanese Americanness by differentiating between Hawai'i and US continental Japanese American communities and considering them two, distinct, US-based cultural centers.[17] Continental Japanese Americans without much direct contact with Hawai'i and its ethnic Japanese population may subsume their Hawai'i counterparts as part of the larger, national Japanese American community. But for those who have had sustained contact with Hawai'i Japanese Americans, it is clear that people raised in Hawai'i have a different cultural framework.

These three views highlight the intersection of ethnic, national, and other place-based differences, all of which are expressed through culture. Japanese Americans are different from Japanese in Japan because of the ways in which they think and act. All three of the views see Japanese Americans as having both American and Japanese traits. But the second view sees "Japanese American culture" as having a separate existence from both Japanese culture and American culture. Comments by my interviewees suggest that before going to Japan, later-generation Japanese Americans saw this difference as additive (Japanese plus American), whereas after living in Japan, they see it as ontologically distinct. Finally, the third view proclaims that in addition, "Japanese American culture" needs to be further separated into continental and Hawai'i variations.

There are two related issues here: 1) individual exposure to and familiarity with contemporary Japanese society as well as contemporary Japanese American culture and 2) related opinions about the ontology, or separate existence, of Japanese and Japanese Americans. An example that teases out these related issues comes from Brian, the sansei/yonsei from California mentioned earlier, who asserts a clear differentiation between Japanese American culture in the United States and Japanese culture in Japan, due to wartime history largely shaped by incarceration in the United States. At the same time, after making this assertion, he admits that he is not familiar with "mainstream" urban Japanese American community and identity. So when he attends an obon festival in the San Francisco Bay Area, he expresses the view that it feels "fake" to him and that he would rather attend a similar festival in Japan.

What Brian says is certainly not representative of most Japanese Americans, but it is theoretically telling because it separates the two related issues I outlined earlier. First is the ontology of Japanese American culture as being different from Japan-based forms. Second is how familiarity with Japanese American culture affects perceptions of it. How one interprets Japanese American community, culture, and identity depends on the lens through which one is looking. If the only knowledge of Japan-related things one has is Japan-based, then everything will be seen through that lens and Japanese cultural forms outside of Japan will look fake. But if one believes that Japanese Americans can develop their own culture as ontologically distinct from that in Japan, in a way that is not "watered down" but rather the development of a new cultural form, then that is a very different perception of the relationship of Japanese Americans to Japan.

In other words, if Japanese Americans grew up in the United States enmeshed in Japanese American community practices, they would likely learn to see them as different from those of mainstream American culture. Moreover, if they then lived in Japan and went back to the United States, they might again notice differences between Japanese American communities and Japanese society. However, if someone has not been exposed to a large Japanese American community and Japanese American culture in the United States, then after living in Japan, the reference point would be comparing it to Japanese society, in which case it would always look "fake." These two interpretations reflect the assumption of different cultural centers as reference points. That is, if Japan is the cultural center, then Japanese Americans are not ontologically independent, but merely a distortion of Japan-based culture. In contrast, if Japanese American communities are the cultural centers, then Japanese American cultures are presumed to be ontologically distinct from Japanese culture in Japan and are authentic in their own way.

## Conclusion

Japanese Americans who have lived in Japan learn how they are not "Japanese" in Japan-based terms. Instead, most realize that they are "Japanese American." But what being "Japanese American" means to them varies by generation, geographic upbringing, and other factors that have shaped their ways of identifying and relating to Japan. Experiences growing up in the United States—including their level of familiarity with mainstream Japanese American culture and exposure to contemporary Japanese society and culture—as well as temporarily living in Japan, contribute to different ontological perspectives on Japanese Americanness.

One group of Japanese Americans focuses on their similarities to *nihonjin* in Japan. It is socialization in the United States that has shaped their thoughts and behavior in ways that make them distinct from their Japanese counterparts. Had their ancestors not emigrated to the United States, they imagine they would be living lives similar to their relatives in Japan.[18] While they view themselves to be "American," this Americanness can include speaking Japanese, having immigrant parents, and maintaining transnational connections to Japan—all of this is what makes them "Japanese American." In other words, in addition to ancestry and phenotype, continued cultural ties to Japan shape their ethnic identity, making it transnational. For this group, the cultural center of Japaneseness is Japan, suggesting a homeland orientation and also making them diasporic.

For a second group a "Japanese American" identity is ethnic, but not transnational or diasporic. In this second perspective, the history of Japanese Americans in the United States includes a wartime disconnection from Japan, both physical and psychological, that has led to a distinctly Japanese American identity and culture ontologically different from that of *nihonjin*. When Japanese American culture is perceived to be ontologically distinct from Japan-based forms (although there can still be interaction between the two), then the cultural center is not Japan, but rather Japanese American communities in the United States. That is, ties to Japan are historical rather than ongoing.

Finally, a third perspective is that within Japanese American communities in the United States, Hawai'i and the US continent need to be separated. Hawai'i Japanese Americans tend to identify with Hawai'i-based forms of culture, including ways of speaking, acting, dressing, and eating. In Hawai'i, they disidentify with their continental counterparts and see their "local Japanese culture" as a third ontological culture.

Interestingly, generations removed from the ancestral homeland are not the determining factor shaping ontological views of Japanese Americanness. Some shin-nisei who have grown up around large Japanese American communities adhere to the ethnic view predominantly espoused by later-generation Japanese Americans. Similarly, some later-generation Japanese Americans who have not grown up around large Japanese American communities do not see the existence of a Japanese American culture beyond their own relatives. Hence, more than generational distance from Japan, structural factors, including exposure to contemporary Japanese society and Japanese American communities while growing up, shape how Japanese Americans view their cultural and ethnic identities in relation to Japan.

# Conclusion

*I think being here is definitely part of the evolution of shaping my identity. I believe that who I am, my cultural, ethnic identity is not a set thing. It's evolving, always. And being in Japan will definitely play a big part in that evolution. And where it will go after being here, or while being here, I'm not quite sure. But overall, I think it's going to have—and it has had—a very big effect.*

—Jordan, *a Japanese American interviewee living in Tokyo*

Japanese American views of themselves and the world around them are altered by the experience of living in Japan. The new perspectives that Japanese Americans develop are a direct result of their interactions with Japanese in Japan, in which their notions of self and what constitutes Japaneseness are confronted and transformed by mainstream Japanese interpretations of Japanese Americans. This book has demonstrated how Japanese American experiences in Japan are shaped by phenotype, generation, gender, and whether one was raised in Hawai'i or on the US continent. Based on these characteristics, in addition to how well their Japanese linguistic, social, and cultural knowledge allows them to navigate daily life in Japan, Japanese Americans encounter shifting boundaries that include and exclude them and develop various strategies to best meet their needs. Through their claiming of "Japanese American," "Hawai'i," and mixed identities, as well as through the use of Japanese alphabets to write their names and the inclusion of middle names, Japanese Americans are able to assert both their socialization outside of Japan and their Japanese ancestry, despite Japanese attempts to place them neatly in the dichotomous categories of "Japanese" and "foreign."

In this Conclusion, I discuss the implications of my findings about Japanese American identity constructions in Japan. I will focus on how the concept of global ancestral groups 1) enables a different way of thinking about the relationship between ancestry, identity, and place; 2) establishes a new paradigm for thinking about ancestral homeland migration; 3) facilitates discussion about how Japanese Americans feel less Japanese in Japan; 4) highlights how differences from within the nation-state can be reconstructed abroad; and 5) provides a framework for this study that challenges the boundaries between Asian American Studies and Asian Studies.

## Global Ancestral Groups: Rethinking the Relationship between Ancestry, Ethnicity, and Identity

The experiences of Japanese Americans and how they identify while living in Japan provide new insight into the relationship between ancestry and identification. I have introduced the concept of global ancestral groups and applied it to people of Japanese ancestry as a way to conceptualize the relationship between global Japanese from the US continent, Hawai'i, and Japan. The concept of global ancestral groups analytically distinguishes between ancestry, culture, ethnicity, race, nationality, and other forms of identification that may overlap in practice.

The fact that my Japanese American interviewees are of Japanese ancestry but lack cultural proficiency in Japan highlights the importance of distinguishing ancestry from ethnicity to draw attention to the multiple forms of culture among people of shared ancestry. Ancestry and ethnicity are often conflated or used interchangeably, but they refer to different phenomena. Ancestry is only about kinship and lineage claims. On the other hand, ethnicity includes claims to ancestry as well as perceived historical ties and shared claims to cultural symbols (Cornell and Hartmann 2007). Using the framework of ethnicity without analytically distinguishing it from ancestry blurs ancestry and culture, effectively conflating them and contributing to the essentialization of a global ancestral group. Thus, by starting with ancestry, it becomes possible to see when culture also matters.

People of Japanese ancestry around the world have developed different communities, identities, and forms of Japanese culture. Each of these communities includes some people who identify with Japan and have diasporic outlooks. But each also includes people who do not identify with Japan. Among those who do not identify with Japan, some do identify with local forms of Japanese culture such as Japanese American culture on the US continent or in Hawai'i.

The different forms of Japanese culture that Japanese Americans identify with reflect different conceptualizations of culture, as national cultural framework and as ethnic cultural center. In this first sense, "Japanese" and "Americans" have different cultural frameworks that they internalize based on growing up in Japan or the United States, respectively. As people born and raised in the United States, Japanese Americans learn to think and act as Americans. The symbolic boundary here is between "Japanese" and "Americans" based on different socialization and regardless of race or ethnicity. At the same time, even though they have American cultural frameworks, Japanese Americans are still connected to Japan as global coethnics. So in the second sense, culture refers to the multiple ethnic cultural centers that people of Japanese ancestry can have. Focusing on global Japanese coethnics, the symbolic boundaries in this case are between Japanese coethnics in Hawai'i, the US continent, Japan, and other places, also based on different socialization but among people of shared ancestry. By analytically separating ancestry from ethnicity, the concept of global ancestral groups highlights the multiple forms of culture among people of shared ancestry not only in terms of different nations (the US versus Japan), but also in regards to branches of the global ancestral group (e.g., US continent, Hawai'i, Japan).

## Ancestral Homeland Migration: Against the Paradigm of "Diasporic Return"

Japanese American experiences in Japan suggest that not all ancestral homeland migration should be interpreted through the dominant paradigm of "diasporic return." Deeming migration to the ancestral homeland a "diasporic return" makes two assumptions: that migrants are part of "the diaspora" and that they are "returning" to the homeland. These assumptions are problematic because 1) the notion of diaspora assumes that the homeland is the ethnic center and causes forms of ethnic culture outside of the ancestral homeland to be seen as less authentic; and 2) the notion of "return" assumes that coethnics go to the ancestral homeland because of ethnic ties, which does not always coincide with the actual experiences or identification of migrants.

My findings that some Japanese Americans view Japanese American culture to be ontologically distinct from Japanese culture in Japan indicate the importance of distinguishing between Japan as the historical center and other contemporary centers of Japaneseness. People of Japanese ancestry have settled all over the world and developed different localized forms of Japanese culture. While Japanese in Japan can claim the oldest version, it is one version of Japanese culture among many. Ethnic Japanese in Hawai'i and the US continent, as well as in other countries, have their own versions, each of which is authentic to each local population. Although Japan is typically viewed as the place from which Japanese culture originates, it is not the contemporary center of Japanese culture for all people of Japanese ancestry.

Before going to Japan, Japanese Americans who grew up identifying with Japanese American culture often perceived "authentic" Japanese culture to be only in Japan because of its significance as the historical center of Japaneseness. But after living in Japan and learning how different contemporary Japanese society and culture are from historical forms that are more central to Japanese American communities in which they grew up, my interviewees came to redefine Japaneseness in terms of a form in Japan which does not fully include them and a form in the United States which better captures their experiences and identities. In other words, Japanese Americans expected to be included within the symbolic boundaries of Japaneseness within Japan but realized through living in Japan that both symbolic and social boundaries often exclude them.

Moreover, for my Japanese American interviewees, ethnic ties were not the central factor shaping their migration to or experiences in Japan. This is due to both structural factors and individual identification. Patterns of migration to the ancestral homeland are not always shaped by ethnic visas. Global coethnics can migrate to their ancestral homelands as global business elites and through work and study programs, such as the Japan Exchange and Teaching (JET) Program participants and college exchange programs. In an age of globalization and international migration made increasingly accessible through advances in technology, lower costs, and shorter travel times, reasons for migrating continue to vary.

Finally, ancestral homeland migrants themselves do not always see this migration as a "return." Migration to a global city rather than an ancestral village in Japan requires a different framework since connections to relatives are not the central motivating factor for the movement. Whether in the ancestral homeland as a long-term resident or as a tourist,[1] global coethnics do not necessarily have homeland orientations—despite their physical migration there.

## Less Japanese in Japan

Ironically, through the experience of living in Japan, Japanese Americans learn to feel less "Japanese," by Japan-based standards. This is ironic because if Japan is perceived to be the cultural center of Japaneseness then a trip to Japan should allow them to refill their cultural vessel. Many of the Japanese Americans I interviewed in Japan learn to feel less Japanese due to their lack of Japanese language ability and social and cultural knowledge of contemporary Japanese society. These findings challenge conventional assumptions that migration to an ancestral homeland simply reaffirms cultural and ethnic identity by replenishing cultural knowledge lost over generations.

CONCLUSION

This is not to say that in Japan Japanese Americans do not increase their knowledge of Japanese language, culture, and society, because they certainly do. Over time, especially through interactions with Japanese people in Japan, all of my Japanese American interviewees came to better understand Japanese society. This was demonstrated by the ways they shifted their strategies of presentation of self as their linguistic ability and social and cultural knowledge of contemporary Japanese society increased. Over time, Japanese Americans undoubtedly broadened their cultural "toolkits" as they navigated Japanese society.

However, the increased knowledge of Japanese culture and society that Japanese Americans obtained in Japan included awareness that there are limits to their acceptance as Japanese in Japan. Though most Japanese Americans I met who had recently arrived in Japan were excited about the possibility of fitting in as a regular Japanese person, over time this excitement waned. As discussed in Chapter Two, long-term residents in Japan, especially those who were fluent (but not native) in Japanese, were less concerned with fitting in as Japanese and were actually more concerned with managing expectations of them by recognizing situations when it was to their benefit to be seen as foreigners.

What these findings reveal, then, is that knowledge of Japanese society, culture, and language are attributed different meanings in different societies. From a US-based perspective, Japanese Americans may go to Japan, learn about Japanese culture, then return "more Japanese." But the experiences in Japan that Japanese Americans have and their exposure to Japan-based categories and expectations makes it a more complicated process than this. As Chapter Five demonstrated, experiences in Japan help Japanese Americans to think more carefully about issues of cultural authenticity. When they returned to the United States after having lived in Japan, rather than simply feeling more Japanese, my interviewees reassessed what it meant for them to be Japanese American, what form of Japanese culture they identified with and where it was located. In this way, my study challenges the notion that the ancestral homeland is the only authentic cultural form and highlights the continued importance of place and social formation in contextualizing the meaning attached to ancestry and culture.

## Transnational Minority Identities

This study has shown how differences from within the nation-state can be reproduced abroad. In one sense, my research supports previous findings that national identities are salient for ancestral homeland migrants, since

Japanese Americans do feel more American in Japan. However, my findings also nuance these previous conclusions to demonstrate how sub-national identities from the premigration context continue to matter, and can be reproduced when a national image does not include the particular characteristics of migrants. Japanese American identity formations in Japan illustrate how minority identities from the US domestic context continue to inform and shape experiences across international borders.

Racial and ethnic meaning intersects with national and other place-based identities as people reconstruct identities abroad. Rather than leaving behind their racial and ethnic minority status in the United States, continental Japanese Americans who phenotypically blend in Japan reconstruct identities in Japan that highlight the persistence of this status as they go abroad. Even though they seem to be part of the racial majority in Japan, at the same time, when they assert national identities as Americans, their minority status in the United States is also reconstructed. Since minority identities are tied to places, claiming place-based identities also reconstructs these minority positionings. In other words, the basic tension that exists for Japanese Americans in the United States in terms of being perceived sometimes as American and other times as not American continues as they go abroad, even as it takes slightly different shapes and forms.

It is important to note that the reconstruction of these minority identities is dependent on both the domestic, hegemonic national image (e.g., the image of Americans within the United States) and on international images of the United States (e.g., in Japan). If Japanese Americans were considered minorities within the United States but consistently acknowledged more generally as Americans within Japan, their experiences and identity formations would be different, highlighting their national identities. The fact that the image of Americans as white is dominant in both the United States and Japan contributes significantly to Japanese American construction of minority identities in both places. In this regard, symbolic boundaries from the United States can coincide with those in Japan.

In addition, the Hawai'i/continental distinction continues to be important for Hawai'i Japanese Americans abroad, supporting Wimmer and Glick Schiller's point that scholars need to challenge the naturalization of the nation-state as the only unit for studying transnational migration and processes. Hawai'i identities remain salient due to a combination of their identity assertions and Japanese acknowledgment of them. But what is a Hawai'i identity? A Hawai'i identity is a claim to a place, but Hawai'i is not recognized as a nation-state. Is it a state or regional identity, similar to a California or

CONCLUSION

New York identity? Or is it a colonial identity, since Hawaiʻi was previously an independent kingdom now annexed (occupied?) by the United States? If it is a colonial identity in the United States, what is it in Japan—neocolonial? Moreover, when Asian immigrants and their descendents claim Hawaiʻi, should we think of them as Asian settlers to recognize their different relationship to Hawaiʻi from Native Hawaiians? Future research could further explore Hawaiʻi identity claims and constructions outside of Hawaiʻi and better theorize what type of identity this is.

Although identities are becoming transnational and deterritorialized as people in faraway places feel connected to one another through globalization, my findings reinforce the persistent importance of place—which is not always a nation-state—in relation to socialization and interpellation. Japanese Americans may feel connected to Japanese in Japan due to shared ancestry and history, but they also feel disconnected due to socialization within different branches of the global ancestral group. These differences are reconstructed when they go to Japan. Sustained interactions with Japanese while residing in Japan teach Japanese Americans about Japanese interpellations of them, encouraging Japanese Americans to identify and assert identities that connect them not to their ethnic background, but rather to where they were raised. Where one has lived and where one currently resides continue to matter in terms of how people think and act, as well as how they choose intelligible labels for describing themselves and connecting to groups of people perceived to be similar.

## Challenging the Boundaries of Asian American and Asian Studies

As a study of the shifting boundaries that Asian American migrants negotiate in their Asian ancestral homeland, it may be fitting that this book challenges what constitutes Asian Studies, and where the boundaries lie between them. As a researcher who is studying a Japanese American population with which she identifies, this project is undeniably part of Asian American Studies. Yet when Asian Americans have been studied in terms of transnational identities and processes, this has tended to presume that Asian people in the United States maintain connections to Asia.

My findings force us to rethink what we mean by Asian American transnationalism by looking at Asian Americans from the United States who migrate to Asia. This inverts the typical migration flow from Asia to the United States and in effect challenges the image of Asian Americans as immigrant foreigners in the United States by instead conceptualizing Asian Americans as immigrants from the United States. While doing so may appear to essentialize Asian American identities by assuming ties to Asia, it actually does the opposite by finding that Japanese Americans develop a better understanding of how they are not Japanese through living in Japan. Moreover, by consciously not framing this migration as a "return," this project challenges the paradigm of "return" and its assumptions about authenticity and interminable attachment to place.

To be clear, studying Asian Americans in Asia is not at all presuming the connectedness of Asian Americans to Asia in an essentialist way. Rather, it is a statement about how American they are as they become more globally oriented and take advantage of international work and study programs that invite US citizens to participate. Studying Asian Americans outside of the United States and examining their ties to Asia as they live in their ancestral homelands challenges us to consider the variety of ways in which Asian Americans are constructing their identities and experiencing the world—including but not limited to experiences in the United States.

More specifically, this book has provided insight into Japanese American communities and identities by demonstrating how various subgroups interpret Japan and Japaneseness differently. For example, scholars of Japanese American Studies are well aware of differences between Japanese Americans from Hawai'i and the US continent. But by comparatively studying these two groups in the same place, specifically the ancestral homeland, I have shown how internalized differences, as well as distinctions people in Japan make, between Hawai'i and the continent continue to affect how Japanese Americans see themselves and their relationships to others. Future research comparatively examining ethnic Japanese from Hawai'i and Japan in the context of the US continent, as well as ethnic Japanese from the US continent and Japan in the context of Hawai'i, might also reveal how gaps in the construction of Japaneseness manifest themselves in particular ways to affect migrant experiences in a different racial formation.

Studying the contemporary experiences of Japanese Americans in their ancestral homeland has also been a way to shift focus away from the dominant discourse of Japanese American experiences in terms of plantations in Hawai'i and incarceration on the US continent to think about new ways that Japanese Americans are creating identities in relation to Japan. The history of plantations and incarceration will always be important to Japanese American communities. But what else does it mean to be Japanese American? How are Japanese Americans of multiple generations, from various parts of the United States, of mixed heritage creatively reconstructing

CONCLUSION

Japanese American community and identity? My hope is that this study can contribute to new developments in Japanese American studies that better reflect the dynamic and incredibly diverse lived experiences of Japanese Americans.

This book on Japanese American experiences in Japan also pushes the boundaries of Japanese Studies. Is Japanese Studies about incidents that occur in Japan that can only be studied by using the Japanese language? Or is Japanese Studies about occurrences within the geopolitical boundaries of Japan, whoever that includes? Or is it about the experiences of "Japanese people" (i.e., *nihonjin*), regardless of where they take place? Does this include anyone of Japanese ancestry? Considering whether or not Japanese American experiences in Japan is a topic within Japanese Studies forces us to ponder what constitutes Japanese Studies and where the boundaries lie. Coming from the United States and speaking English, Japanese Americans in Japan might not be included as being part of Japanese Studies by the scholars who focus on Japanese language as the essential component marking this field.

Some might see Japanese Americans in Japan as part of "the Japanese diaspora" and thus an appropriate topic for Japanese Studies if research includes all people of Japanese ancestry. But if people of Japanese ancestry are studied as part of "Japanese Studies," how much does this essentialize Japaneseness? For example, what is the difference between studying later-generation, US-born and raised Japanese Americans living in Japan and *chuuzaiin* (Japanese citizens temporarily stationed abroad for work) living in the United States? What is at stake by considering them all "overseas Japanese"?

Finally, my findings about the strategies that Japanese Americans develop in Japan highlight assumptions around phenotype, linguistic, social, and cultural knowledge that international migrants of all backgrounds must negotiate as they live in Japanese society. Though they will change depending on the context, effective strategies for interacting with Japanese people consider not only phenotype or linguistic knowledge, but all of a person's characteristics, including where they are from, what languages they speak, their level of social and cultural knowledge of Japanese society, and how their country is represented in Japan. International migration to Japan is an increasingly important topic related to the future of Japanese society as the declining birthrate and rapid aging of the population continue to cause concern about how Japan will maintain an active labor force to support its social security system. In the midst of politicians, scholars, and activists debating the future of Japan as an immigration society that might need to consciously promote multiculturalism, it is critical to continue to pose the question, "What does it mean to be Japanese?" By studying ancestral homeland migrant experiences in Japan and showing how they come to redefine Japaneseness through encounters in Japanese society, we gain a better understanding of not only what it means to be Japanese in Japan, but about larger processes of transnational and ethnic identity construction in a globalizing world.

# Appendix A: Methodology of Studying Japanese American Experiences in Tokyo

To systematically research how Japanese Americans construct identities in Tokyo, I carried out ethnographic fieldwork in the greater Tokyo area, conducting interviews, as well as observing and participating in various Japanese American events between 2004 and 2009. I wanted to understand Japanese American experiences in Japan while they were going through them as opposed to after they left Japan to elicit more detail and reflections about their interpretations of the situation. In 2002, in Hawai'i I interviewed Japanese Americans who had previously lived in Japan and had returned to the United States. I noticed that they were not able to provide much detail about their daily interactions with Japanese people in Japan and I wanted to find out more. So I decided to conduct the majority of my research in Japan to enable me to obtain fresher memories of experiences and more detailed accounts of the strategies Japanese Americans developed for how to present themselves in Japanese society, as well as a deeper sense of the reasons behind their strategies.

I supplemented this fieldwork with interviews and research in the United States to reveal broader Japanese American interpretations of their experiences in Japan. While interviewees in the midst of the experience of living in Japan were able to provide many details about daily interactions, understandably they seemed to have a more difficult time thinking about the overall experience and what it meant to them. Talking with Japanese Americans after they had returned to the United States allowed for more thoughtful discussions about how living in Japan affected their understanding of what it means to be Japanese American.

By being "systematic," I am not claiming that my study represents the experiences of all Japanese Americans in Tokyo. As an ethnographic study that used snowball sampling to have interviewees recommend potential interviewees, my sample was not meant to be representative. Rather, the purpose of this study was to conduct in-depth, qualitative analysis of Japanese American experiences in Japan to understand their "meaning-making" processes (Kim 2008, Spillman 2002), not to provide a statistical overview or any type of quantitative analysis of the entire population. To my knowledge, no statistical data on the population of Japanese Americans in Japan exists. The Japanese government keeps data on foreign national residents and visitors but does not collect information by racial or ethnic background. So there is general information on US citizens living in Japan, but not on Japanese Americans specifically. The U.S. Census does not currently include US citizens overseas. Therefore, any kind of representative study with random sampling would not be possible, even if I wanted to use that type of design.

## Tokyo, Japan

I conducted more than 50 formal semi-structured interviews, as well as many more informal interviews with Japanese Americans who were living in Tokyo between 2004 and 2009. I limited my Tokyo interviewees to people living there or planning to live there for at least one year (those who were in possession of at least a one-year visa) in order to omit tourists. By tourists, I mean US citizens visiting Japan for three months or less on a visa attainable upon entry and requiring no additional planning or paperwork. Omitting tourists allowed me to focus on residents, who are more likely to try adapting to the conventions of Japanese society. In addition, residents are forced to deal with these conventions over a longer period of time, enabling them to develop strategies and opinions about how to deal with them. Most of my interviewees in Tokyo were long-term residents: lawyers, businesspeople, and other highly educated white-collar workers. I also included migrants who stayed in Japan for as little as one year because this subset included college exchange students and Japan Exchange and Teaching (JET) participants, both of which include many Japanese Americans and represent a significant part of Japanese American experiences in Japan.[1]

In terms of occupation and period of stay, Tokyo interviewees tended to fall into two broad groupings.[2] The first grouping included those who were shorter-term, on the above mentioned study and work exchange programs for one- to five-year contracts, typically single and under 30 years of age. The second grouping included those who were living in Japan more permanently, often with families and open-ended contracts pursuing careers. Length of stay in Japan corresponded to occupation: university exchange students stayed for about one year; JETs stayed one to five years (since 2007 the contract system has been extended to five years); and some long-term residents have been in Japan for decades, most established in their careers and married to Japanese nationals.

I located potential interviewees firsthand through attending Japanese American events and other academic and social gatherings in Tokyo or via friends and acquaintances in the Tokyo area who offered to introduce me to someone they knew, once I described my research topic ("Japanese Americans in Japan"). Then I used snowball sampling to find additional informants. Reflecting the transnational nature of the project, I was able to find some interviewees in Japan through personal networks in the United States, such as having my California-based sansei mother forward an email announcement about my research to her network of contacts, including relatives and friends across the country. Occasionally I would meet Japanese Americans (in Japan and the United States) who had heard about my research through someone else, suggesting that Japanese American networks and community were closer and more transnational than I had anticipated.

I also used stratified purposeful sampling to obtain more diverse interview data (Patton 1990). Without stratifying my sample, the majority of my interviewees were men from the US continent who claimed only Japanese ancestry. So I consciously sought out women, people from Hawai'i, and mixed-heritage Japanese Americans since they were harder to find and seemed to have different experiences in Japan. By the end, my Tokyo interviewees included thirteen women, eighteen Japanese Americans who were raised in Hawai'i, and fifteen Japanese Americans who claimed multiple ancestries.

Before I met with interviewees face-to-face, most of them had filled out a five-page questionnaire to acquire basic background information, such as age, where they grew up and had lived, current occupation, exposure in the United States to Japanese language and culture (see Hays 1996). This also served the purpose of informing them of my interests, as well as provoking thoughts about issues to be covered when we met. Interviews lasted anywhere from one to five hours but averaged about two hours. During the interviews, which I audio recorded, I also took notes while reviewing their questionnaire responses and asking follow-up questions.

Respondents ranged in age and generational background. The youngest participant was twenty, while the oldest was sixty-five. Most interviewees were in their thirties and forties (see Appendix B). They included *nisei* (second generation/children of Japanese emigrants), *sansei* (third generation/grandchildren of Japanese emigrants), *yonsei* (fourth generation/great-grandchildren of Japanese emigrants), *gosei* (fifth generation/

great-great-grandchildren of Japanese emigrants) and *shin-nisei* (second generation/specifically the children of postwar Japanese emigrants). Many interviewees were mixed generation (e.g., having a *shin-issei* mother and a *nisei* father).

While I was living in Tokyo, I regularly attended events and meetings held by two groups for Japanese American residents: the Tokyo chapter of the Japanese American Citizens League (JACL) and a Japanese American study group. I joined the "Japan" JACL chapter,[3] becoming a board member for two years and regularly attending and helping to organize meetings and functions (e.g., the Day of Remembrance program, summer BBQs, and happy-hour gatherings). In order to keep my sample as diverse as possible, I did not focus my research on Japan JACL members or events. However, speaking informally with Japanese Americans and others who attended JACL events helped me better understand the intersection of Japaneseness and Americanness in Tokyo. I was also invited to attend Japanese American study group dinner meetings organized by Glen S. Fukushima, which included talks by scholars, businesspeople, and politicians who were primarily Japanese American but also included a Japanese Brazilian and a Japanese person from Japan. At one meeting, I was able to present my tentative research findings to an audience that included several of my interviewees.

In addition, since this study was not centered on organizations, I wanted to meet Japanese Americans who were not involved with Japanese American groups and was able to do this through personal and professional networks, as briefly mentioned above. In addition to social gatherings of friends and my spouse's co-workers, welcome receptions I attended included the following: for a visiting delegation of the American Studies Association; for Crown Prince Akihito scholars; and for the visiting Japanese American Leadership Delegation (JALD) to Japan, a group of "younger Japanese American leaders" annually invited to spend about a week meeting with various Japanese governmental and business leaders.[4] I also participated in several research and study groups, including a Hawai'i research group based at the University of Tokyo, comprised of Japanese scholars who conduct research related to Hawai'i. Through attending many events in Tokyo, I was able to meet different people whose various networks included Japanese Americans whom I eventually met and interviewed.

My Tokyo-area observations are based on one year living in Ishikawa-cho in Yokohama, Kanagawa prefecture, from 2004 to 2005, and four years in Narashino-shi, Chiba prefecture, from 2005 to 2009. The apartment building I lived in in the first location was close to a large homeless and day-worker population and across the station from Chinatown, while my apartment

APPENDIX A

building in the second location was part of a large, suburban public housing complex that particularly welcomed families and seniors. Thus, between living in lower- and middle-class neighborhoods and attending functions at elite institutions, I was able to see a range of daily situations in the context of socioeconomic class. I regularly took buses and trains to Tokyo proper to conduct the aforementioned interviews; attend university-based study groups, symposia, and other campus events; audit graduate seminars at the University of Tokyo; teach classes at Sophia University; meet friends for lunch and dinner; and do my shopping. Finally, while based in Tokyo, I also conducted secondary research in Japanese on Japanese Americans and Japanese society and performed historical research in English at various university libraries to supplement my interview and ethnographic data.

## The United States

Between 2005 and 2015, I also conducted thirty-two formal and many more informal interviews with Japanese Americans who were living in the United States after having returned from Japan. These Japanese Americans were slightly older than my Tokyo-based interviewees, ranging from twenty-four to seventy-six years old. All were college-educated and were in occupations such as business, education, government, and law, including a full-time mother and a retiree. Some were doing Japan-related work, with one who did Japanese American-related community work. One interviewee had a full-time job not related to Japan, but after returning to the United States he had also started his own side business importing products from Japan.

Some of these interviews were second meetings with Japanese Americans I had formally interviewed in Tokyo. Both during visits to the United States while I was living in Japan and after I moved back to the United States, I conducted interviews with people I had met in Tokyo who had moved back to the United States. Specifically, I conducted seven interviews in the United States with Japanese Americans I had previously spoken with in Tokyo. Two of these interviews were conducted in Honolulu.

Twenty-five interviews with Japanese Americans in the United States who had previously lived in Japan were first interviews. I conducted these interviews while I was living in Los Angeles between 2009 and 2014 and in Berkeley since 2014. Ten in-person interviews took place in the San Francisco Bay Area, nine took place in the Los Angeles area, and one took place in Chicago. Reflecting this era in which technology allows connections across place and time, I conducted two interviews via email exchange from Los Angeles with people living in the San Francisco Bay Area and three interviews via Skype from Berkeley with one person living in the Los Angeles area, one person living in New England, and one person living in Honolulu.

Nine of my US-based interviewees had not lived in the Tokyo area, but I spoke with them anyway to get a sense of their Japan experience. They had all been in Japan as JET Program participants in rural areas, college exchange students in the Kansai area (including Osaka and Kyoto), or as private English teachers. It is also worth noting that some of the Japanese Americans that I interviewed in Tokyo, especially the older working professionals, had previously lived in Japan outside of Tokyo as exchange students in the Kansai area and as JET Program participants in rural areas. So speaking with Japanese Americans who had not lived in Tokyo gave me a sense of the particularities of the Tokyo experience, as compared to living in other parts of Japan.

In addition to interviewing Japanese Americans who were living or had lived in Japan, to contextualize Japanese American experiences in Japan, I conducted more than 25 formal and many more informal interviews in Japan and the United States with several groups: non-Japanese American foreign residents in Japan,[5] Japanese people in Japan and in the United States who have Japanese American friends or co-workers, and Japanese Americans who have not lived in Japan. I asked them about their own experiences and about their observations of Japanese Americans in Japan in order to gain perspective on what it means to be "Japanese" and "Japanese American" in Japan and the United States.

## Qualitative Research and Subjectivity

Because qualitative research is consciously interpretive (Denzin and Lincoln 2003, Geertz 1973), a deeper, firsthand knowledge of the people and societies being studied enhances analysis. Having studied Japanese for more than two decades and having lived in multiple parts of Japan (Tokyo, Nagano, Kanagawa, and Chiba prefectures), my social, cultural, and linguistic background was good enough for me to be able to understand Japanese conversations. This background greatly enhanced my research because in the majority of cases when Japanese American interviewees spoke Japanese at a level equal to or less developed than mine, I could also evaluate their comprehension and communication abilities in Japanese.

In addition, as a sansei/yonsei (third generation/fourth generation) who was born and raised in the San Francisco Bay Area, lived for four years in Hawai'i, spent nine years intermittently in Japan, and resided another five years in the Los Angeles area before returning to the San Francisco Bay Area, my lived experiences and observations also greatly informed my research.

APPENDIX A

Growing up as a racial minority in the Bay Area and being asked about where I was "really from," then moving to Hawai'i as an adult and having people assume I must be local, I observed firsthand qualitative and quantitative differences in ethnic Japanese experiences in each place. While attending Japanese American community functions in every city in which I have lived, I have had numerous informal discussions revealing how Japanese Americans relate to Japan and what it means for them to identify as "Japanese American."

Since the Japanese language is used in different ways in different places, being able to observe how Japanese Americans use Japanese in the United States has been useful in understanding how they also used it in Japan. One example is a planning meeting in 2015 for a local, Japanese American community event. In discussing possible activities, what would be considered basic words in Japan such as "taisō" (exercise) and "cosplay" (dressing up in costume, especially as anime or manga characters) came up. Further discussion revealed that several sansei did not know what these words meant, though they did know other Japanese words such as "bento" and "mochi." In another example, I have repeatedly observed an upper middle-class sansei woman ask her toddler if he wants to go to the "benjo," a word which in contemporary Japan would not commonly be used by upper middle-class women (as the connotations are more like "toilet" or "john" rather than "bathroom") (see Asakawa 2015). These types of conversations reminded me about the unnevenness of Japanese knowledge and culture across locations among people of Japanese ancestry and how it should not be assumed that knowing some Japanese foods or words reflects a deeper knowledge of Japanese linguistic or cultural practices.

### Insider/Outsider Dynamics

While a shared background with the people and experiences being studied can be helpful in conducting research and analyzing findings, this familiarity does not automatically make one an "insider." As Lila Abu-Lughod (1991), Kirin Narayan (1993), and others have pointed out, the position of a researcher who is connected to the population s/he is studying is never part of the oversimplified binary of "insider/outsider." Differences along gender, age, occupational, and generational lines emerge as interviewees describe their experiences. Thus, we need to recognize "the multilayered, shifting, and competing similarities and differences between native or insider researchers and their communities—a process that is shaped by simultaneous, ongoing negotiations" (Võ 2000: 19).

At times, I did feel like an insider while conducting this research. My conceptualization of the project emerged from a combination of my own experiences in Japan (as a Japanese American college exchange student in Tokyo, as a participant in the JET Program for three years in Nagano, and living in the Tokyo area for five years) and my background in Japanese Studies and Asian American identity and community. I could relate to college exchange students and JET Program participants because I had gone through those programs myself. My research questions were partly based on my own experiences that I wanted to explore more systematically by seeing how others viewed their migration to Japan and interactions with Japanese people. Moreover, as a US-born Japanese American living in the Tokyo area for at least a year, I also fit the description of people I was interviewing. My interviewees saw this as well, often using inclusive terms such as "we" as they shared their experiences (see Võ 2000).

However, at the same time, I was clearly different from my interviewees. While we shared claims to Japanese ancestry, we differed in terms of gender, class, age, occupation, and generation. As a sansei/yonsei who has studied Japanese as a foreign language for more than 20 years since entering college and has lived several times in Japan, my language abilities were closer to the children of Japanese immigrants. But I did not grow up speaking or hearing Japanese on a regular basis. In fact, once I began taking classes, my Japanese language ability quickly surpassed that of my sansei mother. Thus, I could relate to sansei and yonsei who did not grow up exposed to contemporary Japanese culture or language, yet many of them were struggling to attain fluency in Japanese and to understand Japanese social norms.

Moreover, although I was a former college exchange student and JET Program participant, there were limited ways in which I, as a heterosexual married woman in her thirties, could relate to younger Japanese Americans in a different stage of life. At times, our informal discussions included plans for the future as they struggled to choose careers, consider graduate school, and contemplate having long-term relationships. At the other end of the spectrum, when speaking with elite Japanese American men married to Japanese women and supporting families, I was conscious of my position as a young, female graduate student who was married to another Japanese American. Thus, while my Japanese language ability and previous experiences in Japan greatly influenced my research questions and interpretations of Japanese American experiences in Tokyo, they were also very different from those of most of my interviewees.

Finally, being a "co-ethnic researcher" can present a variety of complications regarding relations with research subjects (Kang 2000).[6] There were several times when I felt like my interviews were therapy sessions, providing a space to talk about the challenges of being Japanese American in Japan (that non-Japanese Americans might not understand) and facing an uncertain future regarding family, work, and where to live. I was happy to be able to provide this service, as it enabled me to feel like the meeting was mutually beneficial. But as Miliann Kang has observed, the personal exchange that can take place between researcher and subject can make fieldwork messy, as it requires "restraining the desire to steer conversations toward those topics that are beneficial to the research agenda and, instead, exercising an openness to engage in conversations that seemingly make no direct contribution to the data" (Kang 2000: 44). Similar to Kang, I found that the benefits outweighed the drawbacks, as I enjoyed helping and getting to know my interviewees and occasionally "unearth[ed] surprising findings that end[ed] up informing the data" (Kang 2000: 45).

### The Choice of Tokyo as a Field Site

Tokyo is the largest urban area in Japan and a "global city" (Sassen 2001), making it a useful field site to explore Japanese American migrant experiences in Japan. As a domestic center, Tokyo attracts more internal migrants than any other prefecture in Japan: 394,116 reported in 2011 (Statistics Bureau 2013b). As an international center, Tokyo also attracts more foreign residents than any other prefecture in Japan: 248,363 as of 2005 (Statistics Bureau 2013a), including a large number of US citizens. More specifically, 36 percent (18,568 of 52,149) of the US citizens living in Japan were reported to reside in the Tokyo area as of 2009 (Statistics Bureau 2012). This means that the greater Tokyo metropolitan area is home to the most populous and diverse population of both Japanese and international migrants in Japan, many of whom are US citizens. Tokyo was the ideal place in which to conduct my research because as Japan becomes an increasingly multicultural nation connected to global flows of people, capital, and ideas, Tokyo will likely be at the center of this social change.

Japanese American migration to Tokyo is significantly different from "roots migrating" to ancestral villages where relatives welcome migrants "home" (Levitt 2002, Louie 2004, Wessendorf 2013).[7] Roots migrating implies a search for relatives as the main goal. This means focusing on genealogy, or connections to people and places in Japan. The relationships and affinities developed through a trip centered expressly on making these connections encourage identity constructions in Japan that are very different from those of people who want to study or work in Tokyo—and who may or may not contact relatives during their stay. A sansei from the US continent told me that when she visited the ancestral village of her mother in Shimane, her relatives told her that she had "come home." When one migrates to the ancestral homeland and lives with relatives in a small town, that is a very different environment from the sea of strangers in metropolitan Tokyo in which most Japanese Americans in my study were immersed.

The fact that in Tokyo most Japanese Americans encounter strangers on a daily basis makes it a useful research site for examining identity constructions and the management of presentations of self (Goffman 1959). In an urban area like Tokyo, Japanese Americans have more first encounters with strangers, opportunities to consider how they are being perceived, and attempts to adjust these perceptions of others. This contrasts with smaller towns which require more sustained contact with local communities and fewer opportunities to try different approaches.

Most Japanese Americans, like other domestic and international migrants to Tokyo, are seeking opportunities for education and work. As the nation's capital and center of business and government, Tokyo is home to more than 75 percent of foreign-affiliated companies in Japan and has more than 200 Japanese colleges and universities (Business Development Center Tokyo). While my Japanese American interviewees mentioned their Japanese heritage to be a relevant factor in their migration to Tokyo, all of them also mentioned at least two or three additional factors which made this choice attractive. For example, an interest in living abroad for the adventure, together with the opportunity to gain international experience, was the most commonly given reason for wanting to move to Tokyo. Many interviewees said they were starting with Japan, then planned to live in other foreign countries in the future (though some never made it past Tokyo).

Similar to those in the larger US population, Japanese Americans in Japan have an interest in studying Japanese culture or society and a desire to build a career in Japan-related work. These people include those in academia, business, politics, and the arts. Although my sample did not include many professional artists, there are some Japanese Americans living in Japan (in Tokyo and elsewhere) to develop their skills in ceramics, textiles, *taiko* (Japanese drumming), the martial arts, and music (see, for example, Dung, Fukami, and Yamada 2006, Nomura 2006). Finally, particularly during Japan's "bubble economy," many of my interviewees were drawn to work in Tokyo by Japan's economic strength, power, and influence.

# Appendix B: List of Japanese American Interviewees Who Have Lived in Japan

| | Name[1] | Sex | Age[2] | Occupation while living in Japan | Ancestry[3] | Generation[4] | Residence prior to age 18[5] |
|---|---|---|---|---|---|---|---|
| 1 | Aaron | M | 21 | College exchange student | Japanese | Shin-nisei | US continent |
| 2 | Alvin | M | 34 | Lawyer | Japanese | Shin-nisei/ yonsei | US continent |
| 3 | Amy | F | 47 | ALT on JET Program (1988–1990), OL (1990–1993) | Japanese | Shin-nisei/ sansei | US continent |
| 4 | Andrea | F | 41 | ALT on JET Program (1994–1997) | Japanese | Yonsei | US continent |
| 5 | Bob | M | 51 | Lawyer | Japanese | Sansei | Hawai'i |
| 6 | Brent | M | 23 | Language student | Japanese, Okinawan | Sansei/ yonsei | Hawai'i |
| 7 | Brian | M | 46 | English teacher | Japanese | Sansei/ yonsei | US continent |
| 8 | Bruce | M | 47 | Lawyer | Japanese | Shin-nisei/ yonsei | Hawai'i |
| 9 | Carol | F | 55 | Tourism industry | Japanese | Sansei | Hawai'i |

*(continued)*

APPENDIX B

| | Name[1] | Sex | Age[2] | Occupation while living in Japan | Ancestry[3] | Generation[4] | Residence prior to age 18[5] |
|---|---|---|---|---|---|---|---|
| 10 | Carrie | F | 46 | Lawyer | Japanese | Yonsei | Hawaiʻi |
| 11 | Chris | M | 36 | ALT on JET Program (2004–2008) | Japanese, Chinese | Yonsei | US continent |
| 12 | Clark | M | 35 | Marketing | Japanese | Sansei | US continent |
| 13 | Craig | M | 49 | Lawyer | Japanese | Yonsei/gosei | Hawaiʻi |
| 14 | Daniel Okimoto | M | 71 | Graduate Research Student (1968–1970) | Japanese | Nisei | US continent |
| 15 | Dave | M | 29 | ALT on JET Program (2007–2012) | Japanese | Yonsei | US continent |
| 16 | Diana | F | 50 | US Diplomat | Japanese | Nisei/sansei | US continent |
| 17 | Edna | F | 33 | Human Resources | Japanese | Shin-nisei/sansei | US continent |
| 18 | Emma | F | 20 | College exchange student | Japanese, Italian, English, Scottish | Shin-nisei | US continent |
| 19 | Erin | F | 33 | ALT on JET Program (2002–2003) | Japanese | Yonsei | US continent |
| 20 | Fred | M | 60 | English teacher (1973–1985) | Japanese | Sansei | US continent |
| 21 | Gary | M | 36 | US military employee | Japanese | Sansei | US continent |
| 22 | George | M | 56 | US military employee | Japanese | Shin-nisei/sansei | Japan |
| 23 | Glen Fukushima | M | 56 | Business person | Japanese | Sansei[6] | US continent, Japan |

*(continued)*

APPENDIX B

| Name[1] | Sex | Age[2] | Occupation while living in Japan | Ancestry[3] | Generation[4] | Residence prior to age 18[5] |
|---|---|---|---|---|---|---|
| 24 Glenn | M | 26 | ALT on JET Program (2011–2014) | Japanese, Filipino | Gosei | Hawai'i |
| 25 Grant | M | 44 | Financial Consulting | Japanese | Shin-nisei/ sansei | US continent |
| 26 Greg | M | | English teacher (1977–1980) | Japanese | Sansei | US continent |
| 27 Henry | M | 36 | Business Management | Japanese | Shin-nisei/ sansei | US continent |
| 28 Hiroshi | M | 21 | College exchange student | Japanese, Irish | Yonsei | US continent |
| 29 Ian | M | 52 | English teacher | Japanese | Sansei | US continent |
| 30 Ida | F | 51 | US military employee | Japanese | Shin-nisei/ sansei | Japan |
| 31 Isabella | F | 42 | ALT on JET Program (1993–1995) | Japanese, Chinese | Yonsei | US continent |
| 32 Jason | M | 50 | Lawyer | Japanese, Greek | Shin-nisei | US continent |
| 33 Jay | M | 25 | CIR on JET Program | Japanese | Yonsei[7] | Hawai'i |
| 34 Jill | F | 25 | ALT on JET Program | Japanese, Okinawan | Sansei/ yonsei | Hawai'i |
| 35 Jim Minamoto | M | 48 | Lawyer | Japanese | Sansei | US continent |
| 36 Jimmy | M | 30 | Finance | Japanese | Shin-nisei/ sansei | Hawai'i |
| 37 Joe | M | 44 | University English Instructor | Japanese | Shin-nisei | US continent |
| 38 Joel | M | 53 | Industrial Engineer | Japanese | Sansei | US continent |

*(continued)*

| Name[1] | Sex | Age[2] | Occupation while living in Japan | Ancestry[3] | Generation[4] | Residence prior to age 18[5] |
|---|---|---|---|---|---|---|
| 39 John | M | 29 | Language student | Japanese, German, Scottish, Native American (Blackfoot Indian) | Yonsei | US continent |
| 40 Jordan | M | 35 | English teacher | Japanese, Italian, Polish, German, Scotts-Irish | Sansei | US continent |
| 41 June | F | 58 | College exchange student (1975–1976) | Japanese | Nisei/Sansei | US continent |
| 42 Karen | F | 41 | College exchange student (1992–1993) | Japanese | Shin-nisei | US continent |
| 43 Kathy Masaoka | F | 66 | College exchange student (1968–1969) | Japanese | Sansei | US continent |
| 44 Ken | M | 45 | US military employee | Japanese, white American | Shin-nisei | US continent, Japan |
| 45 Kenji | M | 28 | CIR on JET Program (2008–2010) | Japanese, Taiwanese | Shin-nisei | |
| 46 Kim | F | 28 | ALT on JET Program (2006–2008) | Japanese | Yonsei | Hawaiʻi |
| 47 Kyle | M | 42 | Lawyer | Japanese | Sansei | Hawaiʻi |
| 48 Leo | M | 24 | College exchange student | Japanese | Yonsei | US continent |

*(continued)*

APPENDIX B                                                                                         171

| Name[1] | Sex | Age[2] | Occupation while living in Japan | Ancestry[3] | Generation[4] | Residence prior to age 18[5] |
|---|---|---|---|---|---|---|
| 49 Mark | M | 39 | Executive Administration | Japanese | Sansei | US continent |
| 50 Martin | M | 26 | Language student | Japanese, Irish, Scottish | Shin-nisei | US continent, Japan |
| 51 Masato | M | 36 | Finance | Japanese | Shin-nisei | US continent |
| 52 Melody | F | 23 | Language student | Okinawan | Yonsei | Hawai'i |
| 53 Michelle | F | 37 | Housewife | Japanese | Sansei/yonsei | Hawai'i |
| 54 Nancy | F | 27 | ALT on JET Program (2006–2008) | Japanese | Yonsei | Hawai'i |
| 55 Naomi | F | 35 | Yoga Instructor | Japanese, white American | Shin-nisei | US continent, Japan |
| 56 Oliver | M | 39 | English teacher | Japanese | Yonsei | US continent |
| 57 Peter | M | 44 | US military employee | Japanese | Shin-nisei | Japan, internationally |
| 58 Phil | M | 47 | US military employee | Japanese, African | Shin-nisei | US continent, Japan |
| 59 Raleigh | F | 41 | English teacher | Japanese | Sansei/yonsei | Hawai'i |
| 60 Rick | M | 43 | Language student | Japanese | Sansei | Hawai'i, US continent |
| 61 Ronald | M | 61 | Education-related | Japanese | Sansei/yonsei | US continent |
| 62 Russell | M | 39 | Publishing | Japanese | Sansei | Hawai'i |
| 63 Ryan Yokota | M | 42 | Language student (2006–2007) | Japanese, Okinawan | Shin-nisei/yonsei | US continent |

*(continued)*

| Name[1] | Sex | Age[2] | Occupation while living in Japan | Ancestry[3] | Generation[4] | Residence prior to age 18[5] |
|---|---|---|---|---|---|---|
| 64 Sachiko | F | 65 | Education-related | Japanese | Nisei/sansei | US continent |
| 65 Sam | M | 55 | Tourism industry | Japanese | Shin-nisei/sansei | Hawai'i |
| 66 Saori | F | 28 | ALT on JET Program (2008–2009) | Japanese | Shin-nisei | US continent |
| 67 Sara | F | 27 | Language student | Japanese, Irish, French, French-Canadian | Shin-nisei | US continent |
| 68 Scott | M | 25 | ALT on JET Program | Japanese, Irish | Yonsei | US continent |
| 69 Sean | M | 30 | English teacher | Japanese, Okinawan, English, Irish, Dutch, Welsh, Scottish, German | Yonsei | Hawai'i |
| 70 Sherman Abe | M | 61 | College Professor and Administrator | Japanese | Nisei | US continent |
| 71 Shin Mune | M | 76 | Farmer, English teacher (1998–2000) | Japanese | Nisei | US continent |
| 72 Stephanie | F | 39 | College exchange student (1995–1996) | Japanese | Yonsei | US continent |
| 73 Steve | M | 44 | Business Management | Okinawan | Sansei/yonsei | US continent |
| 74 Stewart | M | 38 | Public Relations | Japanese | Yonsei | Hawai'i |

*(continued)*

APPENDIX B

| Name[1] | Sex | Age[2] | Occupation while living in Japan | Ancestry[3] | Generation[4] | Residence prior to age 18[5] |
|---|---|---|---|---|---|---|
| 75 Tak | M | 75 | English teacher, visiting relatives (1966–1967) | Japanese | Sansei | US continent |
| 76 Takamori | M | 50 | Lawyer | Japanese | Shin-nisei | US continent, internationally |
| 77 Todd | M | 47 | English teacher (1991–1997) | Japanese, Okinawan | Yonsei | US continent |
| 78 Valerie | F | 58 | College exchange student (1975–1976) | Japanese | Sansei | US continent |
| 79 Ying | M | 22 | College exchange student | Japanese, Taiwanese | Shin-nisei/ Sansei | US continent |

[1] All names are pseudonyms except for respondents listed with last names who have written or been interviewed for publications used as resources.
[2] Age at time of first interview
[3] Although it is not an ancestry, "white American" is used when interviewees described parents this way, unsure of their ethnonational origins. Two interviewees described their ancestry as "Japanese" but in the course of the interview it became clear that their ancestors were from Okinawa so I describe them in this way.
[4] This is my description, not necessarily how they identify.
[5] Official residence up to the age of about 18 and through graduating high school, not including where one spent summers. Some interviewees raised in the US continent spent summers in Hawai'i with relatives.
[6] This interviewee was originally categorized as shin-nisei/sansei. At his request, he was re-categorized as sansei.
[7] His maternal grandparents were issei and nisei, making his mother nisei/sansei. His paternal grandparents were nisei, making his father sansei.

# Notes

## INTRODUCTION

1. Kevin, Cheryl, and Jocelyn are composites based on my Japanese American interviewees, so their information is not listed in Appendix B.

2. Large concentrations of Japanese Americans also reside in a number of areas on the US continent, such as Torrance, California. I met some Japanese Americans who grew up in predominantly Japanese American or Asian American high schools and cities in the US continent and said they felt like part of the majority in certain contexts. This is different from Hawai'i, however, because even when a city on the US continent is predominantly comprised of people of Asian ancestries, the surrounding cities and larger states are not.

3. Migration refers to movement across borders; international migration is movement across international borders. Migrants range in intentions, from temporary to permanent (Castles and Miller 1993), and include people of varied occupations—international students as well as business elites (Favell, Feldblum, and Smith 2006).

4. This is the first book-length systematic study of contemporary Japanese American experiences. A number of books, memoirs, and narratives reflecting on individual experiences have been written. Most of this work focuses on nisei who lived in prewar and wartime Japan (Miyamoto 1957, Sano 1997, Tomita and Lee 1995, Yoshida and Hosokawa 1972), which is understandable since 40,000–50,000 are estimated to have been living in Japan before, during, and after World War II (Azuma 2005, Jin 2013). Essays about experiences serving in the US Military Intelligence Service have documented experiences in postwar Japan of members of the Allied Occupation Forces (Hawaii Nikkei History Editorial Board 1998), and some research has also analyzed MIS experiences in Japan (Azuma 2009, Shibutani 1978). Japanese American memoirs have reflected on more recent experiences in the late 1960s as Japanese society was undergoing intense social, economic, and political change (Okimoto 1971), in the economically booming Japan of the 1980s (Mura 1992), and reflecting on twenty-five years of being married to a Japanese man and raising a family in Japan (Sakayori 2000). The biography of Wally Yonamine describes his experiences as the first American to play professional baseball in Japan in the postwar period (Fitts 2012). In addition, some theses and dissertations have examined Japanese American experiences in prewar and wartime Japan ( Jin 2013, Nisei Survey Committee 1939, Sato 1994), the late 1970s (Uratsu 1977), and more recently (Takamori 2011).

5. Global ancestral group is an abstract concept and the localization of the ancestral group in each society takes on ethnic forms. When referring to members of a global ancestral group, I use "coethnics" and "global coethnics" interchangeably. When discussing the Japanese global ancestral group, I use phrases such as "ethnic Japanese," "Japanese coethnics," and "people of Japanese ancestry" interchangeably.

6. In his well-referenced article discussing the concept of diaspora, William Safran did note that based on the six characteristics he proposed to define diaspora more narrowly than Walker Connor's earlier definition, many of the cases he covered were not clearly diasporas (e.g., some ethnic Polish are diasporic and some are not due to the conditions of their exiting and their maintenance of ties to the homeland). See Safran (1991) and Connor (1986).

7. *Ancestry* is a concept that needs to be used with caution because even though it can imply natural, biological connections, it is a social construction, similar to ethnicity or race. Most research on "ancestry" is conducted by geneticists. Even when based in genetic research, however, "ancestry" is a social construction for at least two main reasons. First, multiple ways of defining ancestry mean multiple systems of categorization, including "genetic ancestry, geographic ancestry, biogeographical ancestry" (Ali-Khan, Krakowski, and Daar 2011: 59), "continental ancestry" and "lineage or family history" (Royal et al. 2010: 661–662). For example, while "continental ancestry . . . assumes the existence of four or five major 'parental' populations that gave rise within the last 100,000 years to existing populations" and is often equated with the concept of race, "biogeographic ancestry" associates "a person's origin . . . with the geographic location(s) of presumed ancestors inferred by comparison with contemporary populations living in these locations" (Royal et al. 2010: 661) and seems to imply ethnic or national origin. Thus, ancestry sometimes refers to smaller areas such as nations, and other times to larger areas, such as continents, making usage of the concept inconsistent and unclear. Second, the places to which ancestry is linked—the categories by which ancestry is defined—are also socially constructed. Even if we were to adhere to a single definition of ancestry as biogeographic, national and other territorial boundaries shift over time. Exactly what "ancestry" refers to is far from clear-cut, despite its association with genetic testing (Royal et al. 2010).

8. The construction of group boundaries assumes similarity and difference—similarity within the group juxtaposed against the difference constructed by the border distinguishing the group from "the other." However, rather than referring to the differentiation that the boundaries of the group represent, the difference I am referring to is the heterogeneity within the group. This internal diversity and sameness can coexist if the latter is understood to be a form of what Spivak calls "strategic essentialism."

9. The benefit of casting likeness as based on the past, rather than the present, is that it can acknowledge divergences in the present and leaves open what may happen in the future without taking away from the possibility of a shared identity and group experience among diverse and geographically distant branches of a global ancestral group. Moreover, it does not make assumptions about the dynamic and ongoing relationship of the past to the present and the future.

10. In Europe, race is generally synonymous with nation (see Banton 2002: 191).

11. For excellent discussions of Asian settler colonialism focusing on North America, see Laura Fugikawa's (2011) fascinating comparative discussion of Japanese American and Native American relocation and Iyko Day's (2016) discussion of the triangulation of Native, alien, and settler positions.

12. Other terms used to refer to when the descendents of emigrants migrate to their ancestral homeland include "ancestral return" and "counter diasporic return" (see King and Christou 2010a and b, King and Christou 2011).

13. Despite using the language of "diaspora" and "return," King and Christou support my point by commenting that "return is perhaps questionable as a defining criterion of diaspora. Some diasporas do not desire to return" (King and Christou 2010a: 171).

14. Of course, "European Americans" are a diverse group. Americans of English, Irish, Italian, and French ancestry, for example, identify with and are associated with their ancestral homelands in varying ways due to the histories of these populations and their relationship to whiteness in the United States (see Brodkin 1994, Jacobson 1998, Lipsitz 2006, López 1996). In addition, the "diaspora" policies of each ancestral homeland government greatly shape this discourse. An example is the creation of an Irish "diaspora minister" in 2014 (O'Shea 2014).

15. In referring to populations in Japan, *nikkeijin* usually includes only the descendants of Japanese emigrants. In referring to populations outside of Japan, *nikkeijin* sometimes also includes Japanese emigrants themselves. See (Yamashiro 2008b).

CHAPTER 1 — JAPANESE AS A GLOBAL ANCESTRAL GROUP: JAPANESENESS ON THE US CONTINENT, HAWAI'I, AND JAPAN

1. In this chapter, when talking about US Census data, people reporting Japanese ancestry include some Japanese citizens and temporary residents, as well as small numbers of ethnic Japanese raised in and with citizenship in other places, such as Japan or Peru. I recognize that these people may not identify as "Japanese Americans," and use phrases such as "people of Japanese ancestry" or "ethnic Japanese" to carefully acknowledge this.

2. The top cities in which Japanese Americans claim residence as of 2009, and their respective percentages of the population are: Los Angeles, CA (19 percent), New York, NY (14 percent), Torrance, CA (8 percent), San Francisco, CA (7 percent), and Seattle, WA (5 percent) (Shinagawa et al. 2011).

3. Within Hawai'i specifically, most Japanese immigrants came from Hiroshima, Yamaguchi, Kumamoto, Okinawa, and Fukuoka prefectures. Concentrated flows from different prefectures varied by emigration period. See (Kimura 1988: 22–23).

4. Hawai'i previously signed treaties with and had its own consuls in Japan (see Okahata 1971: 71).

5. Alan Moriyama describes five periods of migration from Japan to Hawai'i: 1868–1885. as a period when emigration was prohibited by the Japanese government; 1885–1894 as a period of government-sponsored emigrants; 1894–1908 as a period of company emigrants, including those using emigration companies; 1908–1924 as a period of independent emigrants who went on their own; and 1924–the postwar period when Japanese were not allowed into the United States (Moriyama 1985).

6. Japanese workers were offered $1.25 to $1.35 per day to work in fishery operations, canneries, and agriculture on the West Coast. In Hawai'i they were paid only 69 cents per day (Kimura 1988: 14).

7. While I recognize that most academic work on Japanese Americans capitalizes generational terms such as *issei* and *nisei*, in this book, I italicize these terms at first usage but do not capitalize them. It is a standard convention in sociology to not capitalize "white" or "black" so I follow this formatting style.

8. Exceptions include Takahashi (1997) and Befu (2010: 39) who recognizes how "education and socialization in Japan during their formative years set them clearly apart from the Nisei who remained in North America . . . Yet they were a whole generation apart from their parents, putting them in a totally different category either from Issei or so-called pure Nisei."

9. Although Japanese Americans occupy a position of power in the state of Hawai'i, the analogy to whiteness as a majority racial category associated with power has its limits.

Whiteness is associated with power nationally in the United States and globally. So although Hawaiʻi may have a different racial formation, is it still affected by larger national and global contexts where whiteness is associated with power.

10. The racism that Japanese immigrants and their descendents in Hawaiʻi have experienced in earlier periods is well-documented (see, for example, Okamura 2014, Okihiro 1991, Takaki 1983).

11. While "haole" means "foreigner" in the Hawaiian language, in everyday conversation it most often refers specifically to whites from the continental United States. This distinction reflects continental ignorance of Hawaiʻi ways of life and ways of speaking as symbolized by "the mainland haole" and can be understood within a larger history of "imposition" by haoles that can be traced back to the nineteenth century. See Ogawa (1973: 12) and Whittaker (1986).

12. The strong distinction between Hawaiʻi and the US continent has historical roots dating back to the US colonization of Hawaiʻi. People in Hawaiʻi distinguish between these two places in terms of culture, lifestyle, and sometimes, power. The fact that this distinction is made more in Hawaiʻi than on the continent reflects the uneven power relations. The continent-based national government routinely makes decisions that affect Hawaiʻi, including the continued militarization of the islands. Hawaii's economic dependence on tourism can also be attributed to US national interests of having Hawaiʻi as part of its territory—as a convenient domestic vacation spot.

13. The phrase "Asian settler colonialism" has been used by some scholars to highlight the complex history of Asian immigrants in Hawaiʻi who are not the islands' original inhabitants. See Fujikane and Okamura (2008).

14. Interestingly, during the period of the Japanese Empire, the assimilationist policies that the Japanese government adopted resulted in a "mixed nation" discourse that included colonial populations as Japanese citizens. See Oguma 2002.

15. Interestingly, while Ishida is clear about the social construction of national borders and citizenship, it is slightly unclear if he includes himself as believing in this "natural" notion of Japanese.

16. Some scholars distinguish between Japanese war orphans who were children as "*zanryūkoji*" and who were adult women as "*zanryū fujin*." See Ward (2006).

17. Sometimes "*nikkeijin*" includes Japanese emigrants but sometimes it refers only to their foreign-born descendants. In addition to differences in citizenship, the *nihonjin/nikkeijin* distinction usually includes allusion to cultural and social differences that can develop from living outside of Japan.

18. *Burakumin* are people of Japanese ancestry discriminated against due to occupations that deemed them "unpure" (e.g., tanners, butchers). They historically resided in certain areas, or *buraku*, so their descendants continue to be socially marginalized due to this connection.

19. Of course, individual situations matter. While people perceived to be white are generally higher on the racial hierarchy than people perceived to be black, one can imagine that the ambassador of Ghana would be treated with more respect than a white teenager. So race and nation need to be considered along with class, status, age, gender, and other categories of difference.

CHAPTER 2 — DIFFERENTIATED JAPANESE AMERICAN IDENTITIES: THE CONTINENT VERSUS HAWAIʻI

1. While in everyday language race implies genetic differences, scholars have shown how race is a social construction—that there is no evidence to support the belief that genetic differences between races exist. In fact, there is more genetic variation within a single racial group than there is between races. See Koenig, Lee, and Richardson (2008).

2. In contrast, mixed Japanese Americans I interviewed generally spoke more about how context matters in how they are phenotypically interpreted. For example, Martin said that when in a group, whether it be with Japanese friends or foreign ones, he is usually assumed (by Japanese who don't know) to be the same as the rest of the group, i.e., Japanese among a group of Japanese and a foreigner among a group of foreigners. In one-on-one interactions, however, Martin said that people could tell he was a foreigner.

3. Logically speaking, this makes sense, since most foreigners in Japan are of East Asian ancestries. In 2005, Korean nationals were the largest reported foreign national resident population in Japan (598,687) and Chinese nationals were second (687,156). Since 2010, however, Chinese nationals have become the largest reported population (687,156) with Korean nationals second largest (565,989) (Statistics Bureau 2016). Most Chinese nationals are international migrants from China but roughly two-thirds of Korean nationals were born and raised in Japan, not automatically given Japanese citizenship because Japan does not observe a system of *jus soli*, or citizenship based on birth on that country's soil. Ethnic Koreans born in Japan tend to either 1) claim South Korean citizenship through lineage; 2) naturalize to Japanese citizenship; or 3) become stateless if they choose to claim North Korean citizenship, since Japan does not formally recognize or have ties with the Democratic People's Republic of Korea. For more information, see Lee (1981: 148)

4. Interestingly, when Bruce and other Japanese Americans are in Tokyo, they are asked if they are from the countryside. When I lived in a rural part of Nagano prefecture for several years in the late 1990s, I was often asked if I was from Osaka (where the intonation and dialect are different from the Tokyo national standard). Subnational geographical variations contribute to diversity and are a schema for interpreting difference in Japan (Sugimoto 2010: 60–71).

5. Despite the recent "Korea boom," including the popularity of Korean soap operas and foods, mainstream discourse and assumptions about Chinese, Koreans, and other Asians continue to be influenced by Japanese feelings of superiority traced back to the colonization of parts of China, Taiwan, and Korea. In addition, as of December 2015, Chinese are the largest foreign tourist group, due to a combination of a weakened yen and relaxed visa regulations for Chinese citizens from January 2015. (Abkowitz 2015). According to my Tokyo-based Japanese colleague, with this influx a negative image of rude Chinese tourists has developed.

6. Usage of the term "Asian" is different in Japan and the United States. In Japan, "Asian" sometimes includes Japanese when "Asians" are juxtaposed against "Westerners." At other times it excludes Japanese and refers only to people in the rest of Asia.

7. Murders have been committed in Japan by both Japanese Brazilians and Japanese Peruvians. See, for example, "Dairishobatsu de *Nikkeijin* no Otoko Kiso/Hamamatsu no Satsujin/ Burajiru Kensatsu." *Shikoku News*, February 17, 2007, and "Hiroshima murder suspect had poor life, broken home in Peru." *The Japan Times*, Tuesday, December 20, 2005.

8. A few interviewees commented that since September 11, 2001 and subsequent developments in US foreign policy that have been condemned by the global community (e.g., racial profiling), they have felt some embarrassment about being from the United States. One interviewee also recalled incidents of violence against him while in Japan during the Vietnam War era.

9. *Hāfu* refers to the child of one "Japanese" and one "foreign" parent. See Yamashiro (2008a).

10. One Japanese American described how he sometimes identifies as Okinawan in Japan. Steve explained the flow of a typical conversation with a Japanese person. Usually, he will present his namecard to them. Then they comment on his first name, which is Western. He explains that he is *nikkei yonsei* (fourth generation of Japanese ancestry). "When I say that I'm American, they'll ask if my father's American or my mother's American. I say that my passport is American. Even if I say I'm 'American *nikkei*' (not Brazilian), and that it's not my father or mother but my grandfather and great grandfather that emigrated from Japan, they'll usually ask 'are you all Japanese?' and I'll say, 'no, I'm all American.' Then they'll say, 'but you don't really look Japanese' and I'll tell them that that's because my ancestors are from Okinawa." He explains, "I don't have an issue telling people my family is originally from Okinawa, but I think some Japanese still make a distinction."

11. Another example of someone whose background was often misunderstood is a Chinese Malaysian woman who was a friend of a friend. She was third and fourth generation Chinese from Malaysia working for an American company in Tokyo. At first I wondered if she was ever mistaken as a Japanese but she said, "I don't look Japanese" and that she usually spent time in areas where many people speak English, such as Roppongi or Azabujuban. According to my fieldnotes from October 29, 2007, she told me that "when she does have conversations where she tells people that she's Chinese Malaysian, they don't get it. Their image of Malaysians is Muslims with head wraps."

12. One medium-skinned African American interviewee said that most Japanese initially assumed he was from Africa or Latin America. After saying he was American, most Japanese immediately began interpreting him in relation to jazz, Michael Jordan, and rap music, in terms of stereotypes of African Americans. This suggests that although the dominant image of Americans is racialized white, stereotypes of African Americans are also common in Japan.

13. Elsewhere, I have explained this process of the reconstruction of a racial minority identity abroad as "racialized national identity formation." See Yamashiro (2011).

14. As someone of Japanese and Okinawan ancestry who had also lived in Okinawa, Ryan added that people in Okinawa understood his family's diasporic history "very quickly regardless of generation."

15. I analytically differentiate between a "Hawai'i" identity and a "Hawaiian" identity. The former refers to people of any ancestry who identify with Hawai'i. The latter refers to Native Hawaiians, the indigenous people of Hawai'i. Some of my interviewees also made this distinction while some did not.

16. Japanese Americans from the continent also notice the continental/Hawai'i distinction in the context of Hawai'i. Alvin is a Japanese American from Los Angeles who lived in Tokyo and is now living in Honolulu. When I interviewed him in Honolulu, he commented on how he feels like an outsider in Hawai'i, despite being Asian American—similar to most of the population of Hawai'i. He attributed his outsider status to not having his own family in Hawai'i (his wife's family is in Hawai'i) and not having grown up and attended schools in Hawai'i, which placed him outside of most social networks.

17. According to the Hawai'i Tourism Authority 2010 Annual Report, 41.5 percent of Japanese visitors are first time visitors, 58.5 percent are repeat visitors, and the average number of trips Japanese visitors have taken to Hawai'i is 3.81. (Hawai'i Tourism Authority 2011).

18. This awareness, in some ways, can be traced back to when Japanese first began emigrating to the islands in the late 19th century (Yaguchi and Yoshihara 2004:: 83), though it was probably not in the consciousness of the majority of Japanese society.

19. I was able to observe this firsthand at a party hosted by a friend of a friend in the Azabu-juban area of Tokyo in October 2007. The gathering was in a beautiful apartment

building with a view of Tokyo Tower and attendees were a mix of Japanese and foreigners, all of whom seemed to speak English. At one point, I was speaking in English with two other Japanese Americans—one from California and one from Hawai'i, when together we met a Japanese woman for the first time. When she asked where we were from, the other California Japanese American said we were from the United States, then paused and said that he was from California, the other man was from Hawai'i, and I was also from California. The woman paused for a moment then replied, "Wow, Hawai'i, that's nice!"

20. One Japanese American I spoke with said that this type of response was not limited to people in Japan—people he met in Indonesia had also vacationed in Hawai'i and thought of the islands fondly.

CHAPTER 3 — FROM *HAPA* TO *HĀFU*: MIXED JAPANESE AMERICAN IDENTITIES IN JAPAN

1. I avoid using the terms "mixed-race Japanese" and "mixed-ethnicity Japanese" in my analysis, instead describing my interviewees as "mixed Japanese Americans," and Japanese Americans of "mixed ancestry" or of "mixed heritage." I do this because Japanese is considered an ethnicity in the United States but in Japan could also be considered a race, so to avoid confusion I focus on the mixedness itself, rather than on whether this should be understood as mixedness in terms of race or ethnicity. However, when interviewees used terms such as "mixed-race," I retained this language in describing them.

2. Though in this chapter I describe my interviewees as "mixed Japanese Americans," it is worth pointing out that most of them did not identify with the label "Japanese American," instead choosing terms such as *hapa*, *hāfu*, mixed, and Asian American to describe themselves.

3. I use quotes around monoracial, multiracial, and mixed to denote how race is a social construction and racial groupings have no biological or genetic basis, and therefore, multiraciality is also a social construction. In the rest of the chapter, the quotes are omitted for easier reading.

4. While *hāfu* connotes both "Japanese" and "foreign," it also means not completely either and can be seen as providing a "third space" in addition to the traditional bifurcation of "Japanese" and "foreign." As Friere pointed out, having a name is necessary to denote one's existence, Moreover, "having a name and label such as *haafu* or *half Japanese* meant this group of Amerasians existed; it meant the Japanese, the Americans, and they themselves acknowledged their existence as a category of people, and it meant they had successfully negotiated and manufactured an identity where none existed initially" (M.C. Thornton 1983, as cited in Williams 1992: 302, italics in original).

5. The history of mixed Japanese in Japan dates back centuries. See Williams (2016).

6. Mixed Okinawan Americans continue to struggle for social acceptance in Okinawa. Akemi Johnson describes their negotiation of race and class through language: "For someone who looks part white or black or Latino, or has a name like Paola or Shirley or Jack, to not speak English is to risk association with the 'island half' stereotype. Tragic, fatherless, the 'island half' is the product of an affair between a local, lower-class woman of questionable morals and a young no-good serviceman with a 'love-her-and-leave-her' mentality. Sometimes the stereotype extends to an assumption of rape. If a biracial person speaks English, however, this hints at a different picture: a glamorous, international 'half' with loving, married parents and enviable access to the United States" (as cited in Murphy-Shigematsu 2012: 185–186).

7. For more on being mixed black and Japanese, see Houston (1991), Carter (2014), Murphy-Shigematsu (2012).

8. Constructions of race and Japaneseness are different in Okinawa (compared to mainland Japan) due to related factors including a history of colonization by Japanese, experiencing the only land battle on Japanese territory during World War II (and losing approximately a quarter of the local population), occupation by the United States, continued militarization, and economic dependence on tourism.

9. Cynthia Nakashima points out the irony of "people of mixed race" in the US context becoming associated with "attractive physical appearances," since the hybrid degeneracy theory (widely accepted from the end of the Civil War until the mid-1930s) asserted that "multiracial people could inherit 'disharmonious' physical features from their various parent races" (1992: 170).

10. Anecdotally, a book published in 2012 notes a more specific mixed background deemed desirable: "Now in Japan I hear that the best combination is not half and half but three-quarters Japanese and one-quarter white—mostly Japanese, but with just a hint of exotic foreignness" (Murphy-Shigematsu 2012).

11. See http://hafufilm.com/en/about/meaning-of-the-word-hafu. Accessed February 21, 2016.

12. Sato's study also found that, in contrast to depictions in other leading Japanese fashion magazines, the *hāfu* models in ViVi were overwhelmingly in "sensual/sexy" poses, suggesting their hypersexualization and othering in mass media and a shift from sexiness being associated with whiteness to mixedness. In the 176 images she analyzed, Sato found only one of a black model; none were of mixed black and Asian models, suggesting different representations of mixed black/Japanese and mixed white/Japanese in Japan.

13. http://hafufilm.com/en/about/meaning-of-the-word-hafu. Accessed February 1, 2016.

14. For example, in November 2006, I polled forty-nine students at Sophia University about their images of *hāfu* and *nikkei amerikajin* (Japanese Americans). Most described *hāfu* as phenotypically different from Japanese, though some also included people of mixed Japanese-(other)Asian backgrounds who may not be visually distinguishable from Japanese. Almost all students said that their images of *nikkei amerikajin* were of people who looked Japanese but were American in their thinking and behavior.

15. Murphy-Shigematsu has described terms used in Japan since the postwar period to describe people of mixed ancestry. *Ainoko* was used in the period immediately following WWII to refer to mixed Japanese children and is the most blatantly derogatory term, used to describe not only human beings but also the mixing of animal species (Murphy-Shigematsu 2000: 212). *Konketsuji* literally means "mixed-blood child." As war animosities began to subside, this term arose in the post-occupation era as a more politically correct alternative to *ainoko*, though now it is generally seen as politically incorrect and offensive. From the 1960s, another image of mixed Japanese began to emerge in the media that was more popular and exotic: *hāfu*. The expression *hāfu* is said to have become widespread with the rise of a singing group called the *Golden Hāfu* who were popular in the 1970s. *Hāfu* is currently the most commonly used term, though its connotations are also debatable. In October 2007, I went to a pet store in Chiba, a Tokyo suburb, where many dogs were labeled *hāfu* referring to their mixed breeds. From this we can surmise that *hāfu*, like earlier terms, still references both humans and animals.

16. Though not yet heard very often and perhaps used more by the parents of mixed-race children than by the individuals themselves, the implication of empowerment through rearticulation is clear: people are not halves of two groups and less than whole, but rather double and twice as much. In addition to parental ancestries, this term can connote being bilingual and bicultural. None of my interviewees used this term to refer to themselves but all had heard of it, with several saying that younger generations were beginning to use it more often.

17. This notion of blood quantification is similar to the "one-drop-rule" in the United States that has been broadly used to define blackness.

18. The larger category of *hapa* includes both "mixed-race" and "mixed-ethnicity" populations, though who these terms reference change as the definitions of race and ethnicity keep shifting. "Mixed-race" has referred most commonly to having one parent of Asian or Pacific Islander descent and one parent of another group considered a race: white, black, Native American, or Latino/a. Meanwhile, "mixed-ethnicity" has referred to someone with parents from more than one Asian or Pacific Islander group, but not from the other groups considered races. However, the 2000 Census was the first to consider "Asians" and "Pacific Islanders" different races (Dariotis 2003: 114), and, as a result, usage of the terms "mixed-race" and "mixed-ethnicity" varies. The shifting Census classifications of "Asian" and "Pacific Islander" from being part of the same race to being considered different races demonstrates the fluid social construction of race—and of mixed raceness.

19. Increased awareness of and identification with the term *hapa* on the US continent can be partly explained by the growth of *hapa* organizations on college campuses beginning in the early 1990s. In 1992, the Hapa Issues Forum was established at UC Berkeley by mixed-heritage Japanese American students in response to their exclusion from the larger Japanese American community (Leach 2007). The group grew to include mixed-heritage people of other Asian ancestries and expanded to have community-based chapters in San Francisco and Los Angeles, as well as student chapters at Stanford University, UC Irvine, and UC San Diego. Though the Hapa Issues Forum eventually disbanded in 2007, other *hapa* organizations can still be found at numerous colleges and universities (and even at the high school level).

20. The following definitions are provided in a Hawaiian Dictionary: *haole*. nvs. White person, American, Englishman, Caucasian; American, English; formerly, any foreigner (Pukui and Elbert 1986a). *hapa*. 1. nvs. Portion, fragment, part, fraction, installment; to be partial, less. (Eng. half.) . . . 2. nvs. Of mixed blood, person of mixed blood, as hapa Hawai'i, part Hawaiian (Pukui and Elbert 1986b). *hapa haole*. nvs. Part-white person; of part-white blood; part white and part Hawaiian, as an individual or phenomenon (Pukui and Elbert 1986c). Though haole commonly refers to and translates as "white" in contemporary Hawai'i everyday usage, the technical definition usually given is that whites just happened to be the foreigners with whom Native Hawaiians first came into contact. While *hapa* literally refers to parts, the phrase "hapa haole," in Hawaiian, has the connotation of being part white, but also specifically part Hawaiian.

21. Nakashima (2001: 114) points out additional reasons why "a surname is by no means a reliable reflection of a person's ethnicity": conventional patrilineal surnaming practices in the United States mean that maternal heritage is not represented in last names; "Adoption, divorce, and births outside of legal marriage can disrupt the patrilineal naming structure, sometimes bringing in surnames that are not representative of an individual's ethnicity at all"; and name changing with marriage.

22. Even when mixed Japanese people speak Japanese, have Japanese names, and are Japanese citizens, they are often seen as foreign if they appear phenotypically different from most *nihonjin*. See, for example, Fox (2005), Murphy-Shigematsu (2012).

23. More specifically, there is a "hierarchy by color" that is "directly correlated with the present world order," where dark-skinned populations are perceived to be "less qualified to negotiate global issues as equals" (Hall 2003). Indeed, worldwide, "dark skin still correlates with poverty" (Winant 1994: 122).

24. John returned to the United States to finish law school then went back to Tokyo for work. He eventually married a Japanese woman and had two children; he currently lives in Tokyo with his family.

25. When John and I communicated in writing, he included a hyphen in "Japanese-American." Although I do not use a hyphen in "Japanese American," I retained his usage in quotes to reflect his perspective.

26. For mixed Japanese Americans whose phenotypical characteristics are racially ambiguous, blending shifts with context. John and several other interviewees described being able to physically blend into a crowd of Japanese people (e.g., when riding a train) but having their foreignness become salient in one-on-one interactions (e.g., when talking to a store clerk). It was unclear whether this foreignness was due to visual salience or accented Japanese. Either way, John's ability to blend into a crowd is a different experience from the attention that people (mixed or not) perceived to be "white" receive. In addition to phenotype, John pointed out that when he wears a suit he can blend in fairly well, whereas when he is more casually dressed, he is more recognizably foreign. This distinction suggests a socioeconomic class or fashion dimension to the Japanese/foreigner distinction (as opposed to phenotype alone). In Japan, it is a very common practice for businesspeople, men in particular, to wear suits, which makes wearing suits a mainstream marker of white-collar workers. On a related note, John conveyed that he believes he is treated better when he is more noticeably Japanese, in contrast to the bad service he receives when with other international students, such as in restaurants. In regards to sticking out, John thinks that this happens most when he is with other foreigners, when he is by himself but speaking Japanese, or when he is in a new environment and is unsure of the social norms (e.g., asking for the check at a *kaitenzushi*—conveyor belt sushi restaurant).

27. I have retained Emma's spelling of "ha-fu" in quotes to reflect that it differs from the way I write it.

28. Emma pointed out that her last name is white. "I wish I had a Japanese name," she laments. She wanted to change her middle name to her last name—since her middle name is her mother's maiden name. But since her first name can sound Japanese with katakana pronunciation, she says that has helped people to see her as *hāfu* sometimes. Though she had never thought of it before, she now wonders if it was intentional on her mother's part and planned to ask her when she returned home to the United States. When she introduces herself in Japanese, "Emma" sounds Japanese and people ask her about it, giving her a chance to explain her mother's background.

29. Having full Japanese and foreign names is not unique to Sara. The children of Japanese- international marriages often have Japanese first and last names in addition to names that they use in the country of their other parent (e.g., for a second passport, if they have one).

30. Some people distinguish between Chinese and Taiwanese ancestries, but Ying was unsure about his mother's background other than that her family came from Taiwan. In our discussion, he said he was not clear about the difference between Chinese and Taiwanese, so my descriptions of him reflect this ambiguity.

CHAPTER 4 — LANGUAGE AND NAMES IN SHIFTING ASSERTIONS OF JAPANESENESS

1. In addition, all Japanese language schools in California and Hawai'i closed "with the outbreak of war between the United States and Japan" (Morimoto 1997: 117).

2. Sometimes older Japanese women born in the Meiji and Taisho eras (about 1868 to 1926) have first names written in katakana. For discussion of why, see (Tackett 2013).

3. Japanese mestizos, also known as Philippine *nikkeijin*, are mostly the children of prewar, Japanese male overseas migrants and Filipino women. Most of them do not have Japanese last names because they changed their Japanese names to Filipino or Chinese names "and disguised themselves as full-blooded Filipinos or Chinese mestizos" as "a

survival strategy" (Ohno 2007: 248) to avoid harassment and teasing in the Philippines, where anti-Japanese sentiment was understandably high in the postwar period. For more on Philippine *nikkeijin*, see (Iijima and Ohno 2010).

4. Glen S. Fukushima's career in US–Japan relations has spanned academia, journalism, law, government, and business. He might be most well-known for serving as Director for Japanese Affairs (1985–1988) and Deputy Assistant United States Trade Representative for Japan and China (1988–1990) at the Office of the United States Trade Representative (USTR), Executive Office of the President in Washington, D.C, though he has more recently served as President and CEO of companies such as Cadence Design Systems Japan, NCR Japan, and Airbus Japan (Fukushima 2015).

5. In addition, Fukushima described a third "very small group of Japanese Americans . . . who have become so acculturated in Japan that they insist on using kanji and insist on speaking Japanese everywhere." The few people like this that he knows tend to be married to Japanese and to have lived in Japan for more than thirty years, making them "feel quite assimilated into Japanese culture and society." I also met people who fit this description (and, interestingly, were nisei who had Japanese first and last names), but as Fukushima points out, they are a "small exception" and the majority of Japanese Americans living in Japan fit in the aforementioned two larger groups.

6. In contrast, mixed Japanese Americans who are commonly categorized as white or black do not usually idealize their acceptance in Japan in the same way. Those who are racialized white are already a racialized part of the majority in the United States so their experiences in Japan may be the first time they are treated like racial minorities. Those who are racialized black are perceived to be racial minorities in both the United States and Japan.

7. Numerous sources document the experience of Japanese Americans during World War II who volunteered to serve in the US military to prove their Americanness, even as their families were incarcerated.

8. In her research on highly skilled migrants and Japanese corporations in Japan, Nana Oishi reports that "only a few Japanese companies have adopted English as their official language or established a bilingual policy" (Oishi 2012: 1086).

9. As Gary's story demonstrated, it is also related to the US military base presence in Japan.

10. More than just being an English-speaker (as a second or third language), being a native speaker of English is often valued for doing language-related work (e.g., teaching English, doing translation work).

11. According to their website, for a year of tuition at the American School in Japan (ASIJ) from nursery school to grade 12, it costs roughly 2,300,000 yen, or roughly $20,000 per year. See The American School in Japan. "2015-16 Tuition and Fees." Accessed February 28, 2016. http://www.asij.ac.jp/tuition.

12. A few people also had Japanese first names and foreign last names.

13. Martin's father immigrated to the United States from Japan in his late twenties as a graduate student. He became very close to a European American family who had no children and he became their legally adopted son, taking on their last name. Martin's middle name is his father's Japanese family name and his last name is the European name that his father adopted as an adult.

14. By "English," Martin meant the name that he uses when he speaks English, not a British name.

15. In an interview with Adam Komisarof, Glen explains in more detail his decision to continue writing his Japanese last name in katakana: "About 95. percent of my Japanese American friends prefer to use *kanji* for their last names, but I insist on using *katakana* . . . because I don't want people to mistake me as a Japanese citizen. I didn't grow up in the Japanese system. I have studied about Japan and was a teaching fellow for

eminent Japan scholars such as Ezra Vogel and Edwin Reischauer at Harvard. I've also spent a lot of time in Japan, but I wouldn't presume to be a Japanese person, and I would not want to be constrained by rules that Japanese impose on each other but not on non-Japanese" (Komisarof 2012: 141–142).

### CHAPTER 5 — BACK IN THE UNITED STATES: JAPANESE AMERICAN INTERPRETATIONS OF THEIR EXPERIENCES IN JAPAN

1. Findings in this chapter are based primarily on interviews conducted in the Los Angeles area, the San Francisco Bay Area, and the Honolulu area with Japanese Americans who had lived in the greater Tokyo area, as well as other parts of Japan. Since so many Japanese Americans who live in Japan go to rural areas through the Japan Exchange and Teaching (JET) Program, it was important to include their experiences in the provinces, mostly to contextualize the Tokyo experiences as well as highlight their particularities. In addition, the inclusion of these rural experiences shed light on other Japan experiences that helped shape how Japanese Americans think about their relationship to Japan once back in the United States.

2. This refers to the time at which they left Japan; most interviews were conducted years after their return to the United States.

3. Japanese Americans in this first group tended to be in Japan through temporary (one–five year) study and work exchange programs—providing visas and with contracts with end dates and support systems (information about taxes and health insurance, counseling services, etc.) that made it easy and accessible to live in Japan. In the same vein, it also made it easy to leave Japan because to stay would require renewing a contract or, if at the end of their program's period of stay, finding a new occupation and visa.

4. Japanese Americans in this second group tended to be on work-related visas or the "long-term resident" (aka "nikkeijin") or "child or spouse of a Japanese national" status visas, which are renewable.

5. Saori, a shin-nisei interviewee, pointed out how when shin-nisei describe themselves as just "nisei" without the "shin-" prefix, it reflects the way they do not see themselves in relation to the prewar Japanese American community. If they did, she noted, then they would add the "shin-" to distinguish themselves from the prewar nisei.

6. Erin's case is also unusual compared to most sansei and yonsei, however, because in addition to more distant relatives, she also had a US-born and raised uncle and aunt who were living in Tokyo for work.

7. Sonali Jain also found that part of the motivation for second-generation Indian Americans to migrate to India was to develop an independent relationship with the country that was not mediated through their parents. See (Jain 2012).

8. Valerie told me that her relatives "came to America to go to college" before the Japanese tours became popular. She had relatives that had come to the United States just after Commodore Perry went to Japan. Her grandfather attended Keio University, then came with her great uncle to the United States. They intended to westernize then return to Japan, but they lost their businesses and had no choice but to stay. According to Valerie, her great uncle opened a hotel in Little Tokyo and her grandfather became a farmer (though she's not sure why). Also, one of Valerie's grandmothers attended Maryknoll college in Japan before coming over to marry her grandfather. This was very uncommon for women, suggesting a high level of affluence compared to the general population in Japan. When I asked where her family was from in Japan, Valerie said that her great grandfather was the postmaster of Japan so they lived all over the country.

9. His father was born in Japan and raised there until the age of ten, coming to the US in the 1950s. Craig's paternal grandmother was a kibei nisei, born in the US, then went to Japan in the 1930s, returning with Craig's father when he was a child.

10. Within the Japanese American community, "Japantown" is commonly abbreviated to "J-Town" and "Japanese American" is commonly abbreviated to "J.A."

11. This is not to say that Japanese Americans have to go to Japan to make this distinction; going to Japan simply reconstructs the boundaries between Japanese Americanness and Japan-based Japaneseness in particular ways.

12. On the US continent, too, *nihonjin* is sometimes used among Japanese Americans to refer to all people of Japanese ancestry. Growing up in the San Francisco Bay Area, I often heard issei and nisei use this term (now I hear *nikkei* more often). To differentiate between Japanese immigrants and later-generation Japanese Americans, the former are still often referred to as "Japanese nationals" or "Japanese Japanese" versus "Japanese Americans."

13. For an analysis of how this differentiated identity similarly develops for second-generation Korean American tourists to South Korea, see (Kim 2009).

14. In addition to those who identify as "Japanese American," there are some Americans of Japanese ancestry who do not identify with this label because they see it as referencing particular meanings which do not include them: World War II incarceration, cultural distance from Japan, and phenotypical characteristics (Yamashiro 2016).

15. Many of my interviewees viewed this forced separation as unnatural. They commented that they thought the connection that Japanese Americans have to Japan is unusually weak compared to the way other Asian Americans such as Chinese Americans or Korean Americans have stronger connections to China and South Korea, respectively.

16. According to Jonathan Okamura, "the cultural basis of Japanese American ethnic identity is Japanese American culture, not Japanese culture—and certainly not the Japanese culture brought to Hawai'i by the immigrant generation. Japanese American culture has developed over the generations beginning especially with the *nisei* second generation as they were acculturated into American beliefs, values, and norms by their education in Hawaii's public schools and as they socialized with their peers from other ethnic groups. With the continuing development and changes in their culture in Hawai'i, Japanese Americans certainly have become less culturally Japanese (for example, language, religion, and traditional practices), but there still remains a clear affirmation of being Japanese American" (Okamura 2008: 131).

17. See also Ogawa (1973).

18. While later-generation Japanese Americans also note that they might be living lives similar to Japanese relatives had their ancestors not emigrated, the generational distance in addition to the wartime experience in the United States make this connection less concrete.

## CONCLUSION

1. Short tourist trips, too, in and of themselves do not necessarily demonstrate diasporic connections. An example that illustrates this point is the Japanese American Leadership Delegation, which brings Japanese Americans to Japan annually for about ten days to meet with Japanese government and business leaders (see Takeda 2012, forthcoming 2016, Yamashiro 2015).

## APPENDIX A — METHODOLOGY OF STUDYING JAPANESE AMERICAN EXPERIENCES IN TOKYO

1. In this study I use "migrant" and "international migrant" interchangeably to refer to someone who changes her or his country of residence. While people who move for less than one year are also considered international migrants, I focused on people living in Japan or who planned to live in Japan for at least one year for reasons described above. See United Nations (2013).

2. Through a friend stationed in the Tokyo area in the US Air Force, I also met and interviewed several US citizens of Japanese ancestry in the US military. These interviews were helpful to my research because many of them turned out to have been raised internationally, highlighting for me the importance of focusing on Japanese Americans who were born and raised in the United States as people who had internalized one way of thinking about Japaneseness and were encountering a new form in Japan.

3. While the chapter is officially the "Tokyo" chapter, since it is the only chapter within Japan, within Tokyo it is referred to simply as "JACL" and within the United States it is referred to as the "Japan" chapter.

4. The first delegation went to Tokyo in 2000, followed by annual delegations since 2002. The program was proposed by Japanese Americans and received funding from the Japanese Ministry of Foreign Affairs (MOFA) to establish the first delegation. Since 2003 the Japan Foundation Center for Global Partnership (CGP) has also been a financial sponsor. On the US side, delegate pre-departure orientations have been held at the Japanese American National Museum in Los Angeles since around 2010 and the US Japan Council (USJC) has co-sponsored with the CGP a JALD symposium in Japan as part of the trip. The USJC along with the Japanese Embassy and Consulates General in the United States assists in the processing of JALD applications and recommendation of candidates to MOFA, that makes the final decisions about delegates. See Takeda (2012, forthcoming 2016).

5. Interviews with other foreigners included primarily white Americans, an African American, a white Canadian, a white Australian, an Australian of African descent, and a Canadian of Japanese and European ancestry.

6. A couple of times, I experienced cases of mistaken identity. During my first year of fieldwork and interviewing, it turned out that another young female Japanese American researcher was in the Tokyo area studying Japanese Americans in Japan. Once I made arrangements to interview someone who said his friend had told him about me and my research and it was not until we met in person that I realized that he thought that I was her.

7. The majority of Japanese Americans have ancestral ties to southwestern Japan, as prewar immigrants in the late eighteenth and early nineteenth centuries largely originated from Hiroshima, Wakayama, Kumamoto, and Yamaguchi prefectures. Postwar immigration since the 1950s has been more urban and varied, but in smaller numbers.

# Glossary

| | |
|---|---|
| *gaijin/gaikokujin* | foreigner (less polite/polite forms) |
| *hiragana* | Japanese alphabet used with *kanji* in the majority of Japanese writing |
| *issei* | first generation emigrants from Japan |
| *kanji* | Chinese characters commonly used for Japanese names |
| *katakana* | Japanese alphabet used to denote foreign words |
| *kikokushijo* | Japanese returnees |
| *koseki* | family registry |
| *meishi* | business cards |
| *nihonjin* | mainstream Japanese people in Japan |
| *nikkeijin* | the descendents of Japanese emigrants |
| *nisei* | second generation, children of emigrants from Japan |
| *romaji* | Japanese written in roman letters |
| *sansei* | third generation, grandchildren of emigrants from Japan |
| *shin-issei* | "new" postwar wave first generation emigrants from Japan |
| *shin-nisei* | "new" postwar wave second generation, children of emigrants from Japan |

# Bibliography

Abkowitz, Alyssa. 2015. "China Is Now the Top Source of Foreign Tourists to Japan." *Wall Street Journal*, December 2. Accessed February 29, 2016. http://blogs.wsj.com/chinarealtime/2015/12/02/china-is-now-the-top-source-of-foreign-tourists-to-japan.

Abu-Lughod, Lila. 1991. "Writing Against Culture." In *Recapturing Anthropology: Working in the Present*, edited by Richard G. Fox, 137–162. Santa Fe: School of American Research Press.

Adachi, Nobuko, ed. 2006. *Japanese Diasporas: Unsung Pasts, Conflicting Presents, and Uncertain Futures*. London and New York: Routledge.

Alba, Richard D., and Victor Nee. 2003. *Remaking the American Mainstream: Assimilation and Contemporary Immigration*. Cambridge, MA: Harvard University Press.

Ali-Khan, Sarah E., Tomasz Krakowski, Rabia Tahir, and Abdallah S. Daar. 2011. "The Use of Race, Ethnicity and Ancestry in Human Genetic Research." *Hugo J* 5: 47–63.

Ang, Ien. 2001. *On Not Speaking Chinese: Living between Asia and the West*. London and New York: Routledge.

Appadurai, Arjun. 1996. *Modernity at Large: Cultural Dimensions of Globalization*. Minneapolis: University of Minnesota Press.

Asakawa, Gil. 2015. *Being Japanese American: A JA Sourcebook for Nikkei, Hapa . . . & Their Friends*. Second edition. Berkeley, CA: Stone Bridge Press.

Azuma, Eiichiro. 2005. *Between Two Empires: Race, History, and Transnationalism in Japanese America*. New York: Oxford.

———. 2009. "Brokering Race, Culture, and Citizenship: Japanese Americans in Occupied Japan and Postwar National Inclusion." *Journal of American-East Asian Relations* 16 (3): 183–211.

Bachnik, Jane M. 1994. "Uchi/Soto: Challenging Our Conceptualizations of Self, Social Order, and Language." In *Situated Meaning: Inside and Outside in Japanese Self, Society, and Language*, edited by Jane M. Bachnik and Charles J. Quinn Jr., 3–37. Princeton, NJ: Princeton University Press.

Banton, Michael. 2002. *The International Politics of Race*. Cambridge: Polity.

Barth, Fredrik. 1969. "Introduction." In *Ethnic Groups and Boundaries: The Social Organization of Culture Difference*, edited by Fredrik Barth, 9–38. Boston: Little, Brown and Company.

Basch, Linda, Nina Glick Schiller, and Christina Szanton Blanc. 1994. *Nations Unbound: Transnational Projects, Postcolonial Predicaments, and Deterritorialized Nation-States.* Langhorne, PA: Gordon and Breach.

Bashi, Vilna. 2004. "Globalized Anti-blackness: Transnationalizing Western Immigration Law, Policy, and Practice." *Ethnic and Racial Studies* 27 (4): 584–606.

Befu, Harumi. 2002. "Globalization as Human Dispersal: Nikkei in the World." In *New Worlds, New Lives: Globalization and People of Japanese Descent in the Americas and from Latin America in Japan*, edited by Lane Ryo Hirabayashi, Akemi Kikumura-Yano, and James A. Hirabayashi, 5–18. Stanford, CA: Stanford University Press.

———. 2010. "Japanese Transnational Migration in Time and Space: An Historical Overview." In *Japanese and Nikkei at Home and Abroad*, edited by Nobuko Adachi, 31–49. Amherst, NY: Cambria Press.

Bonilla-Silva, Eduardo. 1997. "Rethinking Racism: Toward a Structural Interpretation." *American Sociological Review* 62 (3): 465–480.

Bonnett, Alastair. 2004. *The Idea of the West: Culture, Politics and History.* Houndmils [England]; New York: Palgrave Macmillan.

Boylan, Dan. 1985. "Postwar Booms." In *Kanyaku Imin: A Hundred Years of Japanese Life in Hawaii*, edited by Leonard Lueras, 65–69. Honolulu: International Savings and Loan Association Ltd.

Braziel, Jana Evans. 2008. *Diaspora: An Introduction.* Malden, MA.: Blackwell Pub.

Brodkin, Karen. 1994. *How Jews Became White Folks and What That Says about Race in America.* New Brunswick, NJ: Rutgers University Press.

Brubaker, Rogers. 2002. "Ethnicity Without Groups." *European Journal of Sociology* 43 (2): 163–189.

———. 2005. "The 'Diaspora' Diaspora." *Ethnic and Racial Studies* 28 (1): 1–19.

Bruner, Edward. 1996. "Tourism in Ghana: The Representation of Slavery and the Return of the Black Diaspora." *American Anthropologist* 98 (2): 290–304.

Burgess, Chris. 2012. "'It's Better If They Speak Broken Japanese': Language as a Pathway or an Obstacle to Citizenship in Japan?" In *Language and Citizenship in Japan*, edited by Nanette Gottlieb, 37–57. London and New York: Routledge.

Business Development Center Tokyo. "Business Opportunities in Tokyo." Tokyo Metropolitan Government. Accessed January 8, 2016. http://www.bdc-tokyo.org/en/opportunities/index.html.

Carter, Mitzi Uehara. 2014. "Mixed Race Okinawans and Their Obscure In-Betweeness." *Journal of Intercultural Studies* 35 (6): 646–661.

Castillo, Walbert. 2015. "Asian-American Students Share Their Struggles in #MyBananaStory." *USA Today College*, February 27. http://college.usatoday.com/2015/02/27/asian-american-students-share-their-struggles-in-mybananastory.

Castles, Stephen, and Mark J. Miller. 1993. *The Age of Migration: International Population Movements in the Modern World.* New York: Guilford Press.

Chin, Christina B. 2012. "Hoops, History, and Crossing Over: Boundary Making and Community Building in Japanese American Youth Basketball Leagues." Ph.D. Dissertation Sociology, UCLA.

Chinen, Karleen, and Arnold Hiura, eds. 1997. *From Bento to Mixed Plate: Americans of Japanese Ancestry in Multicultural Hawai`i.* Los Angeles: Japanese American National Museum.

Chuh, Kandice, and Karen Shimakawa, eds. 2001. *Orientations: Mapping Studies in the Asian Diaspora*. Durham, NC: Duke University Press.

Cobas, José A., Jorge Duany, and Joe R. Feagin. 2009. *How the United States Racializes Latinos: White Hegemony and Its Consequences*. Boulder, CO: Paradigm.

Cohen, Robin. 1997. *Global Diasporas: An Introduction*. Seattle: University of Washington Press.

Connor, Walker. 1986. "The Impact of Homelands upon Diasporas." In *Modern Diasporas in International Politics*, edited by Gabriel Sheffer. London: Croom Helm.

Cook-Martín, David, and Anahí Viladrich. 2008. "The Problem with Similarity: Ethnic-Affinity Migrants in Spain." *Journal of Ethnic and Migration Studies* 35 (1): 151–170.

Cooley, Charles Horton. 1902. *Human Nature and the Social Order*. New York: Charles Scribner's Sons.

Cornell, Stephen E., and Douglas Hartmann. 1998. *Ethnicity and Race: Making Identities in a Changing World*, Sociology for a New Century. Thousand Oaks, CA.: Pine Forge Press.

Cornell, Stephen E., and Douglas Hartmann. 2007. *Ethnicity and Race: Making Identities in a Changing World*. Second edition. Sociology for a New Century. Thousand Oaks, CA.: Pine Forge Press, an Imprint of Sage Publication.

Cotterill, Simon. 2011. "Documenting Urban Indigeneity: TOKYO Ainu and the 2011 Survey on the Living Conditions of Ainu outside Hokkaido." *Asia-Pacific Journal* 9 (45).

Creighton, Millie R. 1997. "Soto Others and Uchi Others: Imaging Racial Diversity, Imagining Homogeneous Japan." In *Japan's Minorities: The Illusion of Homogeneity*, edited by Michael Weiner, 211–238. London and New York: Routledge.

Dale, Peter N. 1986. *The Myth of Japanese Uniqueness*. London and Sydney: Croom Helm.

Daniel, G. Reginald, Laura Kina, Wei Ming Dariotis, and Camilla Fojas. 2014. "Emerging Paradigms in Critical Mixed Race Studies." *Journal of Critical Mixed Race Studies* 1 (1): 6–65.

Dariotis, Wei Ming. 2003. "Hapas: The Emerging Community of Multiethnic and Multiracial APAs." In *The New Face of Asian Pacific America: Numbers, Diversity & Change in the 21st Century*, edited by Eric Lai and Dennis Arguelles, 113–121. San Francisco: AsianWeek with UCLA's Asian American Studies Center Press.

Daruma no Gakko. 2015. Accessed September 8, 2015. http://daruma-no-gakko.org/faq.

Day, Iyko. 2016. *Alien Capital: Asian Racialization and the Logic of Settler Colonial Capitalism*. Durham, NC: Duke University Press.

Denzin, Norman K., and Yvonna S. Lincoln. 2003. *Collecting and Interpreting Qualitative Materials*. Second edition. Thousand Oaks, CA: Sage.

Dirlik, Arif. 1999. "Asians on the Rim: Transnational Capital and Local Community in the Making of Contemporary Asian America." In *Across the Pacific: Asian Americans and Globalization*, edited by Evelyn Hu-DeHart, 29–60. Philadelphia: Temple University Press.

Doi, Takeo. 1973. *The Anatomy of Dependence*. Translated by John Bester. Tokyo: Kodansha International.

Donahue, Ray. T. 2002. "Guideposts for Exploring Japaneseness." In *Exploring Japaneseness: On Japanese Enactments of Culture and Consciousness*, edited by Ray T. Donahue, 3–27. Westport, CT: Ablex Publishing.

Dufoix, Stéphane. 2008. *Diasporas*. Berkeley: University of California Press.

Dung, Steven, Dianne Fukami, and Gayle K. Yamada. 2006. *The Spirit of Taiko*. Bridge Media, Inc.

Edles, Laura Desfor. 2004. "Rethinking 'Race,' 'Ethnicity' and 'Culture': Is Hawai'i the 'Model Minority' State?" *Ethnic and Racial Studies* 27 (1): 37–68.

Efird, Rob. 2010. "Distant Kin: Japan's "War Orphans" and the Limits of Ethnicity." *Anthropological Quarterly* 83 (4): 805–838.

Espiritu, Yen Le. 1992. *Asian American Panethnicity: Bridging Institutions and Identities*. Philadelphia: Temple University Press.

Fackler, Martin. 2015. "Biracial Beauty Queen Challenges Japan's Self-Image." *New York Times*, May 29.

Favell, Adrian, Miriam Feldblum, and Michael Peter Smith. 2006. "The Human Face of Global Mobility: A Research Agenda." In *The Human Face of Global Mobility: International Highly Skilled Migration in Europe, North America and the Asia-Pacific*, edited by Michael Peter Smith and Adrian Favell, 1–28. New Brunswick, NJ: Transaction Press.

Feagin, Joe R., and Clairece Booher Feagin. 1999. *Racial and Ethnic Relations*. Sixth edition. Upper Saddle River, NJ: Prentice Hall.

Fitts, Robert K. 2012. *Wally Yonamine: The Man Who Changed Japanese Baseball*. Lincoln: University of Nebraska Press.

Folen, Alana, and Tina Ng. 2007. "The Hapa Project: How Multiracial Identity Crosses Oceans." Accessed February 27. http://www.soc.hawaii.edu/uhtoday/spring2007/j402/alanatina.html.

Foner, Nancy. 2005. *In a New Land: A Comparative View of Immigration*. New York: New York University Press.

Fox, Masahiko Murotani. 2005. *Found in Translation*. Japan and USA: TwinFox Production.

Fry, Rieko. 2009. "Politics of Education for Japanese Returnee Children." *Compare: A Journal of Comparative and International Education* 39 (3): 367–383.

Fujikane, Candace. 2000. "Sweeping Racism under the Rug of 'Censorship': The Controversy over Lois-Ann Yamanaka's Blu's Hanging." *Amerasia Journal* 26 (2): 158–194.

Fujikane, Candace, and Jonathan Y. Okamura, eds. 2000. *Whose Vision?: Asian Settler Colonialism in Hawaii*. *Amerasia Journal* 26 (2).

———. 2008. *Asian Settler Colonialism: From Local Governance to the Habits of Everyday Life in Hawai'i*. Honolulu: University of Hawai'i Press.

Fugikawa, Laura Sachiko. 2011. "Domestic Containment: Japanese Americans, Native Americans, and the Cultural Politics of Relocation." Ph.D. Dissertation, American Studies and Ethnicity, University of Southern California.

Fujita, Yuiko. 2009. *Cultural Migrants From Japan: Youth, Media, and Migration in New York and London*. Lanham, MD: Lexington Books.

Fukuoka, Yasunori. 2000. "Introduction: 'Japanese' and 'Non-Japanese.'" In *Lives of Young Koreans in Japan*, xxxviii. Melbourne: Trans Pacific Press.

Fukushima, Glen S. 1985. "Japanese Americans and US-Japan Relations." *Pacific Citizen*. January 4–11.

———. 2002, "Japanese Americans in the Japanese Media." *Rafu Shimpo*. April 12.
———. 2015. "Glen S. Fukushima." Accessed December 1, 2015. http://glenfukushima.com.
Gans, Herbert J. 1979. "Symbolic Ethnicity: The Future of Ethnic Groups and Cultures in America." *Ethnic and Racial Studies* 2 (1): 1–20.
Gee, Deborah, Herb Wong, Asian Women United of California, Pacific Productions, KQED-TV (Television station: San Francisco, CA), and National Asian American Telecommunications Association. 1995. *Slaying the Dragon*. San Francisco, CA: National Asian American Telecommunications Assn., videorecording.
Geertz, Clifford. 1973. *The Interpretation of Cultures: Selected Essays*. New York: Basic Books.
Giddens, Anthony. 1990. *The Consequences of Modernity*. Stanford, CA: Stanford University Press.
Goffman, Erving. 1959. *The Presentation of Self in Everyday Life*. New York: Doubleday.
Goodman, Roger. 1990. *Japan's "International Youth": The Emergence of a New Class of Schoolchildren*. Oxford and New York: Clarendon Press and Oxford University Press.
Gordon, Milton Myron. 1964. *Assimilation in American Life: The Role of Race, Religion, and National Origins*. New York: Oxford University Press.
Gottlieb, Nanette. 2005. *Language and Society in Japan, Contemporary Japanese Society*. New York: Cambridge University Press.
Graves, Donna, and Gail Dubrow. "California Japantowns." Accessed November 20, 2013. http://www.californiajapantowns.org/index.html.
Guibernau, Montserrat. 2007. *The Identity of Nations*. Cambridge: Polity Press.
"Hafu the film." Accessed February 21, 2016. http://hafufilm.com/en/about/meaning-of-the-word-hafu.
Hagiwara, Shigeru. 2004. "Nihon no terebi kōkoku ni arawareru gaikoku imēji no dōkō [Trends in the appearance of foreign images in Japanese television commercials]." Keio *Media Communication* 54: 5–26.
Hall, Christine C. Iijima, and Trude I. Cooke Turner. 2001. "The Diversity of Biracial Individuals: Asian-White and Asian-Minority Biracial Identity." In *The Sum of Our Parts: Mixed Heritage Asian Americans*, edited by Teresa Williams-Leon and Cynthia L. Nakashima, 81–91. Philadelphia: Temple University Press.
Hall, Ronald E. 2003. "Skin Color as Post-Colonial Hierarchy: A Global Strategy for Conflict Resolution." *Journal of Psychology* 137 (1): 41–53.
Hall, Stuart. 1994. "Cultural Identity and Diaspora." In *Colonial Discourses and Postcolonial Theory*, edited by Patrick Williams and Laura Chrisman, 392–403. New York: Columbia University Press.
Hamabata, Matthews Masayuki. 1990. *Crested Kimono: Power and Love in the Japanese Business Family*. Ithaca, NY: Cornell University Press.
Hawaii Nikkei History Editorial Board. 1998. *Japanese Eyes, American Heart: Personal Reflections of Hawaii's World War II Nisei Soldiers*. Honolulu: Tendai Educational Foundation: Distributed by University of Hawai'i Press.
Hawai'i Tourism Authority. 2011. *Annual Report to the Hawaii State Legislature*. Honolulu: Hawai'i Tourism Authority.
Hayashida, Cullen Tadao. 1976. "Identity, Race and the Blood Ideology of Japan." Ph.D. Dissertation, Sociology, University of Washington.

Hays, Sharon. 1996. *The Cultural Contradictions of Motherhood*. New Haven and London: Yale University Press.

Hazama, Dorothy Ochiai, and Jane Okamoto Komeji. 1986. *Okage Same De: The Japanese in Hawai'i 1885–1985*. Honolulu: Bess Press.

Hein, Laura, and Mark Selden. 2003. "Culture, Power, and Identity in Contemporary Okinawa." In *Islands of Discontent: Okinawan Responses to Japanese and American Power*, edited by Laura Hein and Mark Selden, 1–35. Lanham, MD: Rowman & Littlefield.

Hoeffel, Elizabeth M., Sonya Rastogi, Myoung Ouk Kim, and Hasan Shahid. 2012. *The Asian Population: 2010*. Edited by Economics and Statistics Administration U.S. Department of Commerce. Washington, DC: U.S. Census Bureau.

Holsapple, Stephen. 1999. *Children of the Camps*. San Francisco: Center for Asian American Media.

Houston, H. Rika. 1997. "'Between Two Cultures': A Testimony." *Amerasia Journal* 23 (1): 149–154.

Houston, Velina Hasu. 1991. "The Past Meets the Future: A Cultural Essay." *Amerasia Journal* 17 (1): 53–56.

Hsu, Chien-Jung. 2014. *The Construction of National Identity in Taiwan's Media, 1896–2012*. Leiden: Brill.

Hyodo, Hirosuke. 2013. "The Era of Dual Life: The Shin-Issei, the Japanese Contemporary Migrants to the U.S." *Electronic Journal of Contemporary Japanese Studies* 13 (1).

Ichioka, Yuji. 1988. *The Issei: The World of the First Generation Japanese Immigrants 1885–1924*. New York: The Free Press.

Iijima, Mariko, and Shun Ohno. 2010. "Lives, Citizenships and Identities of Nikkei 'Return' Migrants from the Philippines: The Results of the Nationwide Questionnaire Survey Conducted in Japan." *Bulletin of Kyushu University Asia Center* 4: 35–54.

Inada, Lawson Fusao. 2000. *Only What We Could Carry: The Japanese American Internment Experience*. Berkeley and San Francisco, CA: Heyday Books; California Historical Society.

Ishida, Hiroshi, and David H. Slater. 2010. *Social Class in Contemporary Japan: Structures, Sorting and Strategies*. The Nissan Institute/Routledge Japanese Studies Series. London and New York: Routledge.

Ishida, Takeshi. 1973. *Heiwa to Henkaku no Ronri* [*The Logic of Peace and Change*]. Tokyo: Renga Shobou.

Itoh, Mayumi. 2010. *Japanese War Orphans in Manchuria: Forgotten Victims of World War II*. First edition. New York: Palgrave Macmillan.

Jacobson, Matthew Frye. 1998. *Whiteness of a Different Color: European Immigrants and the Alchemy of Race*. Cambridge, MA: Harvard University Press.

Jain, Sonali. 2010. "For Love and Money: Second-Generation Indian Americans 'Return' to India." Migration Information Source. Accessed July 11, 2011. http://www.migrationinformation.org/Feature/display.cfm?ID=804.

———. 2011. "The Rights of 'Return': Ethnic Identities in the Workplace among Second-Generation Indian-American Professionals in the Parental Homeland." *Journal of Ethnic and Migration Studies* 37 (9): 1313–1330.

———. 2012. "For Love and Money: Second-Generation Indian-Americans 'Return' to India." *Ethnic and Racial Studies* 36 (5): 896–914.
Jenkins, Richard. 2004. *Social Identity*. Second edition. London and New York: Routledge.
Jin, Michael. 2013. "Beyond Two Homelands: Migration and Transnationalism of Japanese Americans in the Pacific, 1930–1955." Ph.D. Dissertation, History, University of California, Santa Cruz.
Joseph, Tiffany D. 2015. *Race on the Move: Brazilian Migrants and the Global Reconstruction of Race*. Stanford, CA: Stanford University Press.
Kang, Miliann. 2000. "Researching One's Own: Negotiating Co-ethnicity in the Field." In *Cultural Compass: Ethnographic Explorations of Asian America*, edited by Martin F. Manalansan IV, 38–48. Philadelphia: Temple University Press.
Kanno, Yasuko. 2000. "Kikokushijo as Bicultural." *International Journal of Intercultural Relations* 24 (3): 361–382.
Kashima, Tetsuden. 2003. *Judgment without Trial: Japanese American Imprisonment during World War II*. Seattle: University of Washington Press.
Kataoka, Hiroko C., Yasuko Koshiyama, and Setsue Shibata. 2008. "Japanese and English Language Ability of Students at Supplementary Japanese Schools in the United States." In *Teaching Chinese, Japanese, and Korean Heritage Language Students*, edited by Kimmi Kondo-Brown and James Dean Brown, 47–76. New York and London: Lawrence Erlbaum Associates.
Kauanui, J. Kēhaulani. 2008. *Hawaiian Blood: Colonialism and the Politics of Sovereignty and Indigeneity, Narrating Native Histories*. Durham, NC: Duke University Press.
Kibria, Nazli. 2002a. *Becoming Asian American: Second-Generation Chinese and Korean American Identities*. Baltimore: Johns Hopkins University Press.
———. 2002b. "Of Blood, Belonging, and Homeland Trips: Transnationalism and Identity Among Second-Generation Chinese and Korean Americans." In *The Changing Face of Home: The Transnational Lives of the Second Generation*, edited by Peggy Levitt and Mary C. Waters, 295–311. New York: Russell Sage Foundation.
Kidder, Louise H. 1992. "Requirements for Being 'Japanese': Stories of Returnees." *International Journal of Intercultural Relations* 16: 383–393.
Kim, Nadia Y. 2008. *Imperial Citizens: Koreans and Race from Seoul to LA*. Stanford, CA: Stanford University Press.
———. 2009. "Finding Our Way Home: Korean Americans, 'Homeland' Trips, and Cultural Foreignness." In *Diasporic Homecomings: Ethnic Return Migration in Comparative Perspective*, edited by Takeyuki Tsuda, 305–324. Stanford, CA: Stanford University Press.
Kimura, Yukiko. 1988. *Issei: Japanese Immigrants in Hawaii*. Honolulu: University of Hawai'i Press.
Kindaichi, Haruhiko. 1988. *The Japanese Language*. First edition, Tuttle Language Library. Rutland, VT: C. E. Tuttle.
King, Russell, and Anastasia Christou. 2010a. "Diaspora, Migration, and Transnationalism: Insights from the Study of Second-Generation 'Returnees.'" In *Diaspora and Transnationalism: Concepts, Theories and Methods*, edited by Rainer Bauböck and Thomas Faist, 167–183. Amsterdam: Amsterdam University Press.

———. 2010b. "Cultural Geographies of Counter-Diasporic Migration: Perspectives from the Study of Second-Generation 'Returnees' to Greece." *Population, Space and Place* 16 (2): 103–119.

———. 2011. "Of Counter-Diaspora and Reverse Transnationalism: Return Mobilities to and from the Ancestral Homeland." *Mobilities* 6 (4): 451–466.

King-O'Riain, Rebecca Chiyoko. 2006. *Pure Beauty: Judging Race in Japanese American Beauty Pageants.* Minneapolis: University of Minnesota Press.

King-O'Riain, Rebecca C., Stephen Small, Minelle Mahtani, Miri Song, and Paul Spickard, eds. 2014. *Global Mixed Race.* New York: NYU Press.

Kingston, Maxine Hong. 1976. *The Woman Warrior: Memoirs of a Girlhood among Ghosts.* First edition. New York: Knopf: distributed by Random House.

Kitano, Harry H. L. 1993. *Generations and Identity: The Japanese American.* Needham Heights, MA: Ginn Press.

Koenig, Barbara A., Sandra Soo-Jin Lee, and Sarah S. Richardson. 2008. *Revisiting Race in a Genomic Age.* Rutgers Series in Medical Anthropology. New Brunswick, NJ: Rutgers University Press.

Komisarof, Adam. 2012. *At Home Abroad: The Contemporary Western Experience in Japan.* Chiba, Japan: Reitaku University Press.

Kondo, Dorinne. 1990. *Crafting Selves: Power, Gender, and Discourses of Identity in a Japanese Workplace.* Chicago: University of Chicago Press.

Kulu, Hill. 2001. "Policy towards the Diaspora and Ethnic (Return) Migration: An Estonian Case." *GeoJournal* 51 (3): 135–143.

Kurashige, Lon. 2002. *Japanese American Celebration and Conflict: A History of Ethnic Identity and Festival, 1934–1990.* Berkeley: University of California Press.

Kurotani, Sawa. 2005. *Home Away from Home: Japanese Corporate Wives in the United States.* Durham, NC: Duke University Press.

Lake, Obiagele. 1995. "Toward a Pan-African Identity: Diaspora African Repatriates in Ghana." *Anthropological Quarterly* 68 (1): 21–36.

Lamont, Michele. 1992. *Money, Morals, and Manners: The Culture of the French and the American Upper-Middle Class.* Chicago: University of Chicago Press.

Lamont, Michele, and Virag Molnar. 2002. "The Study of Boundaries in the Social Sciences." *Annual Review of Sociology* 28: 167–195.

Leach, Emily. 2007. "After 15 Years, Hapa Issues Forum Disbands." *AsianWeek*, September 15, 2007. Accessed October 17, 2007. http://asianweek.com/2007/09/15/after-15-years-hapa-issues-forum-disbands/#.

Lee, Changsoo. 1981. "The Legal Status of Koreans in Japan." In *Koreans in Japan: Ethnic Conflict and Accomodation*, edited by Changsoo Lee and George DeVos, 133–158. Berkeley: University of California Press.

Lee, Helene Kim. 2009. "Bittersweet Homecomings: Ethnic Identity Construction in the Korean Diaspora." Ph.D. Dissertation, Sociology, UCSB.

Lee, Robert G. 1999. *Orientals: Asian Americans in Popular Culture*, Asian American History and Culture. Philadelphia: Temple University Press.

Levitt, Peggy. 2002. "The Ties That Change: Relations to the Ancestral Home over the Life Cycle." In *The Changing Face of Home: The Transnational Lives of the Second Generation*, edited by Peggy Levitt and Mary C. Waters, 123–144. New York: Russell Sage Foundation.

Levitt, Peggy, and Mary C. Waters. 2002. *The Changing Face of Home: the Transnational Lives of the Second Generation.* New York: Russell Sage Foundation.
lewallen, ann-elise. 2008. "Indigenous at last! Ainu Grassroots Organizing and the Indigenous Peoples Summit in Ainu Mosir." *Asia-Pacific Journal* 48 (6).
Lie, John. 2001. *Multiethnic Japan.* Cambridge, MA: Harvard University Press.
Life, Regge. 1995. *Doubles: Japan and America's Intercultural Children.* East Chatham, NY: Global Film Network.
Lim, Youngmi. 2009. "Reinventing Korean Roots and *Zainichi* Routes: The Invisible Diaspora among Naturalized Japanese of Korean Descent." In *Diaspora without Homeland: Being Korean in Japan,* edited by Sonia Ryang and John Lie, 81–106. Berkeley: University of California Press.
Lipsitz, George. 2006. *The Possessive Investment in Whiteness: How White People Profit From Identity Politics.* Rev. and expanded ed. Philadelphia: Temple University Press.
Lise, Marcia Yumi. 2011. *The Hafu Project: Photography and Research.* Pamphlet.
López, Ian F. Haney. 1996. *White by Law: The Legal Construction of Race.* New York: NYU Press.
Louie, Andrea. 2004. *Chineseness across Borders: Renegotiating Chinese Identities in China and the United States.* Durham, NC: Duke University Press.
Lowe, Lisa. 1996. *Immigrant Acts: On Asian American Cultural Politics.* Durham, NC: Duke University Press.
Maher, John C., and Gaynor Macdonald, eds. 1995. *Diversity in Japanese Culture and Language.* New York: Kegan Paul International.
Maira, Sunaina. 2002. *Desis in the House: Indian American Youth Culture in New York City.* Philadelphia: Temple University Press.
Manyika, Sarah. 2003. "Oyinbo." In *Problematizing Blackness,* edited by Percy Claude Hintzen and Jean Muteba Rahier, 65–83. New York and London: Routledge.
McConnell, David L. 2000. *Importing Diversity: Inside Japan's JET Program.* Berkeley: University of California Press.
McIntosh, Peggy. 2007. "White Privilege: Unpacking the Invisible Knapsack." In *Race, Class, and Gender in the United States,* edited by Paula S. Rothenberg, 177–182. New York: Worth Publishers.
Mead, George Herbert. 1934. *Mind, Self, and Society.* Chicago: University of Chicago Press.
Mills, Charles W. 2008. "Global White Supremacy." In *White Privilege,* edited by Paula S. Rothenberg, 97–104. New York: Worth Publishers.
Min, Pyong Gap. 2002. *The Second Generation: Ethnic Identity Among Asian Americans.* Critical Perspectives on Asian Pacific Americans Series. Walnut Creek, CA: AltaMira Press.
Minter, William. 2005. "Invisible Hierarchies: Africa, Race, and Continuities in the World Order." *Science and Society* 69 (3): 449–457.
Miyamoto, Kazuo. 1957. *A Nisei Discovers Japan.* Tokyo: Japan Times Press.
Morimoto, Toyotomi. 1997. *Japanese Americans and Cultural Continuity: Maintaining Language and Heritage.* New York: Garland.
Moriyama, Alan Takeo. 1985. *Imingaisha: Japanese Emigration Companies and Hawaii.* Honolulu: University of Hawai'i Press.

Morris-Suzuki, Tessa. 1998. *Re-inventing Japan: Time, Space, Nation*. Armonk, NY: M. E. Sharpe.

Mouer, Ross E., and Yoshio Sugimoto. 1986. *Images of Japanese Society: A Study in the Structure of Social Reality*. London: Kegan Paul.

Munz, Rainer, and Rainer Ohliger, eds. 2003. *Diasporas and Ethnic Migrants: Germany, Israel and Post-Soviet Successor States in Comparative Perspective*. London: Frank Cass.

Mura, David. 1992. *Turning Japanese: Memoirs of a Sansei*. First Anchor Books edition. New York: Anchor Books.

Murphy-Shigematsu, Stephen. 2000. "Identities of Multiethnic People in Japan." In *Japan and Global Migration: Foreign Workers and the Advent of a Multicultural Society*, edited by Mike Douglass and Glenda S. Roberts, 196–216. London and New York: Routledge.

———. 2001. "Multiethnic Lives and Monoethnic Myths: American-Japanese Amerasians in Japan." In *The Sum of Our Parts: Mixed Heritage Asian Americans*, edited by Teresa Williams-Léon and Cynthia L. Nakashima, 207–216. Philadelphia: Temple University Press.

———. 2012. *When Half is Whole: Multiethnic Asian American Identities, Asian America*. Stanford, CA: Stanford University Press.

Nakane, Chie. 1970. *Japanese Society*. Berkeley: University of California Press.

Nakashima, Cynthia L. 1992. "An Invisible Monster: The Creation and Denial of Mixed-Race People in America." In *Racially Mixed People in America*, edited by Maria P. P. Root, 162–178. Newbury Park, CA: Sage.

Nakashima, Cynthia, Lily Anne Yumi Welty, and Duncan Williams. 2013. Visible and Invisible: A Hapa Japanese American History. Exhibit. Japanese American National Museum.

Nakashima, Daniel A. 2001. "A Rose by Any Other Name: Names, Multiracial/Multiethnic People, and the Politics of Identity." In *The Sum of Our Parts: Mixed Heritage Asian Americans*, edited by Teresa Williams-Leon and Cynthia L. Nakashima, 111–119. Philadelphia: Temple University Press.

Narayan, Kirin. 1993. "How Native is a 'Native' Anthropologist?" *American Anthropologist* 95: 671–686.

Nguyen-Akbar, Mytoan, 2016. "Finding the American Dream Abroad? Narratives of Return among 1.5 and Second Generation Vietnamese American Skilled Migrants in Vietnam." *Journal of Vietnamese Studies*. 11 (23): 96–121.

Nguyen-Akbar, Mytoan. 2014. "The Tensions of Diasporic 'Return' Migration: How Class and Money Create Distance in the Vietnamese Transnational Family." *Journal of Contemporary Ethnography* 43: 176–201.

Nisei Survey Committee. 1939. *The Nisei: A Study of Their Life in Japan*. Tokyo: Keisen Girls' School.

Nomura, Art. 2006. *Finding Home*. DVD. Los Angeles: Arrupe Productions.

O'Shea, James. 2014. "Diaspora Minister Wants Irish Emigrants to Return Home." Accessed February 17, 2016. http://www.irishcentral.com/about.

Odo, Franklin. 2004. *No Sword to Bury: Japanese Americans in Hawai'i during World War II*. Philadelphia: Temple University Press.

Ogasawara, Yuko. 1998. *Office Ladies and Salaried Men: Power, Gender, and Work in Japanese Companies*. Berkeley: University of California Press.

Ogawa, Dennis. 1973. *Jan Ken Po: The World of Hawaii's Japanese Americans*. Honolulu: Obun Printing.

Oguma, Eiji. 1995. *Tan'itsu Minzoku Shinwa no Kigen* [*The Myth of the Homogeneous Nation*]. Tokyo: Shin'yousha.

———. 2002. *A Genealogy of 'Japanese' Self-images*. Melbourne: Trans Pacific Press.

Ohno, Shun. 2007. "Regaining "Japaneseness": The Politics of Recognition by the Philippine Nikkeijin1." *Asian Studies Review* 31 (3): 243–260.

Oishi, Nana. 2012. "The Limits of Immigration Policies: The Challenges of Highly Skilled Migration in Japan." *American Behavioral Scientist* 56 (8): 1080–1100.

Okahata, James. 1971. *A History of Japanese in Hawaii*. Honolulu: United Japanese Society of Hawai'i.

Okamura, Jonathan Y. 1980. "Aloha Kanaka Me Ke Aloha 'Aina: Local Culture and Society in Hawai'i." *Amerasia Journal* 7 (2): 119–137.

———. 1994. "Why There Are No Asian Americans in Hawai'i: The Continuing Significance of Local Identity." *Social Process in Hawai'i: The Political Economy of Hawai'i* 35: 161–178.

———. 2000. "Race Relations in Hawai'i during World War II: The Non-internment of Japanese Americans." *Amerasia Journal* 26 (2): 117–141.

———. 2002a. "Introduction: The Contemporary Japanese American Community in Hawai'i." *Social Process in Hawai'i* 41: ix–xviii.

———., ed. 2002b. *The Japanese American Contemporary Experience in Hawai'i. Social Process in Hawai'i* 41.

———. 2008. *Ethnicity and Inequality in Hawai'i*. Philadelphia: Temple University Press.

———. 2014. *From Race to Ethnicity: Interpreting Japanese American Experiences in Hawai'i*. Honolulu: University of Hawai'i Press.

Okihiro, Gary. 1991. *Cane Fires: The Anti-Japanese Movement in Hawaii, 1865–1945*. Philadelphia: Temple University Press.

Okimoto, Daniel I. 1971. *American in Disguise*. First edition. New York: Walker/Weatherhill.

Omi, Michael, and Howard Winant. 1994. *Racial Formation in the United States: From the 1960s to the 1990s*. Second edition. New York and London: Routledge.

Ono, Kent A., and Vincent N. Pham. 2009. *Asian Americans and the Media*. Cambridge; Malden, MA: Polity.

Osajima, Keith. 2007. "Internalized Racism." In *Race, Class, and Gender in the United States: An Integrated Study*, edited by Paula S. Rothenberg, 138–143. New York: Worth Publishers.

Osaki, Tomohiro. 2015. "Japan's Top Court Upholds Same-Name Rule for Married Couples, Overturns Remarriage Moratorium for Women." *Japan Times*, December 16. Accessed December 17, 2015. http://www.japantimes.co.jp/news/2015/12/16/national/crime-legal/japans-top-court-strikes-rules-divorcee-remarriage/#.VrVSPUKIIyo.

Overman, Stephenie. 1992. "The Right Package—Planning an International Compensation Policy—International Compensation." *HR Magazine*, July.

Palumbo-Liu, David. 1999. *Asian/American: Historical Crossings of a Racial Frontier.* Stanford, CA: Stanford University Press.

Panek, Mark. 2006. *Gaijin Yokozuna: A Biography of Chad Rowan.* Honolulu: University of Hawai'i Press.

Park, Robert E. 1914. "Racial Assimilation in Secondary Groups With Particular Reference to the Negro." *American Journal of Sociology* 19 (5): 606–623.

Parreñas, Rhacel S., and Lok C. D. Siu, eds. 2007. *Asian Diasporas: New Formations, New Conceptions.* Stanford, CA: Stanford University Press.

Patton, Michael Quinn. 1990. *Qualitative Evaluation and Research Methods.* Thousand Oaks, CA: Sage Publications.

Pease, Ben. 2008. "Japantown Atlas." Accessed November 20, 2013. http://japantownatlas.com.

Perez-Takagi, Lara, and Megumi Nishikura. 2013. *Hafu: The Mixed Race Experience in Japan.* DVD. 85 minutes.

Pollock, David C., and Ruth E. Van Reken. 2009. *Third Culture Kids: Growing Up Among Worlds.* Rev. ed. Boston: Nicholas Brealey Pub.

Portes, Alejandro, and Min Zhou. 1993. "The New Second Generation: Segmented Assimilation and Its Variants." *Annals of the American Academy of Political and Social Science* 530 (November): 74–96.

Prieler, Michael. 2010. "Othering, Racial Hierarchies and Identity Construction in Japanese Television Advertising." *International Journal of Cultural Studies* 13: 511–529.

Pukui, Mary Kawena, and Samuel H. Elbert. 1986a. haole. In *Hawaiian Dictionary.* Honolulu: University of Hawai'i Press.

———. 1986b. hapa. In *Hawaiian Dictionary.* Honolulu: University of Hawai'i Press.

———. 1986c. hapa haole. In *Hawaiian Dictionary.* Honolulu: University of Hawai'i Press.

Rabson, Steve. 2012. *The Okinawan Diaspora in Japan: Crossing the Borders Within.* Honolulu: University of Hawai'i Press.

Robertson, Jennifer. 2005. "Biopower: Blood, Kinship, and Eugenic Marriage." In *The Companion to the Anthropology of Japan,* edited by Jennifer Robertson, 329–354. Malden, MA and Oxford: Blackwell.

Rodriguez, Clara E. 2000. *Changing Race: Latinos, the Census, and the History of Ethnicity in the United States.* New York: New York University Press.

Rodriguez, Clara E., and Hector Cordero-Guzman. 1992. "Placing Race in Context." *Ethnic and Racial Studies* 15 (4): 523–541.

Rosa, John P. 2000. "Local Story: The Massie Case Narrative and the Cultural Production of Local Identity in Hawai'i." *Amerasia Journal* 26 (2): 93–115.

Roth, Joshua Hotaka. 2005. "Political and Cultural Perspectives on Japan's Insider Minorities." *Japan Focus* 3 (4).

Roth, Wendy D. 2012. *Race Migration: Latinos and the Cultural Transformation of Race.* Stanford, CA: Stanford University Press.

Rothenberg, Paula S. 2008. *White Privilege: Essential Readings on the Other Side of Racism.* Third ed. New York: Worth Publishers.

Royal, Charmaine D., John Novembre, Stephanie M. Fullerton, David B. Goldstein, Jeffrey C. Long, Michael J. Bamshad, and Andrew G. Clark. 2010. "Inferring Genetic

Ancestry: Opportunities, Challenges, and Implications." *American Journal of Human Genetics* 86 (5): 661–673.

Ryang, Sonia, ed. 2000. *Koreans in Japan: Critical Voices From the Margin*. London and New York: Routledge.

Safran, William. 1991. "Diasporas in Modern Societies: Myths of Homeland and Return." *Diaspora* 1 (1): 83–99.

Sakamoto, Takahiko. 1976. "Writing Systems in Japan." In *New Horizons in Reading*, edited by John E. Merritt, 244–249. Newark, DE: IRA.

Sakayori, Susan S. 2000. "Transcending Cultural Definitions: A Sense of Peace." M.A. Thesis, Teaching, School for International Training.

Sano, Iwao Peter. 1997. *One Thousand Days in Siberia: The Odyssey of a Japanese-American POW*. Lincoln: University of Nebraska Press.

Sassen, Saskia. 2001. *The Global City: New York, London, Tokyo*. Second edition. Princeton and Oxford: Princeton University Press.

Sato, Jonylle S. 1994. "Life in Wartime Japan: A Preliminary Study of Japanese American Experiences During the Second World War." M.A. Thesis, Asian Studies, University of Hawaii.

Sato, Kozue. 2009. "The Representation and Role of Mixed-Race 'Haafu' Models in Contemporary Japanese Female Fashion Magazines." Reconsidering "Race" as a Transnational Construction in Global Japan, Sophia University, Tokyo, November 14, 2009.

"Sawtelle Gets Official Japantown Designation." 2015. *Rafu Shimpo*. February 27.

Schaefer, Richard T. 2011. *Race and Ethnicity in the United States*. Sixth edition. Upper Saddle River, NJ: Prentice Hall.

Sekiguchi, Tomoko. 2002. "*Nikkei* Brazilians in Japan: The Ideology and Symbolic Context Faced by Children of This New Ethnic Minority." In *Exploring Japaneseness: On Japanese Enactments of Culture and Consciousness*, edited by Ray T. Donahue, 197–222. Westport, CT: Ablex Publishing.

Sellek, Yoko. 1997. "Nikkeijin: The Phenomenon of Return Migration." In *Japan's Minorities: The Illusion of Homogeneity*, edited by Michael Weiner, 178–210. London and New York: Routledge.

Seol, Dong-Hoon, and John D. Skrentny. 2009. "Ethnic Return Migration and Hierarchical Nationhood." *Ethnicities* 9 (2): 147–174.

Sheffer, Gabriel. 2003. *Diaspora Politics: At Home Abroad*. Cambridge and New York: Cambridge University Press.

Shibutani, Tamotsu. 1978. *The Derelicts of Company K: A Sociological Study of Demoralization*. Berkeley: University of California Press.

Shinagawa, Larry, Ying Wang, Chang Won Lee, and Yujie Chen. 2011. A Demographic Overview of Japanese Americans. Japanese American Citizens League and the Asian American Studies Program of the University of Maryland, College Park.

Shipper, Apichai W. 2002. "The Political Construction of Foreign Workers in Japan." *Critical Asian Studies* 34 (1): 41–68.

Short, John Rennie. 2001. *Global Dimensions: Space, Place, and the Contemporary World*. London: Reaktion Books/University of Chicago Press.

Siddle, Richard. 1997. "Ainu: Japan's Indigenous People." In *Japan's Minorities: The Illusion of Homogeneity*, edited by Michael Weiner, 17–49. London and New York: Routledge.

———. 2009. "The Ainu: Indigenous People of Japan." In *Japan's Minorities*, edited by Michael Weiner, 21–39. London and New York: Routledge.
Smits, Gregory. 1999. *Visions of Ryukyu: Identity and Ideology in Early-Modern Thought and Politics*. Honolulu: University of Hawai'i Press.
Song, Changzoo. 2009. "Brothers Only in Name: The Alienation and Identity Transformation of Korean Chinese Return Migrants in South Korea." In *Diasporic Homecomings*, edited by Takeyuki Tsuda, 281–304. Stanford, CA: Stanford University Press.
Spickard, Paul R. 1997. "What Must I Be?: Asian Americans and the Question of Multiethnic Identity." *Amerasia Journal* 23 (1): 43–60.
———. 2009. *Japanese Americans: The Formation and Transformations of an Ethnic Group*. Revised edition. New Brunswick, NJ: Rutgers University Press.
Spillman, Lyn. 2002. "Introduction: Culture and Cultural Sociology." In *Cultural Sociology*, edited by Lyn Spillman, 1–16. Oxford: Blackwell.
Statistics Bureau. 2016. Foreign National Residents by Nationality. Tokyo: Minstry of Internal Affairs and Communications.
Statistics Bureau of Japan. 2011. Population Count based on the 2010 Census Released. Tokyo: Statistics Bureau of Japan.
Statistics Bureau, Director-General for Policy Planning (Statistical Standards) & Statistical Research and Training Institute. 2012. 2-15 Foreigners by Prefectures (1920–2005). edited by Ministry of Internal Affairs and Communications. Tokyo.
———. 2013a. Migrants by Prefecture 1995-2011. edited by Ministry of Internal Affairs and Communications. Tokyo.
———. 2013b. Population by Prefecture (1920-2011). edited by Ministry of Internal Affairs and Communications. Tokyo.
Sugimoto, Yoshio. 2003. *An Introduction to Japanese Society*. Second edition. Cambridge: Cambridge University Press.
Swidler, Ann. 1986. "Culture in Action: Symbols and Strategies." *American Sociological Review* 51 (2): 273–286.
Tackett, Rachel. 2013. "Why Old Japanese Women Have Names in Katakana." *Rocket News 24*.
Takahashi, Jere. 1997. *Nisei/Sansei: Shifting Japanese American Identities and Politics*. Philadelphia: Temple University Press.
Takaki, Ronald. 1983. *Pau Hana: Life and Labor in Hawaii*. Honolulu: University of Hawai'i Press.
Takamori, Ayako. 2010. "Rethinking Japanese American 'Heritage' in the Homeland." *Critical Asian Studies* 42 (2): 217-238.
Takamori, Ayako. 2011. "Native Foreigners: Japanese Americans in Japan." Ph.D. Dissertation, Anthropology, New York University.
Takeda, Okiyoshi. 2012. "Japanese American Leadership Delegation Program: The Emergence of a New Network of Japanese Americans Involved in U.S.-Japan Relations." *Imin Kenkyū Nempō (Annual Review of Migration Studies)* 18: 139–150.
———. 2016. "Closing the Gap: The Japanese American Leadership Delegation Program and Increasing Involvement of Japanese Americans in U.S.–Japan Relations." *Japanese Journal of American Studies* 27.
Takenaka, Ayumi. 2009. "Ethnic Hierarchy and Its Impact on Ethnic Identities: A Comparative Analysis of Peruvian and Brazilian Return Migrants in Japan." In *Diasporic Homecomings*, edited by Takeyuki Tsuda, 260–280. Stanford, CA: Stanford University Press.

# BIBLIOGRAPHY

Takezawa, Yasuko. 2005. "Transcending the Western Paradigm of the Idea of Race." *Japanese Journal of American Studies* 16: 5–30.

Tamanoi, Mariko. 2006. "Japanese War Orphans and the Challenges of Repatriation in Post-Colonial East Asia." *Japan Focus*: 4 (8).

Tanaka, Janice. 1992. Who's Going to Pay for These Donuts Anyway? San Francisco: Center for Asian American Media.

Taniguchi, Angela S., and Linda Heidenreich. 2005. "Re-Mix: Rethinking the Use of 'Hapa' in Mixedrace Asian/Pacific Islander American Community Organizing." *Washington State University McNair Journal*: 135–146.

Tannen, Deborah. 1990. *You Just Don't Understand: Women and Men in Conversation*. New York: William Morrow.

Tomita, Mary Kimoto, and Robert G. Lee. 1995. *Dear Miye: Letters Home from Japan, 1939–1946, Asian America*. Stanford, CA: Stanford University Press.

Tomlinson, John. 1991. *Cultural Imperialism: A Critical Introduction*. Baltimore: The Johns Hopkins University Press.

Trumbull, Robert. 1967. "Amerasians." *New York Times*, April 30, 283.

Tsuchiya, Tomoko. 2011. "Interracial Marriages Between American Soldiers and Japanese Women at the Beginning of the Cold War." *Journal of American and Canadian Studies* (29): 59–84.

Tsuda, Takeyuki. 2003. *Strangers in the Ethnic Homeland: Japanese Brazilian Return Migration in Transnational Perspective*. New York: Columbia University Press.

———. 2009a. *Diasporic Homecomings: Ethnic Return Migration in Comparative Perspective*. Stanford, CA: Stanford University Press.

———. 2009b. "Global Inequities and Diasporic Return." In *Diasporic Homecomings*, edited by Takeyuki Tsuda, 227–259. Stanford, CA: Stanford University Press.

———. 2009c. "Introduction: Diasporic Return and Migration Studies." In *Diasporic Homecomings*, edited by Takeyuki Tsuda, 1–18. Stanford, CA: Stanford University Press.

———. 2012. "Disconnected from the 'Diaspora': Japanese Americans and the Lack of Transnational Ethnic Networks." *Journal of Anthropological Research* 68.

Tuan, Mia. 1998. *Forever Foreigners or Honorary Whites?: The Asian Ethnic Experience Today*. New Brunswick, NJ: Rutgers University Press.

Turner, Jonathan H. 2002. *Face to Face: Toward a Sociological Theory of Interpersonal Behavior*. Stanford, CA: Stanford University Press.

United Nations. 2013. "International Migration." Accessed February 9, 2016. http://unstats.un.org/unsd/demographic/sconcerns/migration/migrmethods.htm.

Uratsu, Rod. 1977. "The Sansei Experience in Japan: Observations on Sansei Japanese American College Students in Japan." M.A. Thesis, Sociology, Sophia University.

US Census Bureau. 2013. 2011–2013 American Community Survey 3-Year Estimates edited by US Census Bureau.

Võ, Linda Trinh. 2000. "Performing Ethnography in Asian American Communities: Beyond the Insider-versus-Outsider Perspective." In *Cultural Compass: Ethnographic Explorations of Asian America*, edited by Martin F. Manalansan IV, 17–37. Philadelphia: Temple University Press.

Walker, Brett L. 1999. "The Early Modern Japanese State and Ainu Vaccinations: Redefining the Body Politic 1799–1868." *Past & Present* 163 (1): 121–160.

Wang, Leslie K. 2016. "The Benefits of In-betweenness: Return Migration of Second-Generation Chinese American Professionals to China." *Journal of Ethnic and Migration Studies*.

Ward, Rowena. 2006. "Japaneseness, Multiple Exile and the Japanese Citizens Abandoned in China." *Japanese Studies* 26 (2): 139–151.

Ward Crawford, Miki, Katie Kaori Hayashi, and Shizuko Suenaga. 2010. *Japanese War Brides in America: An Oral History*. Santa Barbara, CA: Praeger.

Waters, Mary. 1990. *Ethnic Options: Choosing Identities in America*. Berkeley: University of California Press.

———. 1999. *Black Identities: West Indian Immigrant Dreams and American Realities*. New York and Cambridge, MA.: Russell Sage Foundation; Harvard University Press.

Weiner, Michael, ed. 1997. *Japan's Minorities: The Illusion of Homogeneity*. London and New York: Routledge.

Wessendorf, Susanne. 2013. *Second-Generation Transnationalism and Roots Migration: Cross-Border Lives*. Surrey and Burlington: Ashgate.

White, Merry. 1988. *The Japanese Overseas: Can They Go Home Again?* Princeton, NJ: Princeton University Press.

Whittaker, Elvi. 1986. *The Mainland HAOLE: The White Experience in Hawaii*. New York: Columbia University Press.

Williams, Duncan, ed. 2016. *Hapa Japan: Constructing Global Mixed Race and Mixed Roots Identities and Representations*. Los Angeles: USC Ito Center and Kaya Press.

Williams, Teresa Kay. 1992. "Prism Lives: Identity of Binational Amerasians." In *Racially Mixed People in America*, edited by Maria P.P. Root, 280–303. Newbury Park, CA: Sage.

———. 1997. "Re-Conceptualizing Race: The Identity Formation of Biracial Japanese European Americans." Ph.D. Dissertation, Sociology, UCLA.

Wimmer, Andreas, and Nina Glick Schiller. 2002. "Methodological Nationalism and Beyond: Nation-State Building, Migration and the Social Sciences." *Global Networks* 2 (4): 301–334.

Winant, Howard. 1994. *Racial Conditions: Politics, Theory, Comparisons*. Minneapolis: University of Minnesota Press.

Wong, Sau-ling C. 1995. "Denationalization Reconsidered: Asian American Cultural Criticism at a Theoretical Crossroads." *Amerasia Journal* 21 (1&2): 1–27.

Yaguchi, Yujin, and Mari Yoshihara. 2004. "Evolutions of 'Paradise': Japanese Tourist Discourse about Hawai'i." *American Studies* 45 (3): 81–106.

Yamamoto, Ryoko. 2004. "Alien Attack?: The Construction of Foreign Criminality in Contemporary Japan." *Japanstudien* 16: 27–57.

———. 2010. "Migrants as a Crime Problem: The Construction of Foreign Criminality Discourse in Contemporary Japan." *International Journal of Comparative and Applied Criminal Justice* 34 (2): 301–330.

Yamanaka, Keiko. 1993. "New Immigration Policy and Unskilled Foreign Workers in Japan." *Pacific Affairs* 66 (1): 72–90.

———. 1996. "Return Migration of Japanese Brazilians to Japan: The Nikkeijin as Ethnic Minority and Political Construct." *Diaspora* 5 (1): 65–97.

Yamashiro, Jane H. 2008a. "Hafu." In *Encyclopedia of Race, Ethnicity, and Society*, edited by Richard T. Schaefer, 569–571. Thousand Oaks, CA: Sage.

———. 2008b. "Nikkeijin." In *Encyclopedia of Race, Ethnicity, and Society*, edited by Richard T. Schaefer, 983–985. Thousand Oaks, CA: Sage.

——. 2008c. "When the Diaspora Returns: Transnational Racial and Ethnic Identity Formation Among Japanese Americans in Global Tokyo." Ph.D. Dissertation, Sociology, University of Hawai'i at Manoa.

——. 2011. "Racialized National Identity Construction in the Ancestral Homeland: Japanese American Migrants in Japan." *Ethnic and Racial Studies* 34 (9): 1502–1521.

——. 2015. "Working Towards Conceptual Consistency in Discussing 'Diaspora' and 'Diaspora Strategies': Ethnicity and Affinity in the Case of Japan." *Geoforum* 59: 178–186.

——. 2016. "The Evolving Japanese American Identity." *Nikkei Heritage*. 26 (1): 4–7, 18.

——. 2017. "From Hapa to Hafu: Reconstructing Mixed Race Japanese Migrant Identities in Japan." In *Hapa Japan: Constructing Global Mixed Race and Mixed Roots Identities and Representations*, Vol. 2, edited by Duncan Williams, 29-57. Los Angeles: USC Ito Center/Kaya Press.

Yamashiro, Jane H., and Hugo Cordova Quero. 2012. "Unequal Transpacific Capital Transfers: Japanese Brazilians and Japanese Americans in Japan." In *Transnational Crossroads: Remapping the Americas and the Pacific*, edited by Camilla Fojas and Rudy P. Guevarra Jr., 403–426. Lincoln: University of Nebraska Press.

Yano, Christine Reiko. 2006. *Crowning the Nice Girl: Gender, Ethnicity, and Culture in Hawaii's Cherry Blossom Festival*. Honolulu: University of Hawai'i Press.

Yano, Christine R. 2008. "Gaze Upon Sakura: Imaging Japanese Americans on Japanese TV." In *Gender and Globalization in Asia and the Pacific: Method, Practice, Theory*, edited by Kathy E. Ferguson and Monique Mironesco, 101–120. Honolulu: University of Hawai'i Press.

Yoshida, Jim, and Bill Hosokawa. 1972. *The Two Worlds of Jim Yoshida*. New York: William Morrow.

Yoshino, Kosaku. 1992. *Cultural Nationalism in Contemporary Japan: A Sociological Enquiry*. London: Routledge.

——. 1998. "Culturalism, Racialism, and Internationalism in the Discourse on Japanese Identity." In *Making Majorities: Constituting the Nation in Japan, Korea, China, Malaysia, Fiji, Turkey, and the United States*, edited by Dru Gladney, 13–51. Stanford, CA: Stanford University Press.

# Index

3/11. *See* March 11, 2011

Abu-Lughod, Lila, 163
adoptee, transnational, 12, 21
African Americans. *See* blacks
*ainoko*, 67, 182n15
Ainu, 12, 102
Akebono, 40
American citizens. *See* US citizens
American: identity abroad, 179n8; identity after returning to the United States, 145; identity as based on place of residence, 20; identity in Japan, 48, 54–57; image of in Japan, 17; use of as a term, xx
American School in Japan (ASIJ), 129–130, 185n11. *See also* international school
ancestral homeland migration, 4–6, 12–16, 20, 149–150; American, 18; and language, 104; definition of, 12; stratification of, 18–19, 40, 53, 63, 109
ancestral homeland as not necessarily the contemporary cultural center, 8–10
ancestral return, 176n12. *See also* ancestral homeland migration
ancestral village, 13. *See also* Japan: urban/rural differences
ancestry: as a social construction, 176n7, 177n13; as different from ethnicity, 148; as different from identification with the ancestral homeland, 6–8; definition of, 7
Ang, Ien, 4, 8
anime/manga, 79, 91, 163

Appadurai, Arjun, 13
Ariyoshi, George, 33
Asian Americans, 7, 11, 13, 16, 26, 54, 70, 79, 84, 90–95, 107, 141; as a racial minority on the US continent, 45–49; connections to Asia, 20–22, 153–154, 187n15; images of in the United States, 16, 25, 26, 47
Asian American Studies, 12, 20–23, 34, 148, 153–155
Asian as a race, 16, 45, 47
Asian settler colonialism, 11, 35, 153, 176n11, 178n13
Asian Studies, 21, 23, 148, 153–156
Asians in Hawai'i. *See* Asian settler colonialism
Asians in Japan, 10, 26, 39, 50–55, 67, 131, 179nn5–6; and *hāfu*, 67
Assistant Language Teacher (ALT). *See* English teachers
authentic cultural center, 9, 127–128, 141–145, 148–150, 151

Bachnik, Jane, 100
Barth, Fredrik, 7, 9
Bay Area. *See* San Francisco Bay Area
Befu, Harumi, 177n8
blacks, 65, 66, 77–78, 178n19; American, 17; capitalization of the term, xix; in Japan, 39, 107, 180n12, 188n5; in the United States, 16, 45, 46, 183n17. *See also* mixed black and Asian; mixed black and Japanese
blackness globally, 77, 183n23
blending into a crowd. *See* phenotype, similar to most Japanese

209

boundaries, ix, 5, 44, 147, 149, 150, 152; 176n8; around *hāfu*, 72; around Japaneseness in Japan, 61–63, 66, 124, 150–151, 155–156; between Asian American and Asian Studies, 20–22, 153–156
Brubaker, Rogers, 6–7
*Burakumin*, 39, 178n18

California, x, 1, 25, 46, 47, 48, 51, 54, 55, 57, 71, 73, 74, 76, 83, 90, 92, 93, 109, 110, 111, 137, 139, 142, 143, 144, 159, 175n2, 177n2, 181n19, 186n1
Carter, Mitzi Uehara, 181n7
census, U.S., 25, 31, 37, 69, 158, 177n1, 183n18
Chiba Prefecture, 130, 160, 162, 182n15
Chinen, Karleen, 34
Chinese: in Japan, 51, 179n3, 179n5; Taiwanese, 184n30. *See also* Asians in Japan
Chinese Americans in China, 13, 18, 21
Chinese Malaysian in Japan, 180n11
Christou, Anastasia, 177n13
citizenship: and *hāfu*, 64, 75, 82, 94; and *zainichi* Koreans in Japan, 179n3; as criteria for being Japanese in Japan, 37, 65, 101, 102; cultural and racial, 13; dual, 40, 98, 140. *See also* US citizens
class, socioeconomic, 38, 65–67, 133, 161, 164
college exchange students: in Japan, 19, 83, 87, 90, 98, 113, 117, 120, 122, 128, 150, 158–159, 162, 164; in the United States, 29, 98
colonialism 153. *See also* Japanese imperialism
Connor, Walker, 176n6
Coordinator of International Relations (CIR), ix
cultural center, authentic. *See* authentic cultural center

Daniel, G. Reginald, 72
Dariotis, Wei Ming, 70, 72
Daruma no Gakko, 30
Day, Iyko, 176n11
diaspora migrants, 4. *See also* ancestral homeland migrants
diaspora, 4, 8, 14, 20, 176n6; and mixed ancestry, 12; framework, limitations of, 5, 9, 12, 14. *See also* global ancestral groups
diasporic identity, 5, 21, 145

diasporic return, 4, 12, 149–150; counter, 176n12. *See also* ancestral homeland migration
Dirlik, Arif, 9, 20
double/*daburu*, 67, 89, 182n16

East Asian phenotype. *See* phenotype, similar to most Japanese
English as a global language, 109, 125
English, native, 1, 19, 98, 109, 185n10
English teachers, 2, 49, 73, 81, 109, 128, 130–131, 124
ethnic groups, 7, 9, 10–11
ethnic migrants, 4. *See also* ancestral homeland migrants
ethnic return migration, 4, 12–13, 19. *See also* ancestral homeland migration
ethnicity. *See* ancestry
European Americans. *See* white: Americans

fifth generation. *See* gosei
first generation. *See* issei
Fojas, Camilla, 72
foreigners. *See* Japanese and foreigners
fourth generation. *See* yonsei
Fox, Masa, 183n22
Fujikane, Candace, 178n13
Fugikawa, Laura, 176n11
Fukuoka Prefecture, 27, 177n3
Fukuoka, Yasunori, 62
Fukushima, Glen S., 105, 112, 115, 122, 160, 185nn4–5, 185–186n15
Fukushima nuclear disaster. *See* March 11, 2011
Fukushima Prefecture, 73

*gaijin*. *See* Japanese and foreigners
Galapagos effect, 137–140
gender, 103. *See also* Japanese American experiences in Japan: as gendered
generation, ethnic, 13–14, 27–28, 34, 64, 91, 96, 100, 132–141, 143, 159–160; capitalization of, xix; italicization of terms, 177n7. *See also* gosei; issei; nisei; sansei; shin-issei; shin-nisei; yonsei
Glick Schiller, Nina, 9, 152
global ancestral groups, 4–12, 20–21, 23, 41, 147–149, 176n5, 176n9; branches, 4, 8–12, 25, 41, 62–63; definition of, 5
globalization, 4, 17, 20, 66, 150, 154
Goffman, Erving, 49; presentation of self 166. *See also* role, Goffman's notion of

gosei, 168, 169. *See also* generation, ethnic

*Hafu* (film), 66, 182n11, 182n13
*hāfu*, ix, 22, 40, 55, 64–68, 71, 72, 73, 74–75, 78–82, 83–90, 95–96, 117, 179n9; as a third space, 181n4; as different from foreigners, 67, 76, 85–86; as different from *nikkeijin*, 67, 81, 182n14; images and stereotypes of in Japan, 182n10, 182n12, 182n14; in Okinawa, 181n6; Japanese confusion about, 55, 68; previous terms for, 182n15
Hall, Stuart, 8
Hamabata, Matthews, 55
haole. *See* white: in Hawai'i
hapa, 22, 64, 68–72, 73–78, 81, 95; as mixed-race and mixed-ethnicity, 183n18; meaning in Hawai'i, 70, 183n20; organizations, 183n19
Hawai'i, x, 2, 50, 51, 52, 56, 108, 113–114, 116, 135, 162; as different from the US continent, 58–59, 60–61, 152–153, 175n2, 178n12, 180n16; interviewing people from, 159; Japanese Americans as different from Japanese, 187n16; Japanese tourists in, 180n17; Japaneseness as different from US continent, 126–127; Japaneseness as different from US continent and Japan, 140–141, 143, 145–146; mixed identities in, 70–71; moving to, 129; parents from, 79- 80; positive image of, 59–61, 180–181nn19–20; postwar rise of Japanese Americans, 32–34; relations with Japan, 177n4; relationship of Japanese to other ethnic and indigenous groups, 11, 31–32, 35; research in, 157, 161, 162, 186n1
Hawai'i identity, 22, 57–63, 152–153; as different from Native Hawaiian identity, 180n15; as different from the US continent, 48–50, 141. *See also* local identity
Hayashida, Cullen, 36
Heidenreich, Linda, 70
hierarchy of foreignness, 38–41, 51–55
*hiragana*, 101
Hiroshima Prefecture, 1, 27, 29, 65, 66, 177n3, 188n7
Hiura, Arnold, 34
Hokkaido Prefecture, 85, 102

homeland orientation, lack of, 6–8, 12
*hoshūkō* (supplementary Japanese schools outside of Japan), 30
Houston, Velina Hasu, 181n7

Ibaraki Prefecture, 55
Ichioka, Yuji, 27
identity: ancestral homeland migrant, 14–16, 17–19; formation as interaction, 14–15, 44, 55, 62; symbolic, 30, 136; transnational racial and ethnic, 16–17
immigration policy: in Japan, 178n17; in the United States, 14, 27
incarceration of Japanese Americans during World War II, 28–29, 32, 57, 68, 70, 88, 91, 100, 126–127, 139, 140, 142, 144, 154; and identity, 187n14; and non-incarceration in Hawai'i, 127; and non-incarceration of postwar wave Japanese Americans, 127
Indian Americans in India, 18, 22, 186n7
Inouye, Daniel, 33
insiders and outsiders, 38, 99, 124; related to research, 163–165. *See also uchi* and *soto*
international and interracial marriage, children of, 65–68, 83–90, 98–99, 118–119
International Christian University (ICU), 1, 98, 117, 133–134
international marriage, ix, 29, 111 (*see also* Japanese Americans with Japanese spouses); children of, 69–72, 75, 82, 90–95, 133, 134–135
international school, 98, 108, 110. *See also* American School in Japan
internment. *See* incarceration of Japanese Americans during World War II
interracial marriage, 106–107; children of, 69–72, 73–83, 103
Ishida, Takeshi, 36, 178n15
Ishihara, Shintaro, 36
Ishii, Craig, 142–143
issei (first generation), xix, 27, 100, 134. *See also* generation, ethnic

Jain, Sonali, 186n7
Japan: as a foreign country, 1, 3, 132, 133; demographic change in, 68, 155; urban/rural differences, 48, 50–51, 162, 165–166, 179n4, 186n1; visits to as children, 87, 132–133, 142

Japan Exchange and Teaching (JET) program. *See* JET Program
Japan Foundation Center for Global Partnership (CGP), 188n4
Japanese American: definition of, xix; as used in US census data 177n1; festivals 127, 138, 139 (*see also* obon); identity, 22, 28–29, 57–58, 68, 79, 80, 81, 84, 87–88, 127, 139–140, 145–146, 154–155, 177n1, 181n2, 187n14
Japanese American Citizen's League (JACL), 88, 91, 160, 188n3
Japanese American experiences in Japan: as Americans, 54–57, 81, 84; as different from white Americans, 54–57, 133–134; as gendered, 23, 110, 111, 113–114, 128, 130–131, 159, 164; causing increased understanding of contemporary Japanese society, 134–136, 151; getting lost, 1–2; in restaurants, 2, 108, 118; on trains, 1–2, 3, 45, 60, 76, 113, 161; perceived as hearing impaired, 53; perceived as mentally challenged, 50–54, 123; with children, 94, 108, 110–111, 125, 128–130, 175n4, 183n24; with taxi drivers, 50, 108; work environment, 108–114
Japanese American Leadership Delegation (JALD), 160, 187n1, 188n4
Japanese American National Museum (JANM), 188n4
Japanese American Studies, 154–155
Japanese Americans: ancestral ties to Japan, 1, 4, 148; and Japanese customs, 73, 132, 137–138; and Japanese food, 73, 83, 90, 91; and relatives in Japan, 133, 150, 186n6; and sports, 73, 91, 126, 127, 142, 143; and the idea of living in Japan permanently, 106, 110, 133; back in the United States, 126–146, 186n1; churches and temples, 126–127, 143; differences based on where they grew up, 23, 41; differences between Hawai'i and the US continent, 18, 25, 41, 43–63, 80; from Hawai'i (*see* Hawai'i: Japanese Americans); prewar and postwar waves, xix, 14, 27–30, 69, 91, 127; reasons for going to Japan, 4, 166; reasons for returning to the United States, 114, 128–131; thoughts about teriyaki, 138
Japanese Americans in Japan: description of interviewees, 158–160; no statistical data on, 158; previous research on, 175n4
Japanese Americans in the United States, 64, 175n2, 187n12
Japanese Americans with Japanese spouses, 108, 112–113, 119–121, 123–124, 129–130, 135, 140, 159, 175n4, 183n24
Japanese and foreigners, x, 1, 35, 38–41, 43–44, 64, 65, 75–76, 101, 102, 115, 121, 124, 147, 155–156, 179n6. *See also* hierarchy of foreigners
Japanese "blood," 2, 35–37, 65, 94, 99
Japanese Brazilians in Japan, 4, 19, 38, 53, 109, 160, 178n17, 179n7
Japanese homogeneity, myth of, 7–8, 11–12, 35–37, 65, 74, 99
Japanese immigrants/emigrants, x, 8, 27, 188n7; to Hawai'i, 27, 177n3, 177nn5–6, 180n18
Japanese imperialism, 26, 51, 53–54, 101, 102, 178n14
Japanese language: ability, 1, 23, 29–31, 64, 67, 87–88, 98–125, 159, 162, 163; and miscategorization in Japan, 50–54; as a heritage language, 29–31, 100–101, 103–104; demotivated to improve, 112–114, 125; improvement as unnecessary, 108–114; schools in the United States, 100, 143, 184n1; used in different ways in different places, 163
Japanese Ministry of Foreign Affairs (MOFA), 188n4
Japanese national identity, 35–36, 50, 65; as mixed nation during Japanese Imperial period, 178n14. *See also* Japanese "blood"; Japaneseness: in Japan; Japanese homogeneity, myth of
Japanese Peruvians in Japan, 53, 179n7
Japanese Studies, 12, 155–156. *See also* Asian Studies
Japanese views of Japanese Americans, 2, 17, 24, 44, 52–54, 55, 57, 60, 64, 162, 182n14
Japaneseness: in Hawai'i, 31–35; in Japan, 26, 35–41, 50, 65, 68, 102, 104, 155–156; in Japan and Japanese Americans, 37–38; in relation to indigenous populations, 11–12; on the US continent, 25–31
Japaneseness, construction of, 7, 8–9, 12, 22, 24–25; as different in different places, 76, 93, 96, 117–118, 136–146, 148–150, 151, 154, 163

INDEX

Japantowns, 126, 139, 140, 187n10; as fake Japanese culture, 139, 140
JET (Japan Exchange and Teaching) Program, ix, 2, 54, 80, 117, 128, 129, 130, 140, 150, 158–159, 162, 164, 186n1
Johnson, Akemi, 181n6

Kagoshima Prefecture, 27, 73
Kanagawa Prefecture, 162
Kang, Miliann, 165
*kanji*, 23, 87, 101, 105, 115–118, 119–121, 123; switch to *katakana*, 122–123
Kansai. *See* Osaka Prefecture
*katakana*, 23, 101–102, 105, 112, 117, 123; first names for older women, 184n2; used to express foreignness, 121–123. *See also kanji*: switch to *katakana*
kibei nisei, 27, 100, 134, 135, 177n8, 186n9
*kikokushijo* (Japanese "returnees"), 37
Kina, Laura, 72
Kindaichi, Haruhiko, 101
King, Russell, 177n13
King-O'Riain, Rebecca Chiyoko, 92
Kingston, Maxine Hong, 83
Kobe City, 53
Koenig, Barbara A., 178n1
*kokusaiji*, 67
Kondo, Dorinne, 50
*konketsuji*, 67, 182n15
Korean Americans in Korea, 18, 21, 187n13
Koreans in Japan, 53, 103, 179n3. *See also* Asians in Japan
*koseki* (family registry), 101
Kumamoto Prefecture, 27, 177n3, 188n7

language, Japanese. *See* Japanese language
Latinos: in the United States, 16; miscategorized as, 84. *See also* Japanese Brazilians; Japanese Peruvians
lawyers, 50, 79, 108, 109, 113–114, 116, 119, 128, 129, 131, 141, 158
Lee, Changsoo, 179n3
Lee, Sandra Soo-Jin, 178n1
life course, stage in, 128
Little Osaka. *See* Japantowns
Little Tokyo, 186n8. *See also* Japantowns
local identity, 34–35, 59, 71, 163
London, 109
Los Angeles, 25, 28, 30, 85, 138, 139, 161, 162, 177n2, 180n16, 186n1

Louie, Andrea, 13
Lowe, Lisa, 9–10

Maira, Sunaina, 137
Manyika, Sarah, 32
March 11, 2011, 129–130
Matsunaga, Spark, 33
McIntosh, Peggy, 32
Mead, George Herbert, 49
*meishi* (business cards), 115, 116, 117, 122–123
methodological nationalism, 152. *See also* Glick Schiller, Nina; Wimmer, Andreas
methods, research, 157–166
migrant, definition of, 175n3, 187n1
military, US, 35, 65, 66, 69, 70, 106, 107, 108, 185n9; interviewing Japanese Americans in the, 188n2; War II Japanese American service in, 185n7
Mink, Patsy Takemoto, 33
minority/majority dynamics, 11, 25, 31–32, 141, 152–153
MIS (Military Intelligence Service), 175n4
mixed Asian Americans in the United States, 115, 119. *See also* hapa
mixed black and Asian, 69
mixed black and Japanese, 40, 66, 96, 181n7, 182n12, 185n6
mixed Japanese Americans, 64–97, 120; and names, 118–119, 122–123; interviewing, 159, 179n2; marginalization of, 8; terminology referring to, xix, 181nn1–3
mixed Japanese and Chinese, 90–95, 96
mixed Japanese and Filipino, 98
mixed Japanese in Japan. *See hāfu*
mixed Japanese in the United States, 69, 82, 85, 89–90. *See also* hapa
mixed Japaneseness, 12
mixed white and Asian, 66, 69, 70–71, 73–90, 185n6
mixed white and Japanese, 40, 66, 147
Miyamoto, Ariana, 66
Moriyama, Alan, 177n5
Mura, David, 47
Murphy-Shigematsu, Stephen, 67, 181n7, 182n15, 183n22

Nagano Prefecture, ix, 162, 164, 179n4; 1998 Winter Olympics, 40

Nagasaki Prefecture, 27, 29, 66
Nakashima, Cynthia, 182n9
Nakashima, Daniel, 71, 115, 118, 119, 183n21
names, 69, 71, 74, 85, 89, 90, 94, 98, 101–108, 114–124, 99, 102–103, 114–124, 183n21; full Japanese and foreign, 184n29; middle, 115–118, 120; white-sounding, 184n28
Narayan, Kiran, 163
Native Hawaiians, 11, 35, 70, 153, 183n20; "Hawai'i" v. "Hawaiian" identity, 180n15
new first generaton. *See* shin-issei
new second generation, 22, 133. *See also* shin-nisei
New York, 25, 46, 48, 109, 119, 177n2
NHK (Japan Public Broadcasting Corporation), 59
*nihonjin*. See Japaneseness: in Japan
*nihonjin* and *gaijin*. *See* Japanese and foreigners
*nihonjinron*, 36, 102
Nihonmachi. *See* Japantowns
nikkei, xx, 78, 79, 80–83
*nikkeijin*, 17, 19, 37–38, 40, 53, 55, 57, 67, 80–81, 117, 141, 177n15, 178n17; definition of, xx; from the Philippines, 184–185n3. *See also hāfu*: as different from *nikkeijin*
nisei (second generation), xix, 27, 73, 100, 134; who use *kanji* for their full names, 185n5. *See also* generation, ethnic

*obāchan*, 52
Obama, President Barack, 65
obon festivals, 137–140
Office Ladies (OL), 130–131
Ogawa, Dennis, 178n11, 187n17
Oguma, Eiji, 178n14
Oishi, Nana, 185n8
Okamura, Jonathan, 33, 35, 71, 178n13, 187n16
Okayama Prefecture, 27
Okinawa, 12, 27, 29, 65, 66, 102, 177n3, 181n6; race and Japaneseness as different in, 182n8
Okinawan American identity, 180n10, 180n14
Onizuka, Ellison, 33
ontology of Japanese Americanness, 23
orphans, 66
Osaka Prefecture, 163, 179n4

Park, Robert, 46
phenotype, different from most Japanese, 66, 67, 73–78, 83–87, 87–90, 95–96, 183n22, 185n6
phenotype, racially ambiguous, 78–83, 95–96, 123, 179n2, 184n26
phenotype, similar to most Japanese, 1, 40, 45–48, 48–57, 61–63, 90–95, 95–96, 99, 106–108, 111–114, 116, 119, 120–123; and from Hawai'i, 48–50; miscategorized as Asian immigrants and marginal Japanese, 50–54
Philippines, the, ix, x, 98; and Japanese mestizos, 184–185n3
policy, immigration. *See* immigration policy
postwar wave Japanese Americans. *See* Japanese Americans: prewar and postwar waves
power dynamics. *See* minority/majority dynamics
prewar wave Japanese Americans. *See* Japanese Americans: prewar and postwar waves
Prieler, Michael, 39

quarter/*kuōta*, 67, 82

race: and global ancestral groups, 10–12; in Europe, 176n10; in Hawai'i, 2, 48–49, 177–178n9 (*see also* white: in Hawai'i); in Japan, 5, 10, 39, 46, 99 (*see also* Asians in Japan; blacks: in Japan; white: in Japan); as a social construction, 178n1, 181n3; as one-drop-rule, 45, 183n17; as phenotype, 45; globally, 77–78, 183n23; in the United States, 10, 16, 45, 46, 56, 69, 70, 93, 99, 183n18; intersecting with culture and nation, 5, 152, 178n19; transnational reconstruction of minority identity, 152–153
racial formations, 5, 10–12, 15, 71
racialization, 10–11, 16, 71, 107, 136; in Japan, 45–57, 60–61, 86–87, 131; in the United States, 20, 26, 45–49, 54, 71
racism, 1, 34, 76, 99; in Hawai'i, 178n10
relationship of Japanese Americans to Japan, 127, 141–145
return migration, 12–13. *See also* ancestral homeland migration; ethnic return migration
return of the diaspora paradigm, 4, 12–13

# INDEX

Richardson, Sarah S., 178n1
Robertson, Jennifer, 36
role, Goffman's notion of, 45, 99. *See also* Goffman, Erving
*romaji*, 101, 123–124
roots migration, 165. *See also* ancestral homeland migration

Safran, William, 176n6
Saga Prefecture, 27
Sakura morning drama, 59–60
San Diego, 1, 138
San Francisco Bay Area, 25, 28, 30, 73, 74, 137, 138, 139, 140, 144, 161–162, 163, 177n2, 186n1, 187n12
sansei (third generation), 73–78, 79, 100, 106, 109, 110, 116, 132, 133–134, 136–137, 140–141, 159, 163, 164, 165. *See also* generation, ethnic; sansei/yonsei
sansei/yonsei, 90–95, 112, 117, 137–140, 144, 162, 164
Sato, Kozue, 182n12
Sawtelle. *See* Japantowns
Seattle, 25, 177n2
second generation. *See* nisei
Sekiguchi, Tomoko, 53
Shimane Prefecture, 165
shin-issei (postwar first generation), 29, 100, 127. *See also* generation, ethnic
shin-nisei (postwar second generation), 29, 83–90, 112, 118, 119–121, 127, 132–133, 139, 141–143, 146, 186n5; and growing up in Japantown, 140. *See also* generation, ethnic; shin-nisei/yonsei
shin-nisei/yonsei, 57, 134–135
Sophia University, 161, 182n14
Statistics Bureau of Japan, 37
students. *See* college exchange students
Sugimoto, Yoshio, 35
sumo, 40

Taiwan, 90, 94–95, 102, 179n5
Takahashi, Jere, 177n8
Takamori, Ayako, 103
Takeda, Okiyoshi, 188n4
Taniguchi, Angela, 70
Tannen, Deborah, 114
tea: green, 2; pouring, 131. *See also* Office Ladies
third culture kids, 99
third generation. *See* sansei
Tohoku Earthquake. *See* March 11, 2011

Tokyo: as a field site, 165–166; as a global city, 109, 165; blending in (*see* Japan: urban/rural differences); research in, 157–161; spelling of, xx
transnational, 4, 5, 44–45, 133, 142, 145, 153–154, 159; framework, 14–17, 20; minority identities, 151–153
Triple disaster. *See* March 11, 2011
Tsuda, Takeyuki, 18
Tsukuba City, 53

US-Japan Council, 188n4
*uchi* and *soto*, 38, 99, 124
University of Tokyo, 160, 161
US citizens: image of abroad, 179n8; in Japan, 19, 158, 165; spouses of (*see* international marriage); use of term, xx
US military. *See* military, United States
USMIS (US Military Intelligence Service). *See* MIS

Vietnamese Americans in Vietnam, 18, 21–22
visas, 4, 19, 150, 158, 186nn3–4
visual blending. *See* phenotype, similar to most Japanese

Wakayama Prefecture, 27, 188n7
Ward, Rowena, 178n16
Waters, Mary, 56
white: Americans, 26, 39, 47, 56 (*see also* mixed white and Asian); and diaspora, 13, 177n14; capitalization of, xix; in Hawai'i, 33, 35, 178n11, 183n20; in Japan, 19, 39, 40, 60–61, 65, 76–78, 90, 106–107, 112, 119, 131, 178n19, 188n5; on the US continent, 16
whiteness, 11, 32, 76–78, 90; Americanness as, 17, 51, 56–57, 58, 152
Whittaker, Evli, 178n11
Williams, Duncan, 181n5
Williams, Teresa Kay, 69
Wimmer, Andreas, 9, 152
women, Japanese American. *See* Japanese American experiences in Japan: as gendered
Wong, Sau-ling, 20

Yaguchi, Yujin, 59
Yamaguchi Prefecture, 27, 87, 177n3, 188n7
Yamashiro, Jane H., 179n9, 180n13
Yokohama, 160

Yonamine, Wally, 175n4
yonsei (fourth generation), 78–83, 120, 122, 123, 132, 135–136, 136–138, 143, 164. *See also* generation, ethnic; shin-nisei/yonsei
Yoshihara, Mari, 59
Yoshino, Kosaku, 36, 52

*zainichi*. *See* Koreans in Japan
*zanryūkoji* (stranded Japanese war orphans in China), 37; and *zanryū fujin* (stranded Japanese war wives in China), 178n16

# About the Author

JANE H. YAMASHIRO is a visiting scholar at the University of California, Los Angeles (UCLA), Asian American Studies Center.

www.ingramcontent.com/pod-product-compliance
Ingram Content Group UK Ltd.
Pitfield, Milton Keynes, MK11 3LW, UK
UKHW041305180426
11947UKWH00009B/693